LAWLER

THE ENGLISH BOOK

Developed by
National Curriculum Publishing, Inc.
Framingham, Massachusetts

Published by Perma-Bound Books
a Division of Hertzberg-New Method, Inc.

Managing Editor
Mary Ellen Snodgrass
Former English Chair
Hickory High School
Hickory, North Carolina

A Perma-Bound Academic Advantage Book

Acknowledgements

The following portions of *The English Book* have been reprinted with permission.

Pages 23, 29
Excerpts from *Louis: The Louis Armstrong Story*, by Max Jones and John Chilton, © 1971 by November Books, Limited. Reprinted by permission of Little, Brown and Company.

Pages 44, 45
Excerpts from *Home Sweet Home: My Canadian Album*, by Mordecai Richler, © 1984 by Mordecai Richler. Reprinted by permission of Alfred A. Knopf, Inc.

Page 51
Excerpt from *The Shadow of Sequoyah*, translated and edited by Jack Kilpatrick and Anna Gritts Kilpatrick, © 1965 by the University of Oklahoma Press. Reprinted by permission.

Cont. on page 250.

(Revised from *The Great American English Handbook*)

Published by PERMA-BOUND
      Vandalia Road
      Jacksonville, Illinois
      62650

ISBN:0-7804-1950-2

Printed in the United States of America

Language is an integral part of your life. Every person who goes to school, talks with friends, asks directions, writes letters, reads a newspaper, watches television, visits a library, or applies for a job needs a vast amount of knowledge. Depending on the nature of the task at hand, you may be called upon to **read, understand, interpret, rephrase, outline, summarize, question,** or **evaluate** — any of a number of **skills** that enable you to get the job done. As you grow and change, your need for language becomes more complex, often demanding specialized information and sophisticated manipulation of words and symbols.

This handbook is designed to provide **ready information** for particular situations. Indexed by numbered paragraphs, each topic appears in several places on the **index page** with references to guide you directly to the facts you need. There are **rules of grammar** to help you select the correct form or structure a forceful sentence. There are rules to help you **spell** difficult or unfamiliar words, such as unusual plural formations, foreign words, contractions, and abbreviations. There are **models** to illustrate the use of awkward or confusing expressions, such as homonyms and colloquial phrases. In addition, this book provides instruction in **punctuation,** the marks that illustrate how words are pronounced and that make sense of your thoughts when you commit them to paper.

As you use this handbook, you will find additional information, such as a brief **history of the English language,** explaining why English possesses a varied vocabulary and intricate twists and turns of phrase, making it a real challenge to non-native speakers. To add to your store of words, there is a section explaining how **root words, prefixes,** and **suffixes** function. With a new awareness of where language comes from, you will be better prepared to define terms in context and to approximate the meaning of new words by breaking them down into manageable units.

To strengthen and expand your ability to express yourself, ***The English Book*** contains a detailed description of the **writing process,** suggesting ways to compose **paragraphs** and **themes,** prepare a **term paper,** write an **outline, business letter, résumé,** or **biographical essay,** a frequent request on college entrance applications. To assist you with language arts classes, the book features vital information on basic **literary terms** and a chronological list of the **periods of literary history,** including the most important titles, authors, and events from each.

The English Book enables you to make the most of **library research,** including a list of **sources of information** to help you locate specialized data, such as the source of a familiar quotation, the names of colleges that offer courses in your chosen field, the definition of an obscure philosophical term, the works of a current cartoonist, a map of the ancient world, or a diagram of a diesel engine. It also provides valuable information about **test-taking** to raise your scoring power and relieve your anxieties when you face major examinations, including the PSAT, SAT, ACT, College Board Achievement Tests, GED, CLEP, and TOEFL. There is also a section that explains how to interpret **graphs, maps,** and **charts,** including weather maps, time zones, a chart of the rulers of England, ancient alphabets, and the stock market report.

At the end of the book are sixteen appendices, guides to specialized areas of language, including:

Appendix A: the **Indo-European Language Tree,** from which most world languages are derived.

Appendix B: a **world map**

Appendix C: **forms of address** which call for formal introductions or addresses

Appendix D: a standard list of **proofreading symbols**

Appendix E: a series of patterns for **diagramming** the four basic sentence patterns

Appendix F: a brief statement of **parliamentary procedure** for the smooth, democratic operations of clubs and organizations

Appendix G: the **presidents of the United States**

Appendix H: the **Constitution of the United States**

Appendix I: the **Declaration of Independence**

Appendix J: the **Gettysburg Address**

Appendix K: a list of the ten most common **errors in logic**

Appendix L: **Roman numerals**

Appendix M: a list of national, traditional, and religious **holidays**

Appendix N: **traffic signs**

Appendix O: **computer terms**

Appendix P: a **timeline of literature**

This handbook is not meant to be read at one sitting or even covered in a year's coursework. The purpose of this book is to provide you with ways and means to utilize language for those occasions when common sense knowledge is not enough, when you need a model or chart or rule to answer a more sophisticated question. Along with your **dictionary** and **thesaurus,** this book should remain at hand, on your desk, alongside your typewriter, or wherever it will be of greatest service. With a useful guidebook like *The English Book,* you will be able to manage demanding language chores, to express yourself clearly, and to understand and interpret the most challenging uses of the English language.

TABLE OF CONTENTS

TABLE OF CONTENTS

TABLE OF CONTENTS

TABLE OF CONTENTS

APPENDICES

PARTS OF SPEECH

1.1 **Grammar** *refers to the way words function in a sentence. The labels which record how those words function are called the **parts of speech,** which are the major word categories that make up language. To be an effective communicator, you must be able to identify these integral parts of language.*

1.2 The **eight parts of speech** include
- NOUNS
- PRONOUNS
- VERBS
- ADJECTIVES
- ADVERBS
- PREPOSITIONS
- CONJUNCTIONS
- INTERJECTIONS

1.3 NOUN

A **noun** names a person, place, thing, or quality. There are five classes of nouns:

- a **common noun** names a **general** class

    neighbor, pond, government, religion

- a **proper noun** names a **specific** person, place, thing, or quality and always begins with a capital letter

    Mr. Burns, Walden Pond, Congress, Catholicism

- a **collective noun** names a **group**

    nation, flock, committee, team

- a **concrete noun** names something that is known through the **five senses** (*seeing, hearing, tasting, touching, or smelling*)

    coin, shriek, coffee, breeze, aroma

- an **abstract noun** names a quality, state, or idea

    humility, doubt, peace, liberalism

1.4   A **noun** has numerous important functions in a sentence:

- **subject of the verb**

  Apples will be scarce after the drought.

- **object of the preposition**

  Only a few snacks are left in my *backpack.*

- **direct object**

  Let's remind *Julio* before he forgets.

- **indirect object**

  Offer the *children* some popcorn, Tina.

- **predicate nominative**

  Myrna is our *nominee* for vice-president.

- **appositive**

  Harry Fields, a *man* of character, heads the campaign.

- **direct address**

  Are you ready for lunch, *Anita?*

- **nominative absolute**

  The chess *match* having ended, the team went home.

- **objective complement**

  Historians call Washington "the *father* of his country."

- **retained object**

  The lucky tot was given a *choice* of surprises.

"It could probably be shown by facts and figures that there is no distinctly native American criminal class except Congress."

— Mark Twain

1.5 Nouns can be replaced in these grammatical functions by several types of **substantives.**

pronoun

- Both *Cam* and Jamie knew about the *plan.*
- Both *she* and Jamie knew about *it.*

gerund

- Miss Newman teaches that type of *gymnastics.*
- Miss Newman teaches that type of *tumbling.*

infinitive

- Aunt Clara likes *handicrafts.*
- Aunt Clara likes *to crochet.*

noun clause

- His hurried steps proved his *tardiness.*
- His hurried steps proved *that he was late.*

1.6 A noun may be either **singular** (denoting one unit) or **plural** (denoting two or more units). It may also show **possession** by the addition of an **apostrophe** to its singular or plural form.

A. USEFUL RULES FOR FORMING PLURALS

1. Add **-s** to the singular form of most words.
   owl, owls; basket, baskets; member, members; canoe, canoes; rose, roses; zebra, zebras

2. Add **-es** to nouns ending in **-s, -sh, -ch, -x or -z.**
   atlas, atlases; ash, ashes; branch, branches; fox, foxes; waltz, waltzes; James, Jameses

3. For nouns ending in a consonant followed by **-y,** change the **y** to **i** and add **-es.**
   pony, ponies; ally, allies; county, counties; penny, pennies; horsefly, horseflies; sky, skies; inquiry, inquiries; victory, victories; gully, gullies

4. For nouns ending in a vowel followed by **-y,** add **-s.**
   valley, valleys; buoy, buoys; bay, bays; toy, toys; guy, guys; jay, jays; foray, forays; alloy, alloys; quay, quays; roadway, roadways; buy, buys

5. For nouns ending in a vowel followed by **-o,** add **-s.**
   ratio, ratios; patio, patios; portfolio, portfolios; tattoo, tattoos; studio, studios; stereo, stereos; cameo, cameos; embryo, embryos; trio, trios

3

6. For most nouns ending in a consonant followed by **-o,** add **-es:**
   echo, echoes; hero, heroes; motto, mottoes; cargo, cargoes;
   tomato, tomatoes; innuendo, innuendoes;
   mosquito, mosquitoes; torpedo, torpedoes

   > Exceptions: words that came from Spanish, Italian, and Japanese:
   > soprano, sopranos; solo, solos; canto, cantos; proviso, provisos;
   > piano, pianos; falsetto, falsettoes; piccolo, piccolos; albino, albinos;
   > gaucho, gauchos; virtuoso, virtuosos; arroyo, arroyos; torso, torsos;
   > tempo, tempos; kimono, kimonos; mikado, mikados

7. Letters, symbols, abbreviations followed by periods, and words used as
   examples add an apostrophe and **-s.**
   m, m's; @, @'s; M.D., M.D.'s; very, very's

   > Note: When needed to avoid confusion, an **'s** may be used with
   > numbers and acronyms. Example: 1900, 1900s or 1900's; VCR,
   > VCRs or VCR's.

8. For most words ending in **-f** or **-fe,** add **-s.**
   staff, staffs; sheriff, sheriffs; belief, beliefs; whiff, whiffs; safe
   safes; reef, reefs

   > Exceptions: some words change -f or -fe to -v or -ve before adding
   > -es:
   > life, lives; leaf, leaves; wharf, wharves; shelf, shelves; thief, thieves;
   > half, halves; scarf, scarves; calf, calves; elf, elves; wife, wives;
   > self, selves

9. Irregular plurals make a change in spelling.
   foot, feet; goose, geese; woman, women; mouse, mice; tooth, teeth;
   child, children; ox, oxen

10. Some nouns have no singular form.
    pants, summons, suds, thanks, scissors, riches, clothes, proceeds,
    trousers, whereabouts, odds, means, news, premises, quarters,
    savings, earnings, winnings, mumps, mathematics, gallows,
    barracks, athletics, economics, pincers, annals, alms, pliers,
    remains, tweezers, tidings, nuptials, tongs, victuals, spectacles,
    particulars, vespers

11. Some nouns use the same form for singular and plural.
    grouse, salmon, moose, sheep, deer, swine, fish, quail, series,
    species, statistics, politics, ethics, gross, headquarters, goods,
    tactics, rendezvous

12. Some foreign words retain their unique plurals.
    alumnus, alumni; automaton, automata; basis, bases; ovum, ova;
    bacterium, bacteria; medium, media; alumna, alumnae; datum,
    data; mademoiselle, mesdemoiselles; criterion, criteria;
    phenomenon, phenomena; analysis, analyses; rendezvous,
    rendezvous; stimulus, stimuli

Exceptions: Some foreign words may take either the original plural or the Americanized version.
antenna, antennae or antennas; formula, formulae or formulas; beau, beaux or beaus; tableau, tableaux or tableaus; cherub, cherubim or cherubs; fungus, fungi or funguses; vertebra, vertebrae or vertebras; vertex, vertices or vertexes; radius, radii or radiuses; cactus, cacti or cactuses; nebula, nebulae or nebulas

13. Compound nouns (single words made from two words) are made plural at the end.
    armful, armfuls; fisherman, fishermen; stepbrother, stepbrothers; standby, standbys; planeload, planeloads; tablespoonful, tablespoonfuls; bookshelf, bookshelves; holdup, holdups; touchdown, touchdowns; bystander, bystanders; bucketful, bucketfuls

14. Hyphenated nouns add the plural ending to the most important element.
    attorney-at-law, attorneys-at-law; cat's-paw, cat's-paws; forget-me-not, forget-me-nots; passer-by, passers-by; son-in-law, sons-in-law; poet-in-residence, poets-in-residence; man-of-war, men-of-war; court-martial, courts-martial (or court-martials); cross-examination, cross-examinations; self-starter, self-starters; man-hour, man-hours

A Great Communicator

Some people consider Mark Twain (whose real name was Samuel Clemens) the Great American Writer. While others might disagree, no one can deny the impact he continues to have on American literature. Ernest Hemingway, himself a great American writer, said: "All modern American literature comes from a book by Mark Twain called *Huckleberry Finn*...It is the best book we've had. All American writing comes from that. There was nothing before. There has been nothing else as good since."
Hemingway sums it up when he says, "There was nothing before." Of course there were American writers before Mark Twain. The literature they produced, though, could just as well have been British literature; there was nothing that made it distinctly American. Mark Twain changed that. People in his books talk like Americans. They use words, phrases, and speech patterns that are distinctly American. No writer of "serious literature" had ever done that before Mark Twain.

B. USEFUL RULES FOR FORMING POSSESSIVE NOUNS

1. For most singular nouns, add **'s.**
   cousin, cousin's; laborer, laborer's; Charles, Charles's; violinist, violinist's; host, host's; forest, forest's; brigadier general, brigadier general's

2. For most plural nouns ending in **-s,** add an apostrophe.
   inhabitants, inhabitants'; carolers, carolers'; laundresses, laundresses'; Thomases, Thomases'; beagles, beagles'; laborers, laborers'

3. For plural nouns that do not end in **-s,** add an apostrophe and **s.**
   feet, feet's; lice, lice's; sheep, sheep's; stepchildren, stepchildren's; chairwomen, chairwomen's; bacilli, bacilli's; millennia, millennia's; nuclei, nuclei's

4. For compound and hyphenated nouns, add an apostrophe and **s** at the end.
   stepmother, stepmother's; workmen, workmen's; attorney-at-law, attorney-at-law's; vice-president, vice-president's; man-eater, man-eater's

5. For joint ownership, put an apostrophe and **s** after the last noun.
   Sue and Melinda's kites
   Snoopy and Trixie's doghouse
   my brother and sister-in-law's first anniversary

6. For two or more persons who own something separately, add an apostrophe and **s** after each name.
   Andy's and Mr. Stevenson's suitcases
   Brahms's and Strauss's waltzes
   Rhonda's and her mother's purses

"Thunder is good, thunder is impressive; but it is lightning that does the work."

— Mark Twain

1.7 **PRONOUN**

A **pronoun** serves as a substitute for a noun. Each pronoun possesses four properties:

A. person	C. number
B. case	D. type

1.8 Person indicates when the person or thing referred to is speaking, spoken to, or spoken about.

A **first person** pronoun takes the place of the speaker's name:
- *I* will telephone Rosa tomorrow.
- *We* need your help on the decorating committee.

A **second person** pronoun takes the place of the person spoken to:
- *You* should not go to bed so late, Sol.
- Are *you* traveling by bus or car this year?

A **third person** pronoun names the person or thing which is spoken about:
- *She* washed the last party glass and dried it.
- *They* will never put this paper airplane together!

1.9 Pronouns are also categorized by **case** or use in the sentence. There are three cases:

The **nominative case** can serve as either the subject or the predicate nominative.
- *He* applied for a new driver's license.
- The only officers present are John and *I*.

The **possessive case** indicates ownership.
- *Their* knocking awakened Uncle Andrew.
- The boat with the blue sails is *hers*.

Note: A possessive pronoun *(its, hers, his, theirs, ours, whose)* never needs an apostrophe.

The **objective** case serves as the object of a verb or a preposition or the subject of an infinitive.

- Lisa wanted *them* here for Christmas.
- Tony spoke with *her* about it.
- My grandparents don't allow *me* to play cards.

1.10 A pronoun has a number. It can be either **singular** or **plural.** Refer to the chart below for the singular and plural forms in each person and case.

Singular	Nominative	Objective	Possessive
1st person	I	me	my, mine
2nd person	you, thou*	you, thee*	your, yours thy,* thine*
3rd person	he, she, it	him, her, it	his, her, hers, its

Plural	Nominative	Objective	Possessive
1st person	we	us	our, ours
2nd person	you, thou*	you, thee*	your, yours thy,* thine*
3rd person	they	them	their, theirs

Note: The starred words — *thou, thee, thy, thine* — are **archaic forms** which often appear in poetry or religious works. In modern English, they have been replaced by *you, your,* and *yours.*

1.11 The word each pronoun replaces is called the **antecedent.** The pronoun must agree with its antecedent in number and gender.

- *Bob* left *his* swim fins by the pool.
- The *attendants* received *their* first salary increase.
- *Tonna* saw an *egret* at the lake; *it* was wading toward *her.*

1.12 A pronoun is classified not only by case and number, but also by **type:**

1. A **personal pronoun,** like the ones in the preceding chart, refers to people and things.
    - Sarah introduced Mavis to three *friends;* Mavis really liked *them.*
    - Mrs. Thompson needs the *ruler.* Do you have *it?*
2. A **relative pronoun** (who, whom, whose, which, that, what, whoever, whomever, whatever) introduces a dependent clause.
    - Sam wants the seat *that* Ed had yesterday. (clause modifies seat)
    - The girl *who* is skating by is my cousin Jo. (clause modifies girl)
    - Mrs. Stein is a neighbor *who* lives near here. (clause modifies neighbor)
    - Give your name and address to *whoever* answers. (clause serves as object of the preposition to)

3. An **indefinite pronoun** usually expresses quantity. (singular: anybody, anyone, somebody, nobody, no one, none, nothing, someone, much, everyone, everything, everybody, each, neither, one; plural: both, few, many, several, others).
    - *Everyone* loved the chocolate mousse!
    - Will *no one* claim this beige umbrella?
    - The Wells twins don't have *any.* Serve them *some,* please.
    - *Few* signed up for canoeing or woods lore.
    - For *many,* America is the land of hope.

4. An **interrogative pronoun** (who, whom, whose, what, which) asks a question:
    - *Who* will go in Gary's place?
    - *Whom* did the new manager hire?
    - Did Mrs. Nathan learn *whose* this is?

Note: When either *what* or *which* precedes a noun, it becomes an interrogative adjective and no longer functions as a pronoun:
- *Which* dog has lost a day-glo orange leash? (modifier)
- *Which* is Midnight's water dish? (pronoun)

5. A **reflexive pronoun** (myself, ourselves, yourself, yourselves, himself, herself, itself, themselves) refers to the subject of a sentence and is combined with the endings -self or -selves.
    - Susan and I will bowl by *ourselves.*
    - Marge cut *herself* on that sharp edge.

Note: Avoid saying *hisself* or *theirselves,* neither of which is a word. Use instead *himself* or *themselves.*

"Courage is resistance to fear, mastery of fear — not absence of fear."

— Mark Twain

6. An **intensive pronoun** shares the same form as the reflexive pronoun, but it either emphasizes or intensifies.
   - Juan *himself* must take care of this problem.
   - The pearls were found by the owners *themselves*.

7. A **demonstrative pronoun** (this, that, these, those) points out particular people or objects.
   - *That* is an excellent drawing, Lola.
   - Could I have a pair of *these* in size 7?

Note: When *this, that, these,* or *those* precedes a noun, it becomes a demonstrative adjective, as in *that licorice, these tents.* Avoid *them* as a demonstrative adjective. Rather than *them rainbows,* say *those rainbows.*

1.13 VERB

A **verb** expresses action or state of being. The **infinitive** is the simple or basic form of the verb, the form listed in the dictionary:
   (to) establish
   (to) argue
   (to) study

1.14   The **tense** of a verb indicates time. All verb tenses **(past, present,** or **future)** begin with the infinitive base, drop the preposition *to,* and add the appropriate ending. In addition to endings, verbs often need an **auxiliary** or **helping** verb.

   - Sean *established* our family's bulb garden. (past)
   - My little brother *is arguing* with Sally. (present)
   - Lester *will study* at music camp this June. (future)

"Grief can take care of itself, but to get the full value of joy, you must have somebody to divide it with."

— Mark Twain

1.15 A verb is either **regular** or **irregular,** depending on how it forms its principal parts.

A regular verb deserves its name because it always follows the rule in forming its **principal parts.**

> **PRESENT:** drop the *to* from the infinitive
> **PAST:** add *-ed* to the base
> **PAST PARTICIPLE:** add *-ed* to the base

- We *call* Grandmother every Saturday. (present)
- Sunny *called* the ducks to the shore. (past)
- *Called* to the telephone, Father left the table. (participle)

Any verb that forms its principal parts by adding other endings (-d, -t, -n, -e, -k, -m, -g) is an irregular verb.
- Kim and I *choose* to go by Pam's house every day. (present)
- The troop *chose* a shorter route through the forest. (past)
- *Chosen* to recite, Chita rose from her place. (participle)

Note: Only about 200 of all English verbs are irregular. The following chart lists the most common.

1.16 IRREGULAR VERBS

present	past	past participle
arise	arose	arisen
bear	bore	born or borne
become	became	become
begin	began	begun
bend	bent	bent
bite	bit	bitten
blow	blew	blown
break	broke	broken
bring	brought	brought
burst	burst	burst
catch	caught	caught
choose	chose	chosen
come	came	come
creep	crept	crept
dig	dug	dug
do	did	done
draw	drew	drawn
drink	drank	drunk
drive	drove	driven
eat	ate	eaten
fall	fell	fallen

present	past	past participle
fight	fought	fought
flee	fled	fled
fly	flew	flown
forget	forgot	forgotten
forgive	forgave	forgiven
freeze	froze	frozen
get	got	got or gotten
go	went	gone
grow	grew	grown
hang (suspend)	hung	hung
hide	hid	hidden
hold	held	held
kneel	knelt	knelt
know	knew	known
lay	laid	laid
lead	led	led
lend	lent	lent
lie	lay	lain
lose	lost	lost
mistake	mistook	mistaken
pay	paid	paid
ride	rode	ridden
ring	rang	rung
rise	rose	risen
run	ran	run
say	said	said
see	saw	seen
set	set	set
sew	sewed	sewn or sewed
shake	shook	shaken
shrink	shrank	shrunk
sing	sang	sung
sink	sank	sunk
sit	sat	sat
slay	slew	slain
slide	slid	slid
speak	spoke	spoken
spend	spent	spent
spring	sprang	sprung
steal	stole	stolen
swear	swore	sworn
swim	swam	swum
take	took	taken
teach	taught	taught
tear	tore	torn
throw	threw	thrown
wake	woke or waked	waked
wear	wore	worn
wind	wound	wound
wring	wrung	wrung
write	wrote	written

1.17 A **verb** is also labeled according to its **function:**

A **transitive verb** needs an object to complete its thought; an **intransitive verb** needs no object. Some verbs function as both transitive and intransitive.
- Incomplete: Uncle Earl *carried.* (transitive verb needing an object)
- Complete: Uncle Earl *carried* hay to the barn. (transitive)
- Complete: A silver haze *formed* over the lake. (intransitive)
- Complete: The potter *formed* several clay dishes. (transitive)

A **linking verb** (am, is, are, was, were, be, being, been, feel, taste, smell, sound, look, appear, seem, become, grow, prove, remain, turn, get) connects a subject to the word or words that describe it or refer to it.
- Judy *seems* tired of algebra class.
- I *will be* a senior this year.
- That blanket *felt* so soft!
- His fever *has grown* worse since yesterday.
- The weather *had turned* cold overnight.
- Walking on loose scaffolding *proved* treacherous.

A **helping** or **auxiliary verb** (am, is, are, was, were, has, have, had, do, did, will, shall, can, could, would, may, might) is added to a main verb to indicate tense, number, person, mood, and voice.
- Ann *will* answer to me for her rude behavior! (tense)
- Operators *are* answering the last calls. (third person plural)
- Hal's secretary *might have* answered the call. (conditional)
- His letter *was answered* on the tenth, I think. (passive)

Note: The **passive voice** weakens writing by omitting the **doer** of the action. Use passive verbs only where you need to emphasize the **receiver** of the action or where you do not know the identity of the doer.

In addition, an **auxiliary verb** can indicate emphasis, action in progress, and action completed in the past.
- "I *did* write down the message," Steve declared. (emphasis)
- The Andersons *are* raking under the willows. (action in progress)
- *Had* you traveled to Maine before? (action completed in the past)

1.18 ADJECTIVE

An **adjective** modifies, describes, or limits the meaning of a noun or substantive. Adjectives can be **descriptive, possessive, numerical, demonstrative, interrogative, proper,** or **predicate.**

- That *tough* steak broke his filling. (descriptive)
- *Arnie's* photos won him two medals. (possessive)
- We saw *two* shows in New York. (numerical)
- Don't go walking in *this* rain, Coretta. (demonstrative)
- *What* time does the performance begin? (interrogative)
- Tomorrow, we'll read our first *Shakespearean* sonnet. (proper)
- The bucket next to the corral is *empty.* (predicate)

1.19 ADVERB

An **adverb** modifies a verb, adjective, or another adverb.

- Matt's mynah bird whistled *cheerily.* (modifies a verb)
- His joke is *really* funny. (modifies an adjective)
- Jo walked *very* cautiously on the gravel. (modifies another adverb)

1.20 Both adjectives and adverbs have **degree.**

Positive is the **basic** form.
- It will take a *small* key to fit that lock.
- The water department announced a *startling* discovery at Lookout Dam.
- Stars *often* seem red or blue in the atmosphere.

Comparative indicates a **greater degree** and compares two things.
- The *smaller* boy will play the part of Hansel.
- The appearance of a kiwi is *more startling* than the taste.
- I can visit *more often* now that I have my driver's license.

Superlative indicates **the greatest degree** and compares three or more things.
- The *smallest* bill I have is a five.
- The *most startling* fact about this painting is that Degas was almost blind when he completed it.
- Accidents occur *most often* in the home.

Note: Avoid using double comparatives or double superlatives such as *more bolder, most tiniest.*

1.21 For the **comparative** form of one-syllable and most two-syllable adjectives and adverbs, add **-er;** for the **superlative**, add **-est.** For adjectives or adverbs of three syllables, use **more** or **less** (comparative) and **most** or **least** (superlative):

Positive	Comparative	Superlative
great	greater	greatest
smooth	smoother	smoothest
lovely	lovelier	loveliest
intelligent	more intelligent	most intelligent
fast	faster	fastest
carefully	less carefully	least carefully

Note: One group of adjectives, called **absolute**, cannot be compared, for example, *unique, sole, white, square, round.*

1.22 IRREGULAR COMPARISON

bad	worse	worst
far	farther, further	farthest, furthest
good	better	best
――	inner	inmost, innermost
late	latter, later	latest, last
little	less, lesser	least
many, much	more	most
near	nearer	nearest, next
old	older, elder	oldest, eldest
――	outer	outermost
top	――	topmost
――	upper	uppermost
well (in health)	better	――

1.23 PREPOSITION

A **preposition** shows the relationship between its object and another word or words in the sentence.

- I know some good stories *about* ghosts.
- Fran, I'm right *behind* you!
- *At* the time, Quita thought the remark was funny.

Some of the most common prepositions include *about, above, across, after, against, among, around, at, before, behind, below, beside, between, beyond, by, during, except, for, from, in, into, near, of, on, over, through, to, toward, under, upon, with,* and *without.*

Some prepositions are composed of two or more words such as *in accordance with, on account of, because of, as to, next to, instead of, due to, across from, down below,* and *in regard to.*

- *In accordance with* state requirements, my family wears seat belts.
- He spoke *in regard to* First Amendment rights.

Note: When a preposition is used without an object, it serves as an adverb.

- The pop fly went *beyond* the outer fence. (preposition)
- I rode Champ to the gully and *beyond.* (adverb)

1.24 A **prepositional phrase** can serve either as an adverb or an adjective.

- The baby birds will be gone *by late spring.* (modifies gone)
- Harriet's jacket is on the chair *by my bed.* (modifies chair)

Classic "Something that everybody wants to have read and nobody wants to read."

— Mark Twain

1.25 CONJUNCTION

A **conjunction** connects words, phrases, or clauses.

A. A **coordinate conjunction** (and, but, or, nor, for, so, yet) connects elements of equal value.
- Jane picked up Will *and* Mrs. Martin. (connects nouns)
- Jog in place *or* around the track. (connects phrases)
- I'll take spaghetti, *but* I'd rather have tacos. (connects clauses)

Note: When a **coordinate conjunction** connects two clauses, a **comma** precedes the conjunction.

B. **Correlative conjunctions** connect words, phrases, or clauses of equal value and are always used in pairs.

both . . . and, either . . . or, neither . . . nor, not only . . . but also, although . . . yet, if . . . then, since . . . therefore, though . . . still

- Fred's new car is *either* royal blue *or* navy. (connects adjectives)
- Sam was *neither* on the patio *nor* in the yard. (connects phrases)
- Flo will *not only* run for president of her class, *but* she will *also* win! (connects clauses)

C. A **subordinate conjunction** connects a dependent clause with an independent clause.

although, because, unless, as if, when, after, that, until, since, whether, if, while

- *Unless* you tell Dad what happened, he can't help you.
- The roof took shape quickly *because* all the workers helped out.
- At the track meet Debbie ran *as if* her life depended on it.

D. A **conjunctive adverb** suggests a specific relationship between the ideas in two independent clauses.

therefore, however, unless, indeed, thus, consequently, nonetheless, nevertheless, moreover, finally, meanwhile, otherwise, next, instead, further

- We traveled for four hours; *finally*, we reached Atlanta.
- The baby lay sleeping in his crib; *nevertheless*, we turned on the radio to hear the news.

Note: Use a semicolon before and a comma after a conjunctive adverb.

1.26 INTERJECTION

An **interjection** communicates strong emotion or surprise and is not grammatically linked to the rest of the sentence.

> • *Oh no!* I forgot to call my sister.
> • Did you see that skier? *Wow!*
> • *So,* Lana got her kite off the ground before anyone else. *Great!*

1.27 Technically speaking, words have no grammatical designation until they are used in a sentence. Some English words have a variety of uses and meanings, depending upon their placement in the sentence and their relationship to surrounding words and phrases. For example, the following sentences illustrate various uses and meanings of the words *past* and *down.*

- Our photo album captures the fun of *past* Christmases. (adjective)
- Grace enjoys movies and books about the *past.* (noun)
- Drive *past* the bridge, turn left, and stop at number 3. (preposition)
- The cardinal flew *past* before I could see its wings. (adverb)
- The most expensive pillows are stuffed with *down.* (noun)
- Little Joe can *down* his orange juice in one gulp. (verb)
- Tim sat *down* to a great Thanksgiving feast. (adverb)
- *Down* the aisle were three vacant seats. (preposition)
- On the *down* stroke the choir joined in. (adjective)

"A powerful agent is the right word. Whenever we come upon one of those intensely right words in a book or newspaper the resulting effect is physical as well as spiritual, and electrically prompt."

— Mark Twain

1.28 VERBAL

A special category of grammatical structures is the **verbal,** a form derived from a verb but used as another part of speech, such as a noun, adjective, or adverb. There are three types of verbals: the **infinitive,** the **gerund,** and the **participle.**

1.29 An **infinitive,** which contains the word *to* followed by some form of verb, has numerous uses in a sentence. It can serve as a substantive, an adjective, or an adverb.

- *To run* the full distance is impossible. (substantive used as a subject)
- Sherry found an old movie *to relieve* my anxiety. (adjective)
- Jan's elderly aunt is unable *to drive* the car. (adverb)

Note: All three examples — *to run, to relieve,* and *to drive* — are followed by objects, *distance, anxiety,* and *car,* respectively.

The **infinitive** retains certain qualities of the verb in that it may take a subject, an object, or a complement.
- "We expect *you to behave,*" his mom said. (infinitive with subject)
- The choirmaster found time *to open the box.* (infinitive with an object)
- Her son wants *to become a priest.* (infinitive with predicate nominative)
- Madelyn likes her kitchen *to look busy.* (infinitive with a predicate adjective)

Although it lacks person, number, and mood, the **infinitive** retains two other characteristics of a verb — **tense** and **voice.**
- Gerry seems *to have spoken too soon.* (infinitive in the present perfect tense)
- Their child needs *to be washed from head to toe.* (infinitive in the passive voice)

1.30 The **gerund** is a verb form which ends in *-ing* and serves as a substantive. Like the infinitive, it retains certain characteristics of a verb, including **tense** and **voice.**

- *Rowing to shore* sapped his energy. (gerund as subject)
- Sylvia rejected *gardening* as a hobby. (gerund as direct object)
- My roommate relaxes by *sketching mountain scenes.* (gerund followed by an object)
- *Being proud* is not necessarily a virtue. (gerund followed by a predicate adjective)

Like the infinitive, the **gerund** possesses two characteristics of the verb — **tense** and **voice.**

- After *having completed first aid,* our friend enrolled in CPR. (gerund in the present perfect tense)
- *Being chosen a Knight of the Garter* is a great honor. (gerund in the passive)

Unlike the infinitive, the **subject** of a **gerund** is in the **possessive** case. For example,

- She objected to *his* chewing ice during the movie.
- The fans will applaud *her* singing the National Anthem.
- *Their* enthusiastic batting made both Jimmy and Lou likely candidates for the Player of the Year award.

1.31 A **participle** is a verbal that serves as an adjective. It may appear in one of two forms: the **present participle** ends in *-ing;* the **past participle** usually in *-ed,* but irregular participles may employ a variety of endings such as *-d, -n, -t, -k, -e, -g,* or *-m.*

> Examples: fled, held, led; sewn, won, spoken; burst, crept, spent; sunk, drunk, stuck; gone, done, borne; sung, wrung, sprung; swum.

Like the two previous types of verbals, the participle may take an object or complement.

- The cover featured a formation of jets *flying above the Bok tower.* (present participle modifying jets)
- Granny offered the *starved* cat a bowl of scraps. (past participle modifying cat)
- The man *lugging the unwieldy toolbox* stopped to wipe his face. (participial phrase containing an object, toolbox)
- Both girls, *being well brought-up,* said thank-you to the hostess. (participle with a complement, brought-up)

Like both the infinitive and the gerund a **participle** possesses two qualities of a verb — **tense** and **voice.**

- *Having eaten his fill,* Lester pushed back from the table. (participle in the present perfect tense)
- The small boat, *lashed by the storm,* leaned toward the rocks. (participle in the passive voice)

A **participle** is often linked to another word by a hyphen to form a single regular adjective.

> wind-swept, full-blooded, far-seeing, far-reaching, far-flung, forward-looking, snow-covered, heart-broken, sweet-tasting, easy-going, ill-gotten.

- The western movie opened on *wind-swept* prairies and *snow-covered* peaks.
- We are seeking a *forward-looking* leader for the Chamber of Commerce.

Participles, like other modifying words or phrases, should be as close as possible to the agent to clarify the relationship between the action and its doer. A **misplaced** or **dangling participle** violates the sense of the sentence.

- I saw silos in the hayfield *riding on the train.* (misplaced)
- *Riding on the train,* I saw silos in the hayfield. (correct)
- *Buoyed by his praise,* another dive was attempted. (dangling)
- Miss Little, *buoyed by his praise,* attempted another dive. (correct)

"Always do right. This will gratify some people, and astonish the rest."

— Mark Twain

CHAPTER 2

SENTENCE SENSE

2.1 The **eight parts of speech** serve as the building blocks of the **sentence**. A **sentence** is a word or group of words which expresses a complete and independent thought. It begins with a capital letter and ends with a period, question mark, or exclamation point.

- Tyro's birthday is on Tuesday. (a simple statement)
- Who needs the tape and scissors next? (a question)
- Hot dogs are my favorite at a cookout! (an exclamatory statement)
- Jump! (a command) [Note: The subject is an unexpressed *you*.]

2.2 Each sentence must have a **subject** and a **predicate.**

A. The **subject** specifies the person, place, or thing being talked about.
- *April* brought cold, wet weather this year. (noun)
- *That* is a great suggestion, Uncle Ed! (pronoun)
- *She and Mrs. Summers* shopped for hours. (compound subject)
- *Underlining in yellow ink* helps me study. (gerund phrase)
- *To learn archery* takes years of effort. (infinitive phrase)
- *That he kept on trying* is commendable. (noun clause)

B. The **predicate** tells what is being said about the subject. A predicate always contains a verb, which expresses either action or a **state of being** and tells what the subject did, does, or will do, is, was, or will be.
- Nathan *will complete these envelopes.* (action)
- The Taylor girls *are members of our troop.* (state of being)

C. The **simple predicate** is the verb by itself, without objects, complements, or modifiers.
- Lately, I *have started* too many projects. (action)
- *Did* Susan *seem* serious about her flute lessons? (state of being)

D. The **complete predicate** consists of the verb plus any words that modify or complete its meaning.
- Most adults *like reunions.* (verb and direct object)
- My teacher *reads aloud quite well.* (verb and modifiers)
- Fresh ground coffee *smells so good!* (verb and predicate adjective)
- Bo *can skate and carry his books at the same time.* (compound verb with direct object)

E. Verbs are often followed by a **direct object,** the receiver of the action that the sentence describes.

- Roy's dog followed the visitor.

  subject verb   direct object

- Campers expect juice at breakfast and cola for lunch.

  subject   verb   direct object   direct object

- Should the girls take their umbrellas today?

  verb   subject   verb direct object

F. Objects can also be **indirect.** The action is done *to* or *for* someone or something.

- Cheryl Thompkins wired her mom and dad a bouquet.

  subject   verb   indirect object   direct object

- The store promised my neighbor a charge account.

  subject verb   indirect object   direct object

Note: If there is an indirect object in the sentence, there must also be a direct object.

"People say to me what do I think of when I'm playing. Well, I just think about my happy days and memories and the notes come out; always had been that way. To me jazz has always got to be happy music. You've got to love it and play it; I can't vouch for anyone else."

— Louis Armstrong

2.3 A **clause** is a group of words which contains a subject and verb. If it is a complete thought, it is also a sentence.

> **An independent clause can stand alone.**
> - Someone will come this way soon.
> - Shouldn't those gates be locked?
>
> **A dependent or subordinate clause does not express a complete thought and therefore cannot stand on its own.**
> - Someone will come this way soon *if we wait long enough.*
> - Shouldn't those gates be locked *before we leave?*

Note: The clause *if we wait long enough* in the first example does not express a complete thought and could never serve as a sentence. The same is true of *before we leave* in the second example. Be cautious in writing sentences which lack one of the three basic elements — a subject, a verb, or a complete thought. Any group of words which lacks one or more of these components is a **fragment.**

- These cans of varnish. (lacks a verb)
- Must remain here. (lacks a subject)
- In the bottom of the box. (lacks a subject and verb)
- These cans of varnish must remain here in the bottom of the box. (complete sentence)

Note: The last example contains all necessary components.

2.4 A **dependent clause** can be either **restrictive** or **nonrestrictive.**

A **restrictive clause** narrows the meaning of the sentence. Without the clause, the sentence would lose its intended meaning. A restrictive clause needs no commas to separate it from the word modified.

- Players *who score frequently* have a chance at the trophy.
- I want to buy a sofa *that can be made into a bed.*

Note: If we remove the restrictive clause in the first example, the sentence would imply that any player has a chance at the trophy, even players who don't score at all. If we did the same in the second example, we would misunderstand the particular piece of furniture the speaker intends to buy.

A **nonrestrictive clause** adds information that is not necessary to the sense of the sentence. A nonrestrictive clause is set off by commas.
  - Miguel, *whose mother works at the market,* won a scholarship.
  - Our VCR, *which we just got for Christmas,* records at three different forward speeds.

Note: In the first example, where Miguel's mother works is additional information which does not affect the basic thought, that Miguel won a scholarship. In the second example, if we removed the commas, we would imply that we owned more than one VCR.

2.5   A **subordinate clause** can have one of three grammatical uses in a sentence.

A **noun clause** may function in place of a noun. The clause is often begun by a relative pronoun.

who, whom, whoever, whomever, whose, which, what, whatever, that, whichever

  - *What he chooses* is his business. (subject)
  - I asked *that she make plans to arrive here by Tuesday.* (direct object)
  - The child talked with *whomever she liked.* (object of the preposition)
  - The question is *whose name should come first.* (predicate nominative)
  - Our quandary — *that no one had brought a key to the closet* — amused the caretaker. (appositive)
  - Tell *whomever you wish* the news about Mandy. (indirect object)

Note: In the last example, *whomever* is in the objective case because it serves as the direct object of *wish*. The whole dependent clause, *whomever you wish,* serves as the indirect object of *tell*.

An **adjective clause** serves as a modifier of a substantive.
  - A tree *that is covered with vines* shades our porch. (modifies *tree*)
  - Sally can draw anyone *whom you can name.* (modifies *anyone*)
  - Mrs. Simmons canned the beans *which we picked.* (modifies *beans*)

An **adverb clause** serves as a modifier of a verb, adjective, or adverb. Some words which frequently introduce adverb clauses include the following.

when	if	since
because	while	as
after	as if	as long as
in order that	provided that	though
unless	as though	where
until	even though	although
than	whenever	before
in that	once	till

- *If you oil your bike*, it will last longer. (modifies *will last)*
- My room is painted darker *than I wanted.* (modifies *darker*)
- The kite rose as rapidly *as we had ever seen it.* (modifies *rapidly)*

Note: An **adverb clause** which precedes an independent clause, as illustrated by the first example, is always set off by a **comma** to prepare the way for the most important idea.

2.6   A **phrase,** like a clause, may be restrictive or nonrestrictive; unlike a clause, however, a phrase is a group of related words that does not contain a subject or a predicate.

- Search *under both beds* for your slippers. (prepositional phrase)
- Students never like *running in place.* (gerund phrase)
- *To tell the truth*, I'm tired too. (infinitive phrase)
- *Trying her best to listen*, May cupped her hand over her ear. (participial phrase)

Note: A **comma** sets off the underlined phrases in the last two examples because they precede the main clause.

2.7 A **sentence** varies according to the intent of the speaker.

A *declarative* sentence makes a statement.
- Derek grows broccoli in his garden.
- Our boat has leaked since last fall.

An *interrogative* sentence asks a question.
- Wouldn't you like a pillow for your head?
- What will an extra night in the hotel cost?

An *imperative* sentence gives a command.
- Wait for me, Marlo.
- Chauncey, stop that barking!

An *exclamatory* sentence expresses strong emotion or surprise.
- Willie's sister said her first word!
- Oh, what a surprise I have for Lon!

2.8 **Sentences** are also categorized according to their degree of grammatical complexity. A sentence may be classified as *simple, compound, complex,* or *compound-complex.*

A **simple sentence** has only one independent clause and no dependent clauses.
- There are no black olives on the shelves.
- Lance and Muffin frolicked and basked in the sun.

Note: Although both subject and verb are compound in the second example, the sentence is still simple because it contains only one independent clause.

A **compound sentence** consists of two or more independent clauses.
- Mother mowed grass; Alice clipped shrubbery; Sam and I raked.
- All day she sits on the dock, but she never gets bored.
- Mr. Hilton works late; however, he's always home on weekends.

Note: A **compound sentence** must be punctuated to show the importance of each clause. The clauses may be separated by • a semi-colon; • a comma plus a coordinate conjunction; or • a semi-colon, a conjunctive adverb, and a comma. A sentence containing independent clauses that are not separated by punctuation is called a **run-on sentence.** A compound sentence which is punctuated by a comma alone is called a **comma splice.** Both the run-on sentence and the comma splice are incorrect.

A **complex sentence** contains an independent clause plus one or more dependent clauses.

- Even if Jay could swim, he still wouldn't appreciate this freezing lake water.
- My cat always knows when I am about to wake up.
- We want another song, Dee, if you don't mind and if you have time.

A **compound-complex** sentence contains compound independent clauses and at least one dependent clause.

- When you find time, write Charley or call his mother.

  dependent   *independent*   *independent*

- Bob mopped, and Jan dusted, even though it was late.

  independent   *independent*   *dependent*

A Great Communicator

By the time he died in 1971, Louis Armstrong's nickname "Satchmo" was an international household word. Millions of people considered him a great entertainer. The fact is he was much more than an entertainer; he was a great and influential American artist. Jazz music has been one of America's most important contributions to the arts. The influence of jazz has forever changed both serious orchestral music and popular music worldwide. No other figure in the early history of jazz had such a profound influence as Louis Armstrong. It is impossible today to listen to the radio without hearing the echoes of musical ideas that were created by Louis Armstrong, even though many modern musicians may have no idea where those ideas originated. The colorful language of jazz and jazz musicians has also become part of our everyday lives. New York City promotes itself as the "Big Apple." Young musicians book "gigs," play "riffs" and "jam." All of these words and expressions were first used by Louis Armstrong and his contemporaries over sixty years ago.

2.9 **Variety** is the key to interesting, readable sentences. A knowledge of grammar and sentence structure makes it easier for the writer to alter a humdrum, simplistic pattern of words to add sparkle and clarity.

- **It was Ann's birthday. Gabe had no ideas for a gift.** (humdrum)
- **What could Gabe buy Ann for her birthday?** He had no idea. (interrogative)
- Gabe, **who was suffering from a lack of ideas,** had bought nothing for Ann's birthday. (adjective clause)
- In order to buy Ann the perfect gift, Gabe needed one thing — **an idea.** (appositive)
- **Because he lacked ideas,** Gabe had not bought Ann a birthday gift. (introductory adverb clause)
- **To buy Ann the perfect birthday gift,** Gabe must have an idea. (infinitive phrase)
- **With no idea in mind,** Gabe had not bought Ann's birthday gift. (introductory prepositional phrase)
- **Gabe had no ideas; Ann still had no birthday gift.** (compound sentence)
- **Hesitating to buy Ann a birthday gift,** Gabe waited for a good idea. (participial phrase)
- **Buying the right birthday gift for Ann** required a good idea from Gabe. (gerund phrase)

"Music's my language. On all those trips all over the world, maybe the musicians can't speak with you, but play *Struttin' With Some Barbecue* and they'll know their parts and chime right in."

— Louis Armstrong

USAGE

3.1 **W**ebster's Third New International Dictionary boasts over six million word definitions! Each time you speak or write, you draw from a vast word reservoir to communicate your exact meaning. In this chapter, you will learn areas of **word choice** and **grammatical structure** which often cause confusion. This discussion will help you make correct choices.

3.2 **Agreement** refers to the balance of number, person, and gender in a sentence. There are several situations which can cause difficulty with agreement.

Nouns determine how a sentence agrees.

Subjects joined by *and* take a plural verb.
- Mark and Jolene *are* volunteers at Central Hospital.
- I thought that Betty and her brother *were* at camp.
- Mr. Rodriguez and his wife *walk* by here each morning.
- Mom, *do* the knife and spoon *go* on the right side of the plate?
- There *are* the cabbage and shredder; start to work!

If two words connected by *and* represent a **single idea** or if both refer to a single person or thing, use a singular verb.
- Peaches and cream *makes* a great summer dessert.
- The Lone Ranger's loyal friend and trusty companion *is* Tonto.
- The Stars and Stripes *has* a long history.
- Three dollars and ten cents *seems* a great price to pay.
- To an Englishman, fish and chips *is* a hearty meal.

Collective nouns, which name a group, rely on the sense of the sentence to govern their verb form. If the words imply that the group acts as a single unit, the verb is singular.

team, audience, navy, fleet, jury, committee, cast, militia, congregation, family, the United States, remainder, rest, half, percent, number, part, human race, wildlife, class, congress, public, assembly, association, board, cabinet, trio, commission, company, corporation, council, counsel, couple, crowd, department, firm, group, majority, minority, press, staff, army, division, platoon, legion, police, herd

- Hurray! Our crew *has won* the silver cup!
- *Does* the cast *expect* to be paid after the last performance?
- Only the jury *knows* why he was found guilty of arson.
- The quartet *enters* from stage left in Act III.

If the collective noun implies that each member acted individually, then a plural verb is needed.
- The fallen enemy *were scattered* over the countryside.
- Notre Dame's squad *choose* their own method of warm-up.
- The flock *feed* at different times of the day.
- The dance troupe *have* individual styles.

Some nouns appear to be plural but take a singular verb.

> mumps, measles, mathematics, economics, physics, ethics, athletics, politics, summons, news, blues, United States

- The news from Wall Street *is* especially cheerful tonight.
- The ethics of the situation *seems* clear-cut.
- The United States *continues* to symbolize liberty to the world.

Also, some nouns look plural and take a plural verb.

> scissors, pliers, pincers, headquarters, shears, whereabouts, odds, wages, pants, tidings, means, assets, earnings, premises, proceeds, quarters, savings, winnings, goods

- The premises of Lawndale Security and Trust *are* closely guarded.
- Abel's scissors *lie* near his ruler and protractor.
- His quarters *seem* unusually stuffy.

Nouns which denote weight, extent, time, fractions, portions, or quantity **taken as a unit** require a singular verb.
- At fifty cents per yard, four yards *costs* two dollars.
- Two hundred pounds *seems* a reasonable estimate of its weight.
- Sixty seconds *equals* a minute.
- Nearly seven-eighths of the total fund *has been spent.*

Some expressions can take either singular or plural verbs, depending on the sense of the sentence.
Half of the punch *goes* to me; half of the cupcakes *go* to you.

> Note: Because punch is a liquid, its parts cannot be counted. Cupcakes, however, are individual units which can be counted. Therefore, the first verb is singular and the second is plural.

3.3   **Pronouns** can also cause problems with agreement.

Relative pronouns, *who, whoever, which,* and *that,* agree with the antecedent or the word for which they stand. If the pronoun is the subject of a verb, then the verb also agrees with the antecedent.
- It is not *we* who *are* to blame, Mrs. Turner.
- The Jason twins belong to the scout *troop* that *volunteers* on Tuesdays.
- The *birds* which *flock* to our feeder are usually wrens.

A Great Communicator

After hearing Marian Anderson sing in 1935, the legendary conductor Arturo Toscanini told her, "Yours is a voice one hears once in a hundred years." Born into a poor family in Philadelphia in 1902, she began singing in a church choir when she was six years old. Her love of music and tremendous talent was easily apparent at this early age, and she began helping support her family by giving concerts after her father died. In 1923 she won a singing contest sponsored by the Philadelphia Philharmonic. In 1929 she gave a recital at Carnegie Hall in New York City. She toured Europe — including the Soviet Union — in the early 1930s and was enthusiastically greeted wherever she appeared. She sang a variety of classical music, but it was the spirituals she performed that drew the loudest applause. Despite her worldwide reputation, she still encountered racial prejudice in the United States. She was denied hotel accommodations and refused service in restaurants. In 1939 the Daughters of the American Revolution refused to let her perform at their Washington, D.C., concert hall. Instead, Anderson gave a free recital at the Lincoln Memorial; over 75,000 people attended. In 1955 Anderson became the first African American to appear at the Metropolitan Opera in New York City. She retired eight years later. For her 75th birthday, Congress ordered a gold medal struck in her honor.

The **indefinite pronoun** can be either singular or plural. Here are some pronouns that are always singular. These words require a singular verb.

> someone, somebody, each, nobody, anyone, anybody, one, everyone, no one, everybody, either, neither, many a

- Everybody *enjoys* a good cowboy movie.
- *Is* no one *going* to eat this last chocolate chip cookie?
- Each *receives* a choice of seating in the assembly hall.
- Many a fisherman *has fished* this trout stream.

Some pronouns are always plural. They require a **plural verb.**

> several, few, both, others, many

- Few *have learned* Chef Wally's salad secret.
- Others *leave* early, but Sylvia always stays to the end.
- Mr. Isaacs, both of these two types of sponge cake *earn* my recommendation.

Some indefinite pronouns can be either singular or plural, depending on the sense of the sentence.

> some, any, none, all, most

- Some of the oil *was dripping* to the pavement.
- Some of the rocks *have* flecks of mica in them.
- All of this bad weather *has begun* since March.
- Oh, Jane! All of my tapes *have been damaged* by the sun.

Note: Because oil is a liquid, its parts cannot be counted. Rocks, however, are individual units which can be counted. Therefore, the first verb is singular and the second is plural.

3.4 The way in which **conjunctions** join subjects can cause confusion.

When singular objects are joined by **or** or **nor,** the verb is singular.
- One or the other *knows* where to find the boat key.
- Neither my house nor yours *is* big enough for a New Year's Eve party.

When a singular and a plural subject are joined by **or** or **nor,** the subject closer to the verb decides the number of the verb.
- Either Mrs. Watts or her sons *rake* the leaves each fall.
- No, Jan, neither the girls nor their brother *has called.*

When the subjects joined by **or** or **nor** are of different person, the subject nearer the verb determines its person.
- The line foreman realized that neither you nor he *has* enough training.
- Mother thinks that either she or you always *leave* the lid off.

33

3.5 **Parallel Structure** refers to the uniform grammatical structure of words, phrases, or clauses that are connected by coordinating conjunctions or are items in a series.

Incorrect: Misty prefers **to lie in the sun or sleeping in the grass.**

Correct: Misty prefers **to lie in the sun or to sleep in the grass.**

Or: Misty prefers **lying in the sun or sleeping in the grass.**

Note: Either infinitive or gerund phrases are correct as the direct object of **prefers** but because the phrases are joined by a coordinating conjunction, they must have the same grammatical structure.

Incorrect: Matt seems gentle, pleasant, and has nice manners.
                     adj.   adj.   predicate

Correct: Matt seems gentle, pleasant, and mannerly.
                 adj.   adj.   adj.

3.6 **Misplaced modifiers** are words or groups of words incorrectly positioned in a sentence. For greatest clarity, modifiers should be placed as close as possible to the word modified. This is particularly true for the following.

just, only, even, almost, hardly, nearly, especially, merely

Misleading: Lola *even* sings in the shower.

Clearer: Lola sings *even* in the shower.

Misleading: Sue gave gifts to the winners *tied in red ribbon.*

Clearer: Sue gave the winners gifts *tied in red ribbon.*

Misleading: The tourist bought a pin made by Mexicans *set with opals.*

Clearer: The tourist bought a pin *set with opals* and made by Mexicans.

Or: The tourist bought *an opal pin* made by Mexicans.

Dangling modifiers are words, phrases, or clauses which have no sensible connection with an agent or doer.

Incorrect: Having arrived early, the usher offered April a seat.

Correct: Having arrived early, April was offered a seat by the usher.

Or: The usher offered a seat to April, *who arrived early.*

3.7 FREQUENTLY MISUSED WORDS AND PHRASES

In addition to understanding how the parts of speech express ideas in a sentence, you need to distinguish among certain words and expressions that are often misused. This area of language is known as **diction.**

accept a verb meaning *receive* or *agree to*
except a verb meaning *exclude* or *leave out*
a preposition meaning *excluding*

> • The pledges *accepted* the fraternity's bid.
> • The committee will *except* all late applicants.
> • Ollie, I have all the folders *except* yours.

affect a verb meaning *influence*
effect a verb meaning *cause* or *bring about*
a noun meaning *an influence*

> • Lack of sleep *affects* my judgment.
> • The raise *effected* a change in Lu's attitude.
> • The *effect* on prices brought joy to investors.

already an adverb meaning *previously*
all ready an adjective phrase meaning *completely ready*

> • James has *already* signed this form.
> • Is the hotel staff *all ready* for opening night?

altogether an adverb meaning *entirely*
all together an adjective phrase meaning *in a group*

> • His remarks were *altogether* unusual for so shy a man.
> • The girls are *all together* for Sue's anniversary dinner.

amount a noun referring to *a quantity*
number a noun referring to *things that can be counted*

> • The *amount* of oil in the tank was negligible.
> • The large *number* of guests required extra chairs.

anxious an adjective meaning *concerned or worried*
eager an adjective meaning *looking forward to*

> • Granny Cater is always *anxious* during electrical storms.
> • The audience was *eager* for his concert to begin.

beside a preposition meaning *close to*
besides a preposition meaning *in addition to*

> • *Beside* our canoe paddled ten ducklings.
> • *Besides* our canoe we're taking a tent and sleeping bags.

between a preposition used with *two persons or items*
among a preposition used with *three or more persons or items*

> • I have nephews who are *between* one and two years of age.
> • There were starlings *among* the various other species.

Note: Avoid using *amongst*, which is an outdated form.

bring a verb used when direction is *toward the speaker*
take a verb used when direction is *away from the speaker*

> • Susan usually *brings* her lunch from home on cloudy days.
> • Would you *take* this form to Mona's office?
> • Please *take* the money to the bank and *bring* me a receipt.

capital a noun meaning *a key city*
capitol a noun meaning a *legislative building*

> • The Smithsonian Institution is located in the nation's *capital*.
> • Take the bus stop to the left of the *Capitol*.

complement a verb meaning *make complete*
compliment a verb meaning *congratulate*

> • A bright tie *complements* a somber business suit.
> • Rob *complimented* Aunt Ethel on her sprightly two-step.

healthy an adjective meaning *having health*
healthful an adjective meaning *bringing or causing health*

> • *Healthy* skin requires protection from the sun.
> • Raisins and nuts are a *healthful* snack.

imply a verb meaning *suggest or hint*
infer a verb meaning *deduce or conclude*

> • The watchman *implied* that the hall is haunted.
> • I *inferred* from his frown that he chose to be alone.

its a possessive pronoun denoting *ownership*
it's a contraction of the pronoun *it* and the verb *is*

> • The speckled puppy wagged *its* tail with glee.
> • I know *it's* here somewhere, Irene.

Note: There is no such word as its'.

lay a transitive verb meaning *place* (The principal parts of *lay* are *lay, laid, laid.*)
lie an intransitive verb meaning *recline* (The principal parts of *lie* are *lie, lay, lain.*)

> • The elderly man *laid* a single coin on the counter.
> • Could Mariel *lie* on this bench for a moment?

Note: *Lay* always takes a direct object. *Lie* never takes an object.

like a preposition denoting *comparison*
as a preposition suggesting *similarity.*
  a conjunction which *introduces a clause.*

> • Luke chose to dress *like* his twin.
> • Ann's mother came disguised *as* a werewolf.
> • *As* Dan was locking his door, the telephone rang.

principal an adjective meaning *main or chief*
  a noun meaning *head of a school*
principle a noun meaning *law, doctrine, truth, or belief*

> • Rent is our *principal* cost
> • Mrs. Bessinger accepted the job as assistant *principal.*
> • Mr. Coonse explained the *principle* of capillarity.

set a transitive verb meaning *put or place* (The principal parts of *set* are *set, set, set.*)
sit an intransitive verb meaning *take a seat* (The principal parts of *sit* are *sit, sat, sat.*)

> • Lou *set* your tape player on the car seat.
> • The doll is *sitting* in its own tiny rocking chair.

Note: *Set* always takes a direct object. *Sit* never takes an object.

than a conjunction used after the *comparative degree of an adjective*
then an adverb used to signify *next or at the same time*

> • They are later *than* usual.
> • We will eat dinner; *then* we will look at your album.

their a *possessive pronoun*
there an adverb indicating *place*
they're a contraction of the pronoun *they* and the verb *are*

> • The trios want *their* names on the program.
> • We put greenery here and *there* among the candles.
> • *They're* coming to see us next weekend, Dad.

3.8 ACCEPTABLE AND UNACCEPTABLE EXPRESSIONS

all right, *not* alright
  All right, I'm ready for a Scrabble match.

anywhere, *not* anywheres
  Put that trunk *anywhere* that it will fit.

aren't or **isn't,** *not* ain't
  Aren't you interested in drawing, Stan?
  This fillet *isn't* what I ordered.

because of, *not* due to
  Father's plane is delayed *because of* fog.

could've, should've, would've, *not* could of, should of, would of
  The officer *should've* identified himself.

enthusiastic, *not* enthused
  My cousins are *enthusiastic* about the auction.

kind of, *not* kind of a
  What *kind of* dog is a shar pei?

off, *not* off of
  I left the telephone *off* the hook temporarily.

reason is that or **because,** *not* reason is because
  The *reason* for our refusal *is that* we are overbooked.
or We refuse *because* we're overbooked.

regardless, *not* irregardless
  Sheryl wants the machine, *regardless* of the cost.

PUNCTUATION AND CAPITALIZATION

4.1   **P**unctuation *refers to the set of symbols used in writing to separate elements and clarify meaning. These marks replace the body language, voice stress, gestures, and facial expressions used in speech. In written language correct punctuation is as necessary as the right words. Symbols and words work together to produce clear, effective, meaningful communication.*

Punctuation performs the following functions:

- separates units
- divides thoughts
- clarifies meaning

Note how punctuation can affect and alter meanings in these examples:

- Our English class thinks Mr. Ames is effective.
- Our English class, thinks Mr. Ames, is effective.
- Our English class thinks; Mr. Ames is effective.

4.2   The following sections illustrate the types and uses of punctuation marks:

• the period	• the colon
• the comma	• the apostrophe
• the semicolon	• quotation marks

4.3   The **period (.)** is used in these situations:

A. at the end of a sentence that makes a statement or gives a command:
- The Gants' woodpile is located between two pine trees.
- Bring in an armload of kindling before supper, James.

B. after an initial or an abbreviation:
- We saw *Dr.* and *Mrs.* Frank G. Wilson at the Charleston festival.
- Tom, *J.W.*, and Meredith are my son's three best friends.
- Even *Gov.* Martin made an attempt to improve education.

C. as a decimal point:
- Will $14.95 be enough to cover lunch expenses?
- The cost is 4.5% above last year's estimate.
- France is spending 24.5 million dollars on improvements.

D. as ellipsis marks to indicate omission in direct quotation:
  - Thoreau said, "Books must be read as deliberately . . . as they were written."
  - President Johnson agreed with Aristotle: "Poverty is the parent of revolution . . . ."

Note: In the last example the *ellipsis* is followed by a period to end the sentence.

E. after numbers and letters in an outline:
  I. Legends
   A. Paul Bunyan
   B. Joe Magarac
   C. Pecos Bill
   D. Calamity Jane
  II. Myths
   A. Pandora
   B. Prometheus
   C. Ariadne

A Great Communicator

When he was twenty years old, Mordecai Richler did what many other young Canadians did — he left Canada and went to England. Twenty years later he returned to Canada. During that time he had written several highly praised novels. One of them, *The Apprenticeship of Duddy Kravitz*, was made into a movie; Richler wrote the screenplay, which was nominated for an Academy Award. This book, like several others Richler has written, draws upon his background of growing up in the Jewish section of Montreal. Besides novels, Richler has written several collections of essays and two very successful children's books, *Jacob Two-Two and the Hooded Fang* and *Jacob Two-Two and the Dinosaur*. Although he is often critical of Canadian society, his outrageous sense of humor has earned him success in his native land as well as the United States and Britain.

4.4 The **comma (,)** signals the reader when to pause and how to divide units of thought. Its uses include:

A. separation of three or more words, phrases, or clauses in a series:
- Richard ordered a *tent, climbing equipment, and more rope.*
- I need *to turn the rug, to air the drapes, and to vacuum.*
- *Who is speaking, who is spoken to, and what is said* are important considerations to a journalist.

Note: The last comma separating items in a series is often omitted, but for clarity's sake, it should be included, as illustrated by this example:

We stocked up on *juice, macaroni and cheese.*

Because *macaroni* and *cheese* can be purchased separately or together, a comma should be included to separate the last two items in the series.

B. separation of coordinate adjectives or adjectives of equal rank that precede a noun and are not joined by a conjunction:
- Setters and spaniels dislike *loud, piercing* noises.
- These *slow, easy* rhythms make good dance music.

Note: In contrast to coordinate adjectives, **cumulative adjectives** are modifiers that require a particular order. Because they are unequal in value they are not separated by a comma. To differentiate between coordinate and cumulative adjectives, insert *and* between the words in question. If the *and* indicates that the words are equal in importance, use a comma to separate them.

- Sarah's *new business* manager has been a great help.
- Mattie should choose a *long winter* jacket and *some snow* boots.

C. setting off words or phrases:
- The upstairs closet, *my favorite hiding place,* is full. (appositive)
- In the pocket Jan found *not only* his key, *but also* some gum drops. (contrasting expressions joined by *not only . . . but also*)
- *Overhead,* the stunt pilot made lazy loops. (introductory adverb)
- *To answer that question,* we needed a few more facts. (introductory infinitive)
- *Swimming to the top,* the guppy nibbled at bits of bread. (introductory participial phrase)
- *After painting,* the Burgesses aired out the house. (introductory prepositional phrase)

Note: In the last example, there is no structural reason to set off a prepositional phrase of fewer than four words. However, the absence of a comma could cause confusion.

D. separating clauses:
- *Before you turn off the computer,* save your work. (introductory adverb clause)
- *When I leave,* Tony will take my place at the booth. (introductory adverb clause)
- Our convertible has two doors, *but* our sedan has four. (independent clauses joined by a coordinating conjunction)
- He laughed, *"I knew it all along!"* (a direct quotation at the end of a sentence)
- *"You left your scarf on the front seat,"* the bus driver yelled. (a direct quotation at the beginning of a sentence)
- *"This,"* Father exclaimed, *"is a great occasion!"* (a direct quotation that is interrupted)

E. setting off parenthetical phrases:
- Oh, *by the way,* I have to fly to Phoenix in May.
- The alternative route, *on the other hand,* is faster and safer.
- *Yes,* Jason and Tom did mention their plans before they left.
- *Well,* the news certainly surprised Lance!
- It was, *on the whole,* a challenging evening.
- You are, *I assume,* the first volunteer.

F. setting off tag questions:
- The new terminal is certainly long, *isn't it?*
- You two are eager to begin, *aren't you?*

G. separating parts of an elliptical sentence:
- The French Club wanted a car wash; the Beta Club, a magazine sale.
- Some people prefer hot sauce on their barbeque; others, cole slaw and onions.

Note: The comma replaces the implied verb *wanted* in the second clause in the first example. In the second example, *prefer* is deleted from the second clause.

H. setting off proper nouns in direct address:
- Gee, *Ann-Louise,* I don't think you should sell the machine.
- Let me hear from you when you reach home, *Phil.*

I. separating nonrestrictive clauses or clauses which are not essential to the meaning of the sentence:
- Amos, *who sailed on the lake last summer,* bought a new sailboard.
- The society installed officers, *who were elected last week.*

Note: Omission of the comma in the last sentence would imply that officers had been elected at more than one time and that the ones who were elected last week were singled out for installation.

J. setting off contrasting expressions:
- I ordered chopped kielbasa, *not frankfurters.*
- This is Friday, *not Thursday.*

K. separating parts of a date:
- *Monday, January 12,* will be soon enough, Phyllis.
- Twyla was born on *April 4, 1964,* and my niece was born the next day.

L. separating parts of a reference:
- I noted a reference from *Volume I, Chapter 26, page 773.*
- Maybe you should reread *page 26, section b, paragraph 22.*

M. separating geographical names which have several parts:
- The Brontë children grew up at *Haworth, Yorkshire, England.*
- During the war my father found work in *Wilmington, Delaware.*

N. separating titles after a name:
- Our speaker this evening is Rolf McNeil, *Jr., Ph.D.*
- Allison Ward, *M.D.,* works as coordinator of emergency medicine.

O. separating parts of an address:
- Send your reply to *Personnel, Conley Associates, Van Buren Plaza, Springport, Rhode Island   66381.*
- Do you still live at *9801-B Spring Avenue, Newton, Massachusetts 02195?*

Note: There is not a comma separating state and zip code, but there is an extra space between them.

P. separating standard parts of a letter:
- Dear Aunt Nancy, (salutation)
- Affectionately yours, (complimentary close)

Note: For more information about correct letter form, refer to Chapter 8

Q. separating parts of numbers larger than three digits:
- The herdsman counted *4,281* sheep to be shorn.
- Deda read that *328,663,000* bottles were sold in one year.

Note: Certain numbers do not require commas, such as zip codes, telephone numbers, page numbers, or serial numbers.

- The zip code for Jacksonville, Illinois, is *62650.*
- For information call *1-800-555-1212.*
- Look on page *2421* in the Registry of Patents.
- My social security number is *241-68-2312.*

4.5   The **semicolon** (;) serves in several capacities:

A. to separate items in a series in which there are commas:
- Sybil should not eat *popcorn, which is hard on her braces; strawberries, which give her hives; or heavily spiced food.*
- The stories were written by *Edgar Allan Poe, a master of suspense; Mark Twain, the great American humorist; and several authors I did not know.*

B. to separate independent clauses when the clauses contain commas:
- *Mr. Miller is right, Matt;* the issue is freedom of the press.
- *The menu lists broccoli, beets, and fruit salad;* I want all three.

C. to separate independent clauses when there is no conjunction:
- The gravy became gummy; the beverages warmed to room temperature.
- Ginny prefers dancing to slow music; Yvette likes quick melodies.

D. to separate a conjunctive adverb or a transitional expression from the preceding clause. Examples include:

accordingly, also, anyhow, as a result, at this time, besides, consequently, finally, first, for example, for instance, furthermore, hence, however, in addition, in conclusion, indeed, in fact, instead, likewise, moreover, namely, nevertheless, on the other hand, otherwise, second, similarly, still, that is, then, therefore, thus

- Judy's recipe lists pine nuts; *however,* I plan to substitute pecans.
- Tonette reserved the tape; *therefore,* Stan must wait his turn.
- Mattie searched each shelf; *as a result,* she was late for the meeting.

Note: Place a comma after a conjunctive adverb or transitional expression if either is followed by an independent clause.

E. to introduce a series begun by **for example** or **namely:**
- Players need three vital skills; *namely,* speed, accuracy, and training.
- Stained glass work requires specialized materials; *for example,* copper stripping, etching liquid, and a glass cutter.

"Going back to my student days, the U.S. has always been something we both loved and resented. Loved, because the novels we consumed with appetite, the intellectual as well as the pop cultural ideas that shaped us, were largely American-made. Resented because to visit New York, brimming with goodwill, and to proffer a Canadian $10 bill was to be told, 'What's that, kid, Monopoly money?' "

—from *Home Sweet Home*
by Mordecai Richler

4.6 The **colon (:)** serves several purposes:

A. the separation of units of time:
- Convocation begins at *11:00* and ends at *11:50*.
- On a twenty-four hour clock, *2:15* p.m. is written as *14:15*.

B. the separation of chapter and verse in a Biblical quotation, a reference to a periodical, or a subtitle:
- At the service, Martin read *Genesis 5:1-4*.
- Mr. McNair framed a copy of *II Kings 12:5-6*.
- The *Readers' Guide* lists *Popular Science 16:23-26*.
- Dad bought a copy of *Walker's Guide to Plants: How to Raise Perennials*.

Note: The second example is read "second Kings twelve, five through six." In the third example, the numbers indicate volume and pages and are read "volume sixteen, pages 23-26." (See Chapter 10 for more information on *The Readers' Guide to Periodical Literature.)*

C. the introduction of a lengthy series:
- The editorial underscored our concerns: *clean air, business opportunities, and better public service for the elderly.*
- Could we order the following: *another bumper, flashers and signal lights, a stronger antenna, and a mirror?*

D. the introduction of an extended appositive or explanation:
- Jefferson's *Testament of Freedom* asserts one major philosophy: *human beings are accorded freedom at birth.*
- This is an unusual request: *a desk of your own near a window.*

"The Yellowknife Golf Club, a typical act of north-of-sixty defiance, has no grass, but is rooted in sand and rock. Until 1947, it was also without a clubhouse. Then an American DC-3 transport crash landed on the course, sluing through the jack pines just short of the airport. It was immediately converted into the golf course's first amenity. It filled that social office until 1952, when an American order recalled DC-3s everywhere. Along came some USAF personnel to screw an engine onto the clubhouse and fly it into battle in Korea."

— from *Home Sweet Home*
by Mordecai Richler

4.7 The **apostrophe (')** has three basic uses:

A. to show possession:
- Mr. Hutto painted *Dad's* car. (singular possession)
- My *sister-in-law's* cat had seven brindle kittens. (singular possession of a compound noun)
- The professor has a problem remembering the *girls'* names. (plural possession of regular nouns)
- *Children's* coats and hats are on the mezzanine. (plural possession of irregular nouns)

B. to indicate omission in a contraction or date:
- Some *can't* get through the snow and ice. (indicates the elision of *can* and *not* and the resulting loss of *n* and *o*)
- The spirit of the *'49ers* is still alive at Sutter's Mill. (indicates the omission of *1800* from the date *1849*)
- Another name for *jack-o'-lantern* is *will-o'-the-wisp*. (indicates the loss of the *f* in *of*)

Note: For more information about contractions, see Chapter 5.

C. to form plurals of letters, symbols and words named as words:
- I wonder why Sheila dots her *i*'s and *j*'s with tiny circles.
- All three notes contain @ 's.
- The §'s stand for sections.
- His confession was riddled with *but*'s and *however*'s.

Note: To avoid confusion, an apostrophe may be used for the plural of numbers.

- Why do all area codes contain *0*'s or *1*'s?

4.8 **Quotation marks (" ")** are always used in pairs and function as follows:

A. to set off direct quotations:
- *"You can't catch me!"* sneered the hare to the tortoise.
- *"Let that be a lesson to you,"* he sighed, *"or you will have to learn the hard way."*

Note: Commas and periods are *always* placed inside the quotation marks, while colons and semicolons belong outside. Other marks of punctuation, including the question mark and the exclamation point, go inside if they apply only to the element that is quoted. If they conclude the overall sentence, they belong outside. For example:

- Jonathan quoted *"Who Am I?"* (The title of the poem is the question.)
- Did the trio sing *"Bye, Bye Blackbird"*? (The title is only a part of the whole question.)

B. to set off a quotation within a quotation, use single quotation marks:
- The boy wrote, "Mr. Lincoln said, 'As I would not be a slave, so I would not be a master. . . .' "
- "The fish said, 'My name is Tayzanne,' " she read.

C. to set off defined or slang words:
- Mr. Roth demonstrated his *"sympathy"* by firing Bobby's mother.
- The Army was not amused by his brand of *"loyalty."*
- If I had my *"druthers,"* I would choose fewer workdays and more holidays.

D. to set off titles to songs, short stories, book chapters, short poems, essays, television program episodes, and articles in magazines or newspapers:
- The children sang "I'm a Little Teapot" and recited "The Calliope."
- This column quotes "A Day to Remember" from the *Readers' Digest.*

Note: The name of the magazine is italicized or, if written in longhand, underlined.

A Great Communicator

Sequoya was a great native American — a Cherokee, who was born in the mid-18th century and died in 1843. Before Sequoya, the Cherokee had no written language. Sequoya was concerned that many Cherokee customs and traditions were not permanently recorded. To prevent their loss, he invented a writing system for the Cherokee language, a project which took twelve years. He subsequently used this system to record Cherokee history, and books and newspapers in the Cherokee language. Today words from Indian languages permeate American English. The Sequoia trees and the Sequoia National Park, for example, are named for Sequoya himself. Countless place names throughout the country are Indian in origin — Mississippi, Illinois, Iowa, Minnesota, to list a few. Toboggan is an Indian word, as is moccasin. Native animals and plants often retain their Indian names, including raccoon, opossum, moose, skunk, woodchuck, hickory, squash, pecan, and potato.

4.9 ADDITIONAL MARKS OF PUNCTUATION

SYMBOL	USAGE	EXAMPLE
asterisk (*)	Indicates that additional information is given.	See below.*
brackets ([ ])	Sets off explanatory material added to a writer's words.	In his autobiography [*My Other Lives*], he wrote about Julia.
dash (—)	Indicates an abrupt change of thought. Note: To make a dash on a typewriter, use two hyphens.	Mother promises — *can you believe it* — a raise in our allowance.
exclamation point (!)	Expresses strong feeling.	Help! I can't swim!
hyphen (-)	Joins the elements of a compound word;	Mr. Loren Thornfield, the *editor-in-chief*, will speak at noon.
	separates compound numbers twenty-one through ninety-nine;	The city council approved an addition of *sixty-one* units.
	separates fractions which are used as adjectives;	The water gauge is nearly *three-fourths* full.
	attaches a prefix, such as anti-, mid-, pre-, post-, ex-, ante-, and un- to proper nouns;	Senator Allran addressed an assembly concerning *un-American* sentiments in the news.
	connects compound modifiers.	So many *bright-eyed four-legged* friends need homes!
parentheses (( ))	Encloses extra material that interrupts a sentence,	Geoffrey Chaucer *(1340-1400)* is sometimes called the father of English.
	encloses the area code in a telephone number.	I dialed *(800)* 555-4078.
question mark (?)	Punctuates a direct question.	What is the reason for his disappearance?
slash (/)	Separates parts of fractions,	*2/3; 11/16*
	separates parts of a choice,	*and/or; Mr./Mrs./Miss/Ms.*
	in abbreviations,	*c/o* (in care of)
	to replace *per.*	*mi./hr.; words/min.; feet/sec.*

underlining (_)	Denotes titles of books, plays, long poems, periodicals, pamphlets, movies, published speeches, television and radio programs, and visual art, as well as names of ships and foreign phrases. Also indicates stress or emphasis. Note: Underlining replaces printed italics.	The flight attendant offered me a choice of <u>Time</u>, <u>Reader's Digest</u>, or an abandoned copy of <u>Great American Short Stories</u>. We accept <u>no</u> checks.

4.10 CAPITALIZATION RULES

RULE	EXAMPLE
First person singular pronoun: I	Danielle and *I* raked and pruned as we had planned.
First word in a sentence	*These* aren't my gloves, Miss Sebastian.
Independent clauses in a list	Mr. Barger made three promises: (1) *He* would finish the season; (2) *His* aide would provide the committee with facts; and (3) *No* one would be disappointed.
Direct quotation	Claire Andrews urged, "*Please* fill these out and return them within the month."
Independent clause following a colon	The board agreed on one change: *A* manager will assume responsibility for publicity.
First word in a complimentary close or salutation	*Sincerely* yours, *Yours* truly, *Dear* Sirs:
Major words in a title: book, play, movie, song Note: Do not capitalize articles (a, an, the) or prepositions, except when they come first or last in a title or are more than four letters. Note: Do not capitalize *the* before the names of newspapers or magazines.	<u>*For Whom the Bell Tolls*</u> <u>*Crime and Punishment*</u> <u>*Rebel Without a Cause*</u> <u>*A Passage to India*</u> the *New York Times*, the *Washington Post*
The first word in a line of of poetry. Note: When a single line is carried over, it is not capitalized.	"*Home* is the place where, when you have to go there, *They* have to take you in."

Names and titles of people	*Professor* McLeod, *Doctors* St. John and Chou, *Archbishop* Fowles, *Ensign* Beach, *Sir* Alec Guinness, *Rabbi* Stern, *Madam* Pompadour, *Father* Hanes, *Governor* Ingle, *Senator* Ray, *Vice-Admiral* O'Sullivan.
Note: Titles of relatives preceded by a possessive word are not capitalized.	*Mother*, my aunt, *Grandmother* Rossi
Abbreviated titles, whether before or after names	*Sgt.* Abercrombie; Lord Avery, *Esq.*; Mayor Julian Adams, *III*
Descriptive titles	William *the Conqueror*, Alexander *the Great*
Abbreviations or acronyms (words composed of the first letters of a phrase)	*NAACP, IRS, WHKY, AIDS, UNICEF, R.S.V.P., D.D.S., L.P.N., Ed.D., Mme.*
Nouns followed by a number	*Act* V, *Scene* 2, *Line* 88; *Room* 210; *History* 101-102; *Hymn* 145; *Aisle* 6; *Laboratory* D
Substitute nouns	The *Company* announced dividends. (AT&T)
Personified nouns	At Gettysburg the *Blue* and the *Gray* fought valiantly. (the Union and the Confederate armies)
Races, nationalities, languages	*Caucasian, Swahili, Urdu, Tagalog*
Note: This rule applies to proper adjectives as well as nouns.	*English, French, Vietnamese, Mongolian*
Buildings and monuments	the *Empire State Building*, the *World Trade Center*, the *Washington Monument*
Documents	the *Magna Charta*, the *Constitution*, the *Mayflower Compact*
Religious names	*Genesis, Moses*, the *Great Spirit*, the *Tao*, the *New Testament*, the *Holy See*, *Brahma*, the *Talmud*, *Allah*, *Muslims*, the *Koran*, the *Buddha*
Geographical names: cities, avenues, countries, bodies of water, celestial bodies	*Lake James*, the *Chattahoochee River*, *Lookout Dam*, *Frenchman's Reef*, *Fifth Avenue*, *Sri Lanka*, *County Mayo*, *Mount McKinley*, the *West*, *Saturn*, the *North Star*, *Ursa Minor*, west of *San Antonio*
Note: Do not capitalize north, south, east, or west when used to name directions.	
Brand names and names of companies	*Band-Aid, Polaroid, Northwestern Bank, R.J. Reynolds, Metro-Goldwyn-Mayer*

| Holidays, days, and months of the calendar | *Friday, February, Columbus Day, Martin Luther King Day, American Education Week, Hannukah* |
| Note: Do not capitalize the seasons. | fall, summer, autumn, spring |

| Governmental bodies | *Superior Court, Ways* and *Means Committee* |

| School courses, but not subjects | *Modern Civilization, Weight-lifting*, algebra |

| Laws | the *Stamp Act*, the *Fourteenth Amendment* |

| Historical eras and events | *D-Day*, the *Battle* of the *Bulge*, the *Stock Market Crash* of 1929, the *Bronze Age*, *Renaissance* |

| Organizations and clubs | *Royal Order of Moose, Girl Guides*, the *Parent-Teacher Organization, Veterans of Foreign Wars, Knights of Columbus*, the *Elks* |

| Specific vehicles | the *Challenger, Apollo II*, the *Titanic*, the *Concorde*, a *Comet* sedan, the *Silver Chief* |

"Now! I have taken your heart;
I just took your breath.
Your heart has just entered into me:
I have just taken your thought.
Change your heart, and put it into the very middle
of my soul!"
> — *A love incantation translated from*
> *Sequoya's Cherokee written language*

SPELLING

5.1 The **English language** grew from a long history of power struggles. After the Angles and Saxons drove the Celts from their strongholds in England in the Fifth Century, the Celtic language ceased to be used in the major cities of England. **Anglo-Saxon** or **Old English** grammar became the basis upon which the modern English language formed.

When William the Conqueror of France invaded in 1066, two influential languages added a wealth of vocabulary — the French of the nobles and the Latin of church officials and courts of law. By 1385, when Geoffrey Chaucer was writing his Canterbury Tales, the language of England, called **Middle English,** possessed a blend of terms from three sources — Anglo-Saxon, French, and Latin.

Other periods of growth and development brought new vocabulary, such as Latin and Greek words during the Renaissance; the Germans and the Japanese have contributed, for example, with ersatz, kindergarten, kimono, and honcho. When English settlers and explorers brought their language to the New World, **American English** evolved into a separate branch with the addition of Native American terminology and Spanish, Portuguese, Cajun, Gullah, and Creole words, such as moccasin, rodeo, tornado, gumbo, and goober.

As English-speaking nations grow, their need for language continues. The expansion never stops as people find words to describe new inventions and altered social situations, such as fiber optics, microwave, palimony, and condominium. However, as terms are added to the language, others fall into disuse, first as archaic and ultimately as obsolete language, for example, names for ancient weapons, armor, tools, and architecture, such as hauberk, greaves, adze, dibble, and portcullis. Like a living plant, the language adapts itself to the environment.

5.2 When children first learn to speak English, they use mostly **Anglo-Saxon** derivatives such as foot, hand; cow, pig; shirt, shoe; plate, cup; stop, go; fast, slow; in, out; I, you.

These short, monosyllabic terms provide a primitive vocabulary for simple communication needs. By the time children reach school, they have begun adding more complicated terms from Latin and French, such as absence, presence; poultry, beef; entrance, exit. *Consequently their vocabulary is capable of answering more sophisticated communication needs.*

The **reading vocabulary** *of most human beings is the largest list of known words, followed in descending order by the* **listening, speaking,** *and* **writing vocabularies.** *Because a literate person must visualize a word in order to write it, there are often errors during a first attempt at written vocabulary, for example, a mistake in a* **homonym,** *such as* aught *for* ought *or* bear *for* bare. *Therefore, spelling is an essential adjunct to the mastery of composition.*

5.3　　**Spelling** *was not a problem for early writers until the invention of the printing press. Printers began to systematize spelling, or orthography, as it is more properly known. William Caxton's press, which began production of printed texts in England around 1475, did more to* **standardize** *English words than any teacher or grammarian. Because the words that he printed came from varied sources, they follow many sets of rules. It is this rich assortment of linguistic patterns that challenges the speller of English today.*

The following list of English spellings for a single sound gives you some idea of the variety of **letter combinations** *which makes standardized phonetic spelling impossible.*

a	**c**at, pl**ai**d, l**au**gh
aw	c**a**ll, **au**thorize, p**aw**, f**ough**t, br**oa**d
ay	l**a**ke, tr**ai**n, g**au**ge, gr**ay**, b**ei**ge, fr**eigh**t, br**ea**k, v**ei**l, bouqu**et**, ob**ey**
ch	**c**ello, **ch**ap, for**t**une, fe**tch**, inven**ti**on
eh	m**a**ny, **ae**sthetic, s**ai**d, s**ay**s, s**e**ll, r**ea**d, h**ei**r, l**eo**pard, fri**e**nd, b**u**ry, g**ue**ss
ee	C**ae**sar, qu**ay**, th**e**, p**ea**ch, tr**ee**, c**ei**ling, p**eo**ple, k**ey**, mach**i**ne, y**ie**ld, chass**is**, am**oe**ba
er	**ear**th, p**er**, chauff**eur**, **err**, s**ir**, w**or**sen, c**our**age, c**ur**, zeph**yr**
f	**f**air, sta**ff**, tou**gh**, pam**ph**let
g	**g**rain, a**gg**regate, **gh**ost, ro**gue**

53

h	**h**elp, **wh**o
ih	ba**gg**age, pr**e**tty, b**ee**n, forf**ei**t, tr**i**p, marr**ia**ge, misch**ie**f, w**o**men, b**u**sy, b**ui**ld, s**y**stem
i	**ai**sle, **aye,** kal**ei**doscope, g**ey**ser, p**i**pe, p**ie,** th**igh,** b**uy**er, sp**y, r**y**e**
j	gra**d**ual, ri**dg**e, sol**di**er, ga**g**e, exa**gg**erate
k	**c**ape, a**cc**ord, a**cqu**aint, bis**c**uit, **k**it, **ch**oral, si**ck,** li**q**uid, sa**cque,** Ira**q**
m	ta**m**e, to**mb,** su**mm**it, hy**mn**
n	fi**n**e, ru**nn**er, **gn**at, **kn**it, **pn**eumatic
ng	ra**ng,** dri**nk,** to**ngue**
oh	rest**au**rant, band**eau, s**ew,** c**oo**perate, s**oa**p, t**oe, oh,** br**oo**ch, dep**o**t, s**ou**l, r**ow**
oi	c**oi**l, pl**oy,** b**uoy**ant
oo	b**oo**k, c**ou**ld, p**u**t
oo	man**eu**ver, wh**o,** can**oe,** f**oo**l, tr**ou**pe, fl**u**ke, bl**ue,** s**ui**t
ow	r**ou**t, b**ough,** c**ow**
r	ca**r**t, ca**rr**y, **rh**ythm, **wr**iter
s	ra**c**e, **ps**ychic, tea**s**e, **sc**enic, **sch**ism, pa**ss,** gli**st**en
sh	o**c**ean, offi**c**ial, ma**sh, sch**nauzer, con**sci**ence, propul**si**on, ti**ss**ue, aggre**ssi**on, pa**ti**ent
t	chopp**ed, pt**omaine, si**t, th**yme, pat**t**er
u	be**au**tify, f**eu**dal, f**ew, vi**ew**er, t**u**ne
uh	s**ea**son, d**oe**s, bl**oo**d, t**ou**ch, f**u**nny
y	**u**nion, halleluj**ah, Y**ule
z	doe**s,** sci**ss**ors, **x**ylophone, ra**z**e, fi**zz**y
zh	gara**g**e, mea**s**ure, divi**si**on, vi**zi**er, a**z**ure

5.4 HOW TO IMPROVE YOUR SPELLING

- Pay attention to the **arrangement of letters** in any new word you meet. Write it several times until you feel comfortable with it.
- **Pronounce** words carefully. Some words are misspelled because they are mispronounced, such as *united, arctic, government, probably, supposedly, precipitation,* and *chimney.*
- Keep a **mental list** of words that stump you. Review your list from time to time. Watch for these words in your writing.
- **Proofread** carefully. Read your work from end to

beginning, word by word, so that you will concentrate on spelling and not on composition. Trade papers with someone else for a second opinion.

- Keep a **dictionary** handy at your work place and refer to it whenever the spelling of a word seems questionable.
- If you have no dictionary, **test** a word by writing it in both longhand and block or printed letters.
- Be on the alert for English words from **foreign sources,** which may follow a different set of rules, for example; *rajah, chaise longue, khaki, lei, kayak, carafe, chassis, sukiyaki, phenomena,* and *samovar.*
- Familiarize yourself with the various ways to spell a single **sound,** for example, *weigh* and *say.*
- Learn the **rules** that govern spelling. Practice the **exceptions** until you have memorized them.

5.5 BASIC SPELLING RULES

This list covers the most useful patterns of spelling. However, most **rules** have their **exceptions.** These violations of standard practice must be memorized — there is no other way to conquer them. (Note: For rules governing plural nouns, refer to Chapter 1.)

A. The **ie / ei** rule. The diphthong **ie** is predominant.

achieve	fiend	mien	shield
ancient	fierce	mischief	shriek
believe	fiery	mischievous	siege
bier	financier	niece	sieve
brief	friendly	orient	species
brier	frontier	piece	thief
cashier	grief	piedmont	thievery
chief	handkerchief	pier	view
convenient	hieroglyphics	pierce	wield
diesel	liege	priest	yield
diet	lien	relieve	
field	lieutenant	retrieve	

B. Its counterpart, **ei,** is used after c:

ceiling	conceive	perceive	receive
conceit	deceit	receipt	

and in certain exceptions, such as words that contain an **ay** sound:

beige	feint	neigh	sleigh
chow mein	freight	obeisance	veil
eight	heinous	reign	vein
eighteen	heir	reindeer	weigh
eighty	inveigh	seine	weight
feign	neighbor	skein	

CHAPTER 5

caffein or caffeine	forfeit	leisure	seizure
counterfeit	heifer	neither	sheik
either	height	protein	their
feisty	kaleidoscope	seize	weird
foreign			

or when **c** is pronounced **sh:**

ancient	deficiency	prescient
conscience	efficient	sufficient

C. The **ceed** / **cede** rule. The root word -cede is the more common.

accede	cede	intercede	recede
antecedent	concede	precede	secede

The root word -ceed appears in three examples:

exceed	proceed	succeed

EXCEPTION:
supersede

D. Adding **prefixes** to a root word. The root word usually remains the same:

admit	depose	malcontent	postnasal
ambidextrous	diameter	misconstrue	preternatural
antedate	disconnect	misspell	quadriplegia
antidote	expressive	monorail	reconstitute
approval	extraterrestrial	multiply	semicircle
archbishop	forerunner	offspring	submarine
arise	hydrophobic	overlook	subterfuge
bejewel	hypodermic	paramount	superhuman
bisect	interscholastic	paraphrase	suppress
circumference	income	pericardium	telepathy
compress	irreverent	perspire	transcontinental
counteract	juxtaposition	phonograph	unchanging

EXCEPTIONS:

biennial	exigent	perennial

E. Adding **suffixes** to a root word. There are several rules governing the addition of an ending. If the word ends in a **consonant plus y** change the **y** to **i** before adding a **suffix.**

city / citified	geometry / geometric	pretty / prettiest
comply / complies	glory / glorious	ready / readily
creamy / creamier	happy / happiness	rely / reliance
defy / defiant	merry / merriment	secretary / secretarial
fortify / fortification	mercy / merciful	vary / variable
fry / fried	ply / pliant	

EXCEPTIONS:

bounty / bounteous	lady / ladylike	sky / skyward
baby / babyhood	shy / shyness	sly / slyly

Note: This rule does not apply to **suffixes beginning with i,** as in

fry / frying	glory / glorying	hurry / hurrying

F. If the word ends in a **vowel plus y,** make no change before adding a **suffix.**

array / arrayed	convey / conveyance	obey / obeyed
boy / boyish	employ / employee	play / playwright
buy / buyer	joy / joyous	way / wayward

EXCEPTIONS:

day / daily	gay / gaily	pay / paid
gay / gaiety	lay / laid	say / said

G. If the word ends in **e**, drop the **e** when adding a **suffix beginning with a vowel.**

bake / baker	pile / piling	seize / seizure
ice / icy	prime / primary	serve / service
irritate / irritable	procure / procurator	style / stylize
live / liven	rate / rated	universe / universal
nerve / nervous		

EXCEPTIONS:

acre / acreage	die / dying	mile / mileage
advantage /	dye / dyeing	notice / noticeable
advantageous	grade / gradient	peace / peaceable
change / changeable	marriage / marriageable	singe / singeing
courage / courageous	fire / fiery	tie / tying

Also words ending in **ee** or **oe,** such as

hoe / hoeing	see / seeing	shoe / shoeing

Note: Words that end in **ce** or **ge** retain the **e** in order to soften the **consonant** sound. Contrast the **g** sound in *prestigious* and *analogous*, and the **c** sound in *advancement* and *practical*. When either **g** or **c** is followed by **i** or **e**, the **consonant** has a soft sound.

H. If the word ends in **e**, make no change before adding a **suffix beginning with a consonant.**

atone / atonement	home / homeward	piece / piecemeal
awe / awesome	love / lovely	plane / planeload
care / careless	nine / ninety	side / sideways
fore / foremost	peace / peaceful	whole / wholeness

EXCEPTIONS:

ample / amply	double / doubly	simple / simplicity
argue /	due / duly	three / thirteen
argumentation	introduce / introduction	true / truly
cone /	judge / judgmental	whole / wholly
coniferous	nine / ninth	wise / wisdom
define / definition		
divide / divisible		

I. If a word ends in a **consonant-vowel-consonant** arrangement and the **stress** falls on the last syllable, double the final letter.

concur / concurrence	pan / panned	remit / remitting
dispel / dispelling	prod / prodded	stop / stopper
forbid / forbidden	regret / regrettable	transfer / transferring

EXCEPTIONS:

Words ending in **x** or **w** —

box / boxing	flaw / flawed	tow / towed
fix / fixer	plow / plowing	wax / waxer

Note: When the **stress** shifts from the final syllable, the letter is not doubled, as in *confer / conference*.

J. If a word ends in a **consonant-vowel-consonant** arrangement and the **stress** does not fall on the last syllable, make no change when adding a **suffix.**

accredit / accredited	debit / debiting	label / labeler
benefit / benefiting	deposit / depositing	lighten / lightened
budget / budgeter	happen / happened	
cancel / canceler		

K. If a word ends in **two or more vowels followed by a consonant,** make no change when adding a **suffix.**

bureau / bureaucrat	four / fourteen	pour / pouring
clear / clearance	heat / heating	rain / rained
droop / drooped	keep / keeper	wait / waited

EXCEPTIONS:
four / forty

L. **-able / -ible** endings. Words ending in these two **suffixes** should be memorized.

-ABLE:

acceptable	considerable	imaginable	peaceable
adaptable	controllable	implacable	personable
advisable	detachable	indispensable	predictable
agreeable	despicable	irritable	probable
applicable	disagreeable	justifiable	reasonable
approachable	distinguishable	knowledgeable	reliable
available	durable	manageable	suitable
believable	employable	memorable	taxable
changeable	excitable	navigable	unbearable
comfortable	fashionable	noticeable	valuable
conceivable			

-IBLE:

accessible	edible	irresistible	possible
admissible	extendible	legible	responsible
audible	feasible	permissible	reversible
compatible	flexible	negligible	sensible
contemptible	forcible	perfectible	terrible
convertible	horrible	permissible	visible
digestible	invincible	plausible	

M. **-cy / sy** endings. Words ending in these two suffixes should be memorized:

-CY:

accuracy	dependency	fallacy	infancy
consistency	efficiency	illiteracy	prophecy
			tendency

-SY:

autopsy	ecstasy	heresy	jealousy
biopsy	embassy	hyprocrisy	pleurisy
courtesy	epilepsy	idiosyncrasy	prophesy
curtsy	fantasy		

N. **-eous, -eus, -ious, -ius, -ous, -uous, -us** endings. Words ending in these seven **suffixes** should be memorized.

-EOUS:

advantageous	erroneous	igneous	nauseous
beauteous	gaseous	instantaneous	righteous
courageous	gorgeous	miscellaneous	simultaneous
courteous			

-EUS:
nucleus

-IOUS:

anxious	delirious	ingenious	repetitious
atrocious	fictitious	laborious	sacrilegious
cautious	flirtatious	mysterious	sagacious
conscientious	furious	officious	superstitious
conscious	gracious	precious	suspicious
contagious	gregarious	rebellious	usurious
curious	harmonious	religious	various
delicious	industrious		

-IUS:

genius	radius

-OUS:

analogous	grievous	ominous	torturous
circuitous	humorous	onerous	tremendous
desirous	mischievous	ponderous	tyrannous
disastrous	momentous	porous	unanimous
enormous	mountainous	ridiculous	viscous
famous	numerous	synonymous	zealous
generous			

-UOUS:

ambiguous	conspicuous	ingenuous	sumptuous
assiduous	continuous	innocuous	tortuous
contemptuous	fatuous	strenuous	

-US:

alumnus	colossus	focus	stimulus
bacillus	consensus	humus	stylus
bonus	cumulus	locus	terminus
circus	discus	prospectus	virus

O. **-efy / ify.** Most English words end in **-ify.** The exceptions are listed below.

-EFY:

liquefy	putrefy	rarefy	stupefy

P. **-ance / -ence.** Most English words end in **-ence.** Common words ending in **-ance** are included in this list:

-ANCE:

abhorrance	arrogance	entrance	performance
abundance	assistance	guidance	radiance
acceptance	attendance	hindrance	significance
acquaintance	brilliance	ignorance	tolerance
admittance	clearance	importance	utterance
allowance	defiance	maintenance	vengeance
appearance	dominance		

Note: This rule applies to the **-ant / ent, -ancy / ency** variations of these words — arrogant, arrogance, dependent, dependency.

9. **-ary / -ery.** Most English words end in **-ary.** The list of words ending in **-ery** is very short.

-ERY:

buttery	distillery	nursery	stationery
cemetery	millinery	scenery	summery
confectionery	monastery	shrubbery	winery
creamery			

EXCEPTION:
penitentiary

R. **-sion / -tion.** Words ending in -sion usually contain a **zh** sound, as in abrasion, fusion, illusion.

EXCEPTIONS:

aggression	discussion	extension	omission
apprehension	dissension	intercession	propulsion
compulsion	expression	mission	

S. Most English words end in **-er.** The following list contains the few that end in **-or.**

-OR:

ambassador	endeavor	mayor	refrigerator
bachelor	governor	mirror	splendor
calculator	honor	operator	sponsor
debtor	humor	professor	visitor
elevator	liquor		

EXCEPTIONS:

beggar	chauffeur	entrepreneur	grammar
burglar	connoisseur	familiar	nuclear
cashier			

T. **-ch / -tch.** Use **-tch** in one-syllable words with a short vowel sound.

-TCH:

batch	hutch	retch	wretch
catch	itch	stretch	watch
crutch	match	thatch	witch
fetch	patch		

Note: This rule applies to compounds of these **root words,** such as attachment, richness, wretchedly.

-CH:

attach	each	peach	sandwich
beach	impeach	reach	screech
detach	leech		

EXCEPTIONS:

cinch	parch	rich	which
lynch	pinch	such	wrench
much			

U. Certain English words have a different **British spelling,** such as:

advertise / advertize	favor / favour	offense / offence
bark / barque	fiber / fibre	pigmy / pygmy
center / centre	fuse / fuze	plow / plough
check / cheque	gray / grey	program / programme
cipher / cypher	jail / gaol	quartet / quartette
connection / connexion	honor / honour	reflection / reflexion
curb / kerb	kilogram / kilogramme	story / storey
defense / defence	lackey / lacquey	sty / stye
draft / draught	medieval / mediaeval	theater / theatre
esthetic / aesthetic	mold / mould	traveler / traveller
exercise / exercize	molt / moult	wagon / waggon

5.6 HOMOPHONES

Homophones or **homonyms,** are words identical in sound but different in meaning. For this reason, they present a special spelling problem. It is often useful to determine which homophone belongs in a particular situation by the **context clues** which surround it. For example: The *hart* (an animal) arched its neck, gazed into the brush, then bounded into the *heart* (the central core) of the forest.

For maximum success with spelling, learn to spell and define each of these pairs of homophones.

Note: The pairs that cause the most confusion are starred (*).

aisle / isle
all / awl
altar / alter
arc / ark
ascent / assent
ate / eight
aught / ought
bail / bale
ball / bawl
bare / bear*
base / bass
be / bee
beach / beech
beat / beet
beau / bow
been / bin
beer / bier
bell / belle
berth / birth
blew / blue
hoard / bored
born / borne*
bough / bow
brake / break
buy / by / bye
canvas / canvass
capital / capitol*
ceiling / sealing
cell / sell
cellar / seller
cent / scent / sent
cereal / serial
choir / quire
chord / cord / cored
clause / claws
coarse / course
colonel / kernel
council / counsel*
creak / creek
currant / current
dear / deer
dew / due

die / dye
done / dun
earn / urn
faint / feint
fair / fare
feat / feet
fir / fur
flea / flee
flew / flu / flue
flour / flower
for / fore / four
foul / fowl
freeze / frieze
gait / gate
grate / great
groan / grown
guessed / guest
hail / hale
hair / hare
hall / haul
hart / heart
heal / heel
hear / here
heard / herd
heir / ere / air
hew / hue
hoes / hose
hole / whole
holy / wholly
hour / our
idle / idol
in / inn
its / it's*
knead / need
knew / new
knot / not
know / no
lain / lane
lead / led*
lessen / lesson
lie / lye
load / lode

made / maid
mail / male
main / mane
manner / manor
mantel / mantle
meat / meet
medal / meddle
metal / mettle
miner / minor*
moan / mown
muscle / mussel
night / knight
none / nun
one / won
pail / pale
pain / pane
pair / pare / pear
pause / paws
peace / piece*
peal / peel
plain / plane*
pore / pour
pray / prey
pride / pried
principal / principle*
profit / prophet
rain / reign / rein
raise / raze
read / reed
real / reel
reek / wreak
rest / wrest
rhyme / rime
right / rite / write / wright
ring / wring
road / rode / rowed
role / roll*
rose / rows / roes
rough / ruff
rye / wry
sail / sale

scene / seen
sea / see
seam / seem
seine / sane
sew / so / sow
sight / site / cite*
slay / sleigh
sleight / slight
soar / sore
sole / soul
some / sum
son / sun
staid / stayed
stair / stare
stake / steak
stationary / stationery*
steal / steel
stile / style
straight / strait
suite / sweet
tail / tale
their / there / they're
threw / through
throne / thrown
to / too / two*
toe / tow
vail / vale / veil
vain / vane / vein
vice / vise*
wade / weighed
waist / waste*
wait / weight
ware / wear
warn / worn
waive / wave
way / weigh
weak / week
which / witch*

5.7 A LIST OF FREQUENTLY MISSPELLED WORDS

absence
acceptance
accessible
accidentally
accommodate
accustom
ache
acknowledgment
acquaint
acquired
adjacent
advantageous
adviser
allot

all right
already
ambitious
analysis
analyze
annihilate
answer
antecedent
antidote
anxious
apparatus
apparent
appreciation
appropriate

arctic
arguing
argument
ascent
athlete
attendance
author
autumn
auxiliary
awful
balloon
beautiful
beggar
beginning

believing
beneficial
breathe
bulletin
business
calendar
catastrophe
cemetery
changeable
chiefly
chocolate
clothes
college
colonel

61

column	forty	naive	restaurant
commission	fourteen	necessarily	rhyming
compatible	gaiety	neighbor	rhythm
competence	gauge	nickel	ridiculous
conceded	ghetto	niece	righteous
conceivable	government	noticeable	sacrilege
conscience	grammar	nuclear	safety
conscious	guaranteed	nuisance	scene
consensus	guard	occasion	scenic
consistent	handicapped	occur	schedule
controlled	harass	occurred	scientific
convenience	height	official	seize
corroborate	hindrance	omitted	sergeant
counterfeit	hoarse	opponent	separate
criticize	hoping	origin	several
current	hygiene	pamphlet	severely
deceive	hypocrisy	parallel	shepherd
defendant	idol	parliament	similar
defense	immediately	pastime	sincerely
descendant	inconsistent	peaceable	strength
descent	inconvenience	perceived	subtle
desperate	ingenious	permanent	succeed
destroy	insistent	perseverance	sufficient
develop	interference	perspire	sugar
difference	irrelevant	petroleum	superintendent
dilemma	irresistible	phenomena	supersede
disappointed	jealousy	physician	symphony
discipline	jeopardize	playwright	tariff
disease	jewelry	possession	technique
disastrous	kerosene	practice	temperament
divine	laboratory	precede	thorough
dominant	leisure	preferable	tournament
efficiency	library	prevalence	trespass
eighty	license	privilege	truly
elementary	lieutenant	probably	twelfth
eligible	lightening	proceed	tyranny
eliminate	literature	procedure	unable
embarrass	livelihood	psychology	unanimous
endeavor	loathsome	pursue	unnecessary
environment	loneliness	query	usage
equipped	lovable	questionnaire	vacuum
essential	maintenance	receipt	valley
exaggeration	management	receive	variety
excessive	maneuver	reciprocal	vengeance
excellent	mathematics	recognition	veteran
existence	medieval	recommendation	vicinity
experience	miniature	reference	villain
familiar	miscellaneous	referred	visible
fatigue	mischievous	regretted	Wednesday
feasible	missile	reign	weird
February	misspell	relevant	wrench
fictitious	mortgage	religious	yield
fiery	municipal	reminisce	zealous
foreign	musician	repetition	

5.8 CONTRACTIONS

Contractions are words or groups of words shortened by the omission of letters *(o'clock* for *of the clock; dep't.** for *department)* or by the elision of two words into one *(isn't* for *is not).* The apostrophe stands for letters which are omitted in the formation of these two types of contractions. Note: Contractions are acceptable in informal writing, such as friendly letters, dialogues, diaries, and personal essays, but should be avoided in formal writing, including research papers or formal essays or speeches.

*Note: This form is gradually being replaced by dept.

Examples of contractions:

n't for not
aren't, can't, couldn't, didn't, doesn't, don't, hadn't, hasn't, haven't, isn't, mightn't, mustn't, shan't (for *shall not),* shouldn't, wasn't, weren't, won't, (for *will not),* wouldn't

's for is
he's, it's, she's, that's, there's, what's, where's, who's

'd for should, would, had
he'd, I'd, it'd, she'd, they'd, we'd, you'd

'll for shall or will
he'll, I'll, it'll, she'll, they'll, we'll, you'll

've for have
I've, they've, we've, you've

' for v
e'er, e'en, ne'er, ne'er-do-well, o'er, Hallowe'en

're for are
they're, we're, you're

't for it
'tis, 'twas, 'twere

'm for am
I'm

o' for of
cat-o'-nine-tails, tam-o'-shanter, will-o'-the-wisp, o'clock, jack-o'-lantern

ABBREVIATIONS

6.1 **Abbreviations** *are shortened words or phrases which speed up the process of communicating. Most abbreviations are used in business or scientific writing, but some have entered our speech, such as* p.c. *and* c.o.d. *Most abbreviations require periods to indicate that the letters stand for words. For example* p.c. *stands for personal computer;* c.o.d. *stands for cash on delivery.*

Some, however, form new words called **acronyms.** *These are written and/or spoken as though they were words, for example* AWOL, UNICEF, NATO, sonar, radar, *and* laser. *Other phrases, such as* non seq., pro tem., *and* et al., *contain whole words as well as abbreviations and require periods only after the abbreviated terms.*

The following examples of **standard abbreviations** *are divided into categories: titles, time, geography, publications and media, business, government and civic organizations, post office, and scientific terms.*

6.2 TITLES

ABBREVIATION	MEANING	EXAMPLE
A. B. (or B. A.)	bachelor of arts	Karl Brooks, **A. B.**
Adm.	admiral	**Adm.** Lacey Cambridge
Amb.	ambassador	**Amb.** Sol Abrams
Atty.	attorney	**Atty.** William R. Houck
Br.	brother	**Br.** Jacques Verlune
B. S.	bachelor of science	Sandra Thompson, **B. S.**
Capt.	captain	**Capt.** Bea Summers
Cmdr.	commander	**Cmdr.** Vic Lestrade
Col.	colonel	**Col.** Jake Allison
Com.	commissioner	**Com.** Jannette Small
D. D.	doctor of divinity	Jerry Campbell, **D. D.**
D. D. S.	doctor of dental surgery	Augusta Leigh, **D. D. S.**
Dr.	doctor	**Dr.** Joseph P. Hester
Ed.	editor	Gary Roberts, **Ed.**
Ed.-in-Chief	editor-in-chief	Rolf Timmons, **Ed.**-in-Chief
Ed. D.	doctor of education	Jeanne Avery, **Ed. D.**
Ens.	ensign	**Ens.** Joan O'Hara
Esq.	esquire	Lord Hanley, **Esq.**
Fr.	father	**Fr.** Ralph Davies
Gen.	general	**Gen.** Timothy A. Jones, Jr.
Gov.	governor	**Gov.** James Houser
Hon.	honorable	**Hon.** Thurgood Marshall
Jr.	junior	Rayford Spence, **Jr.**
Ll. D.	doctor of laws	Trevor Hampton, **Ll. D.**
Lt.	lieutenant	**Lt.** Jean Wilson
Lt. Col.	lieutenant colonel	**Lt. Col.** A. T. Wyatt
Lt., j.g.	lt., junior grade	**Lt.** Art Baker, **j.g.**
M. A.	master of arts	Juan Tomas Gonzales, **M. A.**

M. B. A.	master of business administration	Vince Lefler, **M. B. A.**
M. D.	medical doctor	Jacky Levine, **M. D.**

Note: When M. D. follows a name, **Dr.** is not used before the name. The reverse is also true.

M. F. A.	master of fine arts	Martha Maynard, **M. F. A.**
M. S.	master of science	Etta Mason, **M. S.**
Maj.	major	**Maj.** Tonya King
Maj. Gen.	major general	**Maj. Gen.** Lawrence Jett, III
Messrs.	plural of **Mr.**	**Messrs.** Bart, Long, and Miles
Mme.	madam or madame	**Mme.** Annette Duval
Mmes.	plural of **Mme.** or **Mrs.**	**Mmes.** Renoir and Dubois
M. P.	member of parliament	Charles Thackeray, **M. P.**
Mr.	mister	**Mr.** Glenn C. Little
Mrs.	mistress	**Mrs.** Sarah Whisnant
Ms.	an adult woman	**Ms.** Katrina Brown
Msgr.	monsignor	**Msgr.** Paul Mueller
M. Sgt.	master sergeant	**M. Sgt.** T. T. Friedman
Ph. D.	doctor of philosophy	Suzette Stokes, **Ph. D.**
Pres.	president	**Pres.** Martin Van Buren
Prof.	professor	**Prof.** Jan Oglesby
pro **tem.**	*pro tempore* (for the time being)	Mayor Pro **Tem.** Alice Watts
Pvt.	private	**Pvt.** Lester Grant
Rep.	representative	**Rep.** Eric Samson
Rev.	reverend	**Rev.** Conrad Johnson
R. N.	registered nurse	Jacob Andrews, **R. N.**
Sec.	secretary	**Sec.** C. W. Lee
Sen.	senator	**Sen.** Avery Longines
Sgt.	sergeant	**Sgt.** Barry Crump
Sr.	senior	C. Charles Moss, **Sr.**
	sister	**Sr.** Hannah Soames
Supt.	superintendent	**Supt.** Margaret Best
Treas.	treasurer	**Treas.** Lottie Cameron
Vice **Adm.**	vice admiral	Vice **Adm.** L. C. Young
V. Pres. (or **V. P.**)	vice president	**V. Pres.** Richard Simpson

6.3 TIME

A. D.	*anno domini* (or in the year of our Lord)	**A. D.** 449

Note: Because the phrase would read *in the year of our Lord 449*, A. D. precedes the figure for the year.

A.M. (or **a.m.**)	*ante meridiem* (or before noon)	7:38 **A.M.**
approx.	approximately	**approx.** 3:00 **P.M.**
Apr.	April	**Apr.**-May
ARR.	arrival	**ARR.** on schedule
Aug.	August	July-**Aug.**
B. C.	before Christ	100-44 **B. C.**
cent.	century	fifteenth **cent.**
d.	day(s)	3rd **d.** of each **mo.**
Dec.	December	**Dec.** 7, 1941

DST	Daylight Savings Time	the effect of **DST**
EDT	Eastern Daylight Time	9:00 P.M., **EDT**
EST	Eastern Standard Time	9:00 P.M., **EST**
ETA	estimated time of arrival	His **ETA** is 5:15 A.M.

Note: The preceding four examples are customarily written without periods.

Feb.	February	**Feb.** 22, 1789
hr.	hour(s)	1 each **hr.**
Jan.	January	**Jan.** 2, 1945
Jun.	June	Saturday, **Jun.** 5
Jul.	July	the third of **Jul.**
Mar.	March	**Mar.**-June
min.	minute(s)	6 **mins.**
mo.	month(s)	6th **mo.** of the 2nd **yr.**
Mon.	Monday	**Mon.**, July 27
Nov.	November	**Nov.** 15
Oct.	October	**Oct.** 30, 1917
P.M. (or **p.m.**)	*post meridiem* (or after noon)	7:38 **P.M.**
Sat.	Saturday	**Sat.**, **Mar.** 7
sec.	second(s)	1 **sec.** intervals
Sept.	September	**Sept.** 10
Sun.	Sunday	**Sun.**, April 16
Thurs.	Thursday	**Thurs.** September 22
Tues. or **Tue.**	Tuesday	**Tues.**, October 1
Wed.	Wednesday	**Wed.**, December 18
wkly.	weekly	a **wkly.** journal
yr.	year(s)	every 3-5 **yrs.**

Note: There is no abbreviation for May.

A Great Communicator

Harper Lee has written only one novel, *To Kill A Mockingbird,* but this single work has been one of the most successful books in American literature. First released in 1961, the book, set in a small Southern town during the 1930s, is about a six-year-old girl whose father is a lawyer defending a black man accused of raping a white woman. Published during the growing national debate over civil rights, the novel was both timely and enlightening. A descendant of Confederate General Robert E. Lee, the novelist, who grew up in a small town in Alabama, used her child narrator to expose the ugliness and stupidity of bigotry. She relied heavily on her own experiences for the book; the narrator's father, for example was based on her own father. Another character was based on Lee's close childhood friend, Truman Capote. *To Kill A Mockingbird* won a Pulitzer Prize and was made into an Academy Award-winning film.

6.4 GEOGRAPHY

Ala.	Alabama	Montgomery, **Ala.**
Alas.	Alaska	Anchorage, **Alas.**
Apt.	apartment	**Apt.** 227-C
Ariz.	Arizona	Tucson, **Ariz.**
Ark.	Arkansas	Little Rock, **Ark.**
Ave.	avenue	27th **Ave.**
Bldg.	building	the Lutz **Bldg.**
Blk.	block	**Blk.** C
Blvd.	boulevard	Grandview **Blvd.**
Calif.	California	San Diego, **Calif.**
Co.	county	Clarc **Co.**
Colo.	Colorado	Yancey, **Colo.**
Conn.	Connecticut	White Mountain, **Conn.**
C. Z.	Canal Zone	the **C. Z.** authority
D. C.	District of Columbia	**D. C.** Parks and Recreation
Del.	Delaware	Wilmington, **Del.**
Dist.	district	88th **Dist.**
Dr.	drive	Montrose **Dr.**
Fla.	Florida	Pelican Harbor, **Fla.**
Ft.	fort	**Ft.** Myers
Ga.	Georgia	Stone Mountain, **Ga.**
Ida.	Idaho	Boise, **Ida.**
Ill.	Illinois	Park City, **Ill.**
Ind.	Indiana	Longview, **Ind.**
I., Is., or **Isl.**	island	Jackson **Is.**
Kans.	Kansas	Gulch City, **Kans.**
La.	Louisiana	Gulf City, **La.**
lat.	latitude	40 degrees of **lat.**
long.	longitude	82 degrees of **long.**
Mass.	Massachusetts	Salem, **Mass.**
Me.	Maine	Dangor, **Mo.**
Md.	Maryland	Harbor Isle, **Md.**
Mich.	Michigan	River City, **Mich.**
Minn.	Minnesota	St. Simeon, **Minn.**
Miss.	Mississippi	Shreveport, **Miss**
Mo.	Missouri	Lake Wylie, **Mo.**
Mont.	Montana	Settler's Rest, **Mont.**
Mt.	Mount; mountain(s)	**Mt.** Mitchell
Natl.	national	Sunshine **Natl.** Park
N. C.	North Carolina	Hickory, **N. C.**
N. D.	North Dakota	Lake James, **N. D.**
Neb.	Nebraska	Lincoln, **Neb.**
Nev.	Nevada	Lake Tahoe, **Nev.**
N. H.	New Hampshire	Canton, **N. H.**
N. J.	New Jersey	Greenview, **N. J.**
N. M.	New Mexico	Taos, **N. M.**
N. Y.	New York	Bronx, **N. Y.**
O.	Ohio	Trent, **O.**
Okla.	Oklahoma	Cherokee, **Okla.**
Ore.	Oregon	Mt. Ida, **Ore.**
Pa.	Pennsylvania	Harrisburg, **Pa.**
Pen.	peninsula	Escada **Pen.**
Pk.	park	La Costa **Pk.**
	peak	Pike's **Pk.**
P. R.	Puerto Rico	St. Juan, **P. R.**
Prov.	province	Northwest **Prov.**
Pt.	point	Danvers **Pt.**
Rd.	road	Bayshore **Rd.**
R. I.	Rhode Island	Cape Crown, **R. I.**
Rte.	route	**Rte.** 11
S. C.	South Carolina	Converse, **S. C.**
S. D.	South Dakota	Walker Valley, **S. D.**

Sq.	square	Calla **Sq.**
St.	street	Longchamps **St.**
Tenn.	Tennessee	Nashville, **Tenn.**
Terr.	territory	Yukon **Terr.**
Tex.	Texas	El Paso, **Tex.**
Ut.	Utah	Salt Lake City, **Ut.**
Va.	Virginia	Caroline County, **Va.**
Ver.	Vermont	Lexington, **Ver.**
V. I.	Virgin Islands	Charlotte Amalie, **V. I.**
Wash.	Washington (state)	Olympia, **Wash.**
W. Va.	West Virginia	**W. Va.** Council of Governments
Wis.	Wisconsin	Lawing, **Wis.**
Wyo.	Wyoming	Conover, **Wyo.**

Note: Guam, Hawaii, and Iowa have no traditional abbreviations.

6.5 PUBLICATIONS AND MEDIA

ABC	American Broadcasting Company	brought to you by **ABC**
anon.	anonymous	"The Chapel Rose," **anon.**
AP	Associated Press	an **AP** dateline
b. f.	boldface	Replace italics with **b. f.**
bibliog.	bibliography (a list of works)	**bibliog.** provided
biog.	biography; biographical	include **biog.** data
bull.	bulletin	monthly **bull.**
c. or **ca.**	*circa* (around)	**ca.** 1830
cap.	capital letter	**Cap.** all chapter headings.
CBS	Columbia Broadcasting System	a **CBS** production
ch or **chap.**	chapter	p. 77, **Ch.** IV
CNN	Cable News Network	a service of **CNN**
ed.	edition	modern **ed.**
	editor	Sarah Carey, **Ed.**
	edited	**ed.** version
e.g.	*exempli gratia* (for example)	**e. g.** General Grant
equiv.	equivalent	the line or its **equiv.**
et al.	*et alii* (and others)	Lydia Robinson, **et al.**
etc.	*et cetera* (and the rest)	many placards, papers, **etc.**
fac.	facsimile (a copy)	**fac.** edition
ff.	following	pages 77 **ff.**
fict.	fiction, fictional	history or **fict.**
fl.	*floruit* (flourished)	**fl.** 500-525 B. C.
gloss.	glossary	**gloss.** and index
gov. or **govt.**	government	the **gov.** representative
grat.	gratis (free)	received **grat.**
hist.	history, historical	**hist. fict.**
ibid.	*ibidem* (in the same place)	**Ibid.**, pp. 34-35
i. e.	*id est* (that is)	the victim, **i. e.** Sadie Willis
ill. or **illus.**	illustrated	Audubon's biography, **illus.**
incl.	including; inclusive	**Ch.** V-IX, **incl.**
intro.	introduction; introductory	Add an **intro.** to paragraph 13
ital.	italics	Use **ital.** sparingly.
l.	line	**l.** 83
ll.	lines	**ll.** 224-306
l. c.	lower case	Use **l. c.** for page headings.
ms.	manuscript	the following **ms.** pages
n. b.	*nota bene* (note well)	**n.b.:** Use only ink.
NBC	National Broadcasting Company	an **NBC** series

no.	number	**Vol.** V. **No.** 17
nonfict.	nonfiction	**nonfict.** section
p.	page	**p.** 77, section B
paren.	parentheses	place in **paren.**
PBS	Public Broadcasting Service	a **PBS** public service message
poet.	poetic	a **poet.** version
pp.	pages	**pp.** 88-104
pseud.	pseudonym	Twain, **pseud.** for Clemens
pub.	published, publisher	first **pub.** 1858
RCA	Radio Corporation of America	an affiliate of **RCA**
ref.	reference	no **ref.** included
sc.	scene	Act I, **sc.** 4
spec.	specific	no **spec.** title given
UPI	United Press International	a **UPI** feature
viz.	*videlicet* (namely)	**viz.** the King of England
vol.	volume(s)	**Vol.** 88 of the series

6.6 BUSINESS

acct.	account, accounting	**acct.** department
adv.	advertisement,	a paid **adv.**
	advertising	**adv.** manager
amt.	amount	specified **amt.**
assn.	association	Thompson **Assn.**
aud.	auditor, auditing	Wexler **Aud.** Co.
ave.	average	monthly **ave.** to date
bal.	balance	trial **bal.**
B/L	bill of lading	enclosed **B/L**
bbl.	barrel(s)	$4.75 per **bbl.**
bros.	brothers	Latham **Bros.**, Inc.
C.E.O.	chief executive officer	A. Thomas Samuels, **C. E. O.**
chgd.	charged	amount **chgd.**
c/o	in care of	**c/o** L. T. Williams
C. O. D.	cash on delivery	Please send **C. O. D.**
CPA	certified public accountant(s)	Rogers and Dearborn, **CPA**
corp.	corporation	a **corp.** officer
dept.	department	the advertising **dept.**
disc.	discount	price with **disc.**
div.	dividend	declared **div.**
	division	northwestern **div.**
ea.	each	$45.35 **ea.**
encl.	enclosure	printed **encl.**
est.	established	**Est.** 1850
	estimated	**est.** daily average
F. O. B.	free on board	**F. O. B.** price guaranteed
frt.	freight	**frt.** entrance
fwd.	forward	please **fwd.** amount due
inc.	incorporated	J. N. Hook, **Inc.**
int.	interest	**int.** penalty
inv.	invoice	**inv.** enclosed
IOU	I owe you	a signed **IOU**
ltd.	limited	Brown Implement, **Ltd.**
max.	maximum	**max.** efficiency
mdse.	merchandise	damaged **mdse.**
memo.	memorandum	transcribed **memo.**
mfg.	manufacturing	Warren **Mfg.**
min.	minimum	**min.** capacity
misc.	miscellaneous	**misc.** charges
mkt.	market	foreign **mkt.** analysts
m. o.	money order	send cash or **m.o.**

mtge.	mortgage	**mtge.** payments
mun.	municipal	**mun.** bonds
o / s	out of stock	parts **o / s**
P & L.	profit and loss	**P & L.** graphs
per **an.**	per annum (yearly)	a per **an.** audit
rec.	receipt	second copy of **rec.**
recd.	received	payment **recd.**

6.7 GOVERNMENT, CIVIC, AND LABOR ORGANIZATIONS

AAUW	American Association of University Women	a caucus of the **AAUW**
AFL-CIO	American Federation of Labor and Congress of Industrial Organizations	a meeting of the **AFL-CIO**
AWOL	absent without leave	court martial for being **AWOL**
BSA	Boy Scouts of America	members of the **BSA** council
CIA	Central Intelligence Agency	**CIA** investigations
DEA	Drug Enforcement Agency	a **DEA** raid
FBI	Federal Bureau of Investigation	an **FBI** probe
FDA	Food and Drug Administration	tested by the **FDA**
fed.	federal, federation	the **fed.** budget
FICA	Federal Insurance Contributions Act (commonly called Social Security)	an **FICA** deduction
GOP	Grand Old Party	a **GOP** convention
GSA	Girl Scouts of America	**GSA** headquarters
hdqrs.	headquarters	party **hdqrs.**
H. M. S.	His or Her Majesty's Ship	the **H. M. S.** Britannia
ILGWU	International Ladies Garment Workers Union	made by the **ILGWU**
IRS	Internal Revenue Service	agents from the **IRS**
j.p.	justice of the peace	a **j.p.** officiated
KGB	Russian security police	a **KGB** officer
MIA	missing in action	search for **MIA's**
NAACP	National Association for the Advancement of Colored People	spokesman for the **NAACP**
NASA	National Aeronautics and Space Administration	**NASA** engineers
NATO	North Atlantic Treaty Organization	member nations of **NATO**
NOW	National Organization of Women	the officers of **NOW**
NRC	Nuclear Regulatory Commission	guidelines from **NRC**
OPEC	Organization of Petroleum Exporting Countries	price quotes from **OPEC**
Pat. Off.	Patent Office	**Pat. Off.** approved
POW	prisoner of war	**POW** families
TVA	Tennessee Valley Authority	a project of the **TVA**
UMW	United Mine Workers of America	president of the **UMW**
UN	United Nations	a **UN** delegate
U. S. M. C.	United States Marine Corps	the **U. S. M. C.** headquarters
U. S. N.	United States Navy	the **U. S. N.** Academy

U. S. S.	United States Ship	the **U. S. S.** Enterprise
U. S. S. R.	Union of Soviet Socialist Republics (Russia)	a **U. S. S. R.** regulation
VA	Veterans Administration	the **VA** office
VFW	Veterans of Foreign Wars	the **VFW** Club
VISTA	Volunteers in Service to America	recruiters for **VISTA**
WHO	World Health Organization	leaflets from **WHO**

"Mockingbirds don't do one thing but make music for us to enjoy. They don't eat up people's gardens, don't nest in corncribs, they don't do one thing but sing their hearts out for us. That's why it's a sin to kill a mockingbird."

— from *To Kill a Mockingbird*
by Harper Lee

6.8 POST OFFICE

AL	Alabama	Tuscaloosa, **AL**
AK	Alaska	Fairbanks, **AK**
APO	army post office	an **APO** address
AR	Arkansas	Jonesboro, **AR**
AZ	Arizona	Phoenix, **AZ**
CA	California	Laguna Beach, **CA**
CO	Colorado	Aaron's Dome, **CO**
CT	Connecticut	Greenview, **CT**
DC	District of Columbia	Washington, **DC**
DE	Delaware	Whiteville, **DE**
DLO	Dead Letter Office	assignment to the **DLO**
FL	Florida	Key West, **FL**
GA	Georgia	Savannah, **GA**
G. P. O.	General Post Office	in care of the **G. P. O.**
HI	Hawaii	Kauai, **HI**
IA	Iowa	Thornton, **IA**
ID	Idaho	Pine Lake, **ID**
IL	Illinois	Sheridan, **IL**
IN	Indiana	Indianapolis, **IN**
KS	Kansas	Kansas City, **KS**
KY	Kentucky	Lawrence, **KY**
LA	Louisiana	Lake Ponchartrain, **LA**
MA	Massachusetts	Boston, **MA**
MD	Maryland	Baltimore, **MD**
ME	Maine	Taylors Ferry, **ME**
MI	Michigan	Lake Point, **MI**
MN	Minnesota	Crown, **MN**
MO	Missouri	River Bend, **MO**
MS	Mississippi	Biloxi, **MS**
MT	Montana	Cedar Valley, **MT**
NE	Nebraska	Nebraska City, **NE**
NC	North Carolina	Rhodhiss, **NC**
ND	North Dakota	Great Falls, **ND**
NH	New Hampshire	Logan, **NH**
NJ	New Jersey	Tanner, **NJ**
NM	New Mexico	Santa Fe, **NM**
NV	Nevada	Reno, **NV**
NY	New York	Buffalo, **NY**
OH	Ohio	Cincinnati, **OH**
OK	Oklahoma	Oklahoma City, **OK**
OR	Oregon	Taylor, **OR**
PA	Pennsylvania	Philadelphia, **PA**
pc(s).	pieces	4 **pcs.** shipped
P. P.	parcel post	send **P. P.**
RFD	rural free delivery	**RFD** 8
RI	Rhode Island	South Point, **RI**
SC	South Carolina	Rock Hill, **SC**
SD	South Dakota	Indian Lake, **SD**
TN	Tennessee	Cleveland, **TN**
TX	Texas	Abilene, **TX**
UPS	United Parcel Service	received via **UPS**
UT	Utah	Cannon, **UT**
VA	Virginia	Hopewell, **VA**
VT	Vermont	Jennings, **VT**
WA	Washington	Walla Walla, **WA**
WI	Wisconsin	Madison, **WI**
WV	West Virginia	Dennison, **WV**
WY	Wyoming	Grant, **WY**

6.9 SCIENTIFIC TERMS

a. c.	air conditioning	with a. c.
	alternating current	measurement of a. c.
alt.	alternate	alt. method
	altitude	alt. 9298 feet
AM	amplitude modulation	20.89 AM
amp(s).	ampere	20 amps.
at. wt.	atomic weight	at. wt. chart
ave.	average	ave. intensity
avdp.	avoirdupoir	avdp. weight scale
bu.	bushel	40 bu. per day
c.	carat	4 c. stone
C	Celsius	11 degrees C
c. c.	cubic centimeter	one c. c. of serum
cm.	centimeter	a pound per cm.
cwt.	hundredweight	$5.85 per cwt.
d. c.	direct current	measurements of d. c.
doz.	dozen	$8.00 per doz.
F	Fahrenheit	degrees F
FM	frequency modulation	on 98.6 FM
ft.	foot	90 ft. cable
gal(s).	gallon	70 gal. tank
gpm	gallons per minute	5 gpm pump capacity
ht.	height	6 feet in ht.
in.	inch	33 in. line
IQ	intelligence quotient	IQ spans of 80-95
K	Kelvin	degrees K
km.	kilometer	five km. track
kwhr.	kilowatt hour	$.075 per kwhr.
L	liter	2.8 L per unit
lb(s).	pounds	100 lbs.
liq.	liquid	liq. measure
mg.	milligram	89 mg.
mi.	mile	4 mi. lengths
non seq.	non sequitur (it does not follow)	the conclusions (non seq.)
oz(s).	ounces	16 oz. size
p. p. m.	parts per million	standard rate of p. p. m.
pr.	pair	$3.50 per pr.
pt.	pint	half pt. cartons
q. e. d.	quod erat demonstrandum (which was to be proved)	complete, q. e. d.
qt.	quart	1.5 qt. package
rm(s).	ream	seven rm. package
r. p. m.	revolutions per minute	at 50 r. p. m.
std.	standard	std. weight
temp.	temperature	maintain temp.
tbsp.	tablespoon	2 tbsp. per hour
tsp.	teaspoon	3 tsp. per dose
wt.	weight	computed wt.
yd.	yard	30 yd. rolls

PREFIXES, SUFFIXES, AND ROOT WORDS

7.1 **A**n *understanding of the building blocks from which words are constructed can lead to a wider vocabulary, better spelling, stronger diction, and a greater appreciation of the history of the English language.*

Example:	**in · cred · ible**
Prefix:	**in = not**
Root:	**cred = believe**
Suffix:	**ible = capable of**
Definition:	**incredible — not capable of being believed**

7.2 **A prefix** is a word segment placed at the beginning of a word to modify its meaning. A word can have more than one prefix, as in *presuppose* and *readmit*. The following chart explains how prefixes join roots to form new words.

Prefix	*Meaning*	*Examples*
a	• on, in, at, towards • up, out, of, from, away • of	abed, aboard, afire ago, arise, awake akin
ab	from, away, off	absolve, abhor
ad, af, al, ap, ar, at	to, toward	adhere, afford, allege, appraise, arrange, attach
ambi	about, on both sides	ambidextrous, ambiguous
amphi	both, on both sides, about	amphibious, amphitheater
ana	up, back, again	analogy, anachronism
ante	before	antedate, antecedent
anti	opposite, against	antidote, antipathy
apo	off, from, detached	apoplexy, apogee
auto	self, one's own	automobile, autograph
be	• by, about • all over, around • make, cause to • affect, treat	because, before, below bedeck, belay, beseige, becalm bedim, befoul, belittle befriend, beguile, bewitch
bene	kindly, good	benefit, benediction
bi	two, twice, double	biennial, bilateral
circum	around, about	circumference, circumscribe
col, com, con, cor	with, together	collect, combine, contact correction
contra	against, contrary to	contradict, contraband
counter	opposite, in opposition to	counteract, countersign
de	down, from, away	depend, detract
deca	ten	decade, decagram

di, dia, du	two, twice	dilemma, diameter, duplex
dis	the reverse of, not	disconnect, disagree
epi	upon, above	epidemic, epidermal
ex	out, forth	exclude, exit
extra	beyond, outside of	extraordinary, extrasensory
for	way, off, apart	forget, forgive
fore	in front	forecourt, foreground
geo	earth	geology, geometric
hemi	half	hemisphere, hemipod
hetero	another, different	heterodoxy, heterosexual
homo	same	homogeneous, homogenize
hydro	water	hydroplane, hydrofoil
hyper	over, excessive	hypercritical, hyperactive
hypo	under, less	hypothalamus, hypothesis
in	• in, within, on	income, inland, inlay
il, im, in,	• not	illegible, impede, insecure
ir		irregularity
inter	between, among	interact, interbreed
intra	within	intracranial, intramural
juxta	near, alongside, next	juxtapose
macro	large	macrobiotic, macrocosm
mal	bad, evil, ill	malcontent, malfunction
mega	great, large, powerful	megascopic, megaphone
meta	along with	metatarsal, metabolism
micro	small	microbe, microsurgery
mid	in the middle of	midline, midterm
milli	thousand	millipede, milliliter
mini	small	minimal, minuscule
mis	wrong, bad, amiss	misspell, misfit
mono	one, single, sole	monologue, monorail
multi	much, many	multitude, multicolored
neo	new, recent	neonatal, neolithic
non	not	nonstandard, noncommittal
ob	against	obscene, obdurate
off	off, from, away	offset, offshoot
omni	all	omniscient, omnibus
out	beyond, better than	outgoing, outstrip
over	above, over	overlook, overlord
pan	all, complete, entire	panacea, panorama
para	beside, beyond	paradox, parapsychology
per	through, by	perambulator, perforate
peri	around	periscope, peritonitis
poly	many	polyphonic, polygon
post	after, behind	postdate, postpone
pre	before	preamble, preconceive
pro	forward	protect, proponent
proto	first	prototype, protozoan
pseudo	false, fake	pseudonym, pseudopod
quadr	four	quadrangle, quadruped
re, retro	again, back	recycle, retrograde
semi	half, partially	semicivilized, semicircle
sub, subter,	under, beneath	submarine, subterfuge
sup		suppose
super	above, beyond	supersede, superiority
syl, sym,	with, together	syllogism, symposium,
syn		synonymous
tele	afar	telekinesis, telepathic
trans	across, beyond	transcontinental, transfix
tri	three	triangular, tricolor
ultra	beyond, to the extreme	ultramarine, ultraviolet
un	not	unknown, unlikely
under	insufficient	underweight, underdone
uni	one	universal, unicycle
zo	animal	zoology, zodiac

CHAPTER 7

7.3 **Roots** — The English language grew from many different languages. There are traces of Anglo-Saxon, Celtic, Latin, Scandinavian, French, and Greek *root words,* to name a few. (See — **Indo-European Language** Chart, Appendix A)

Underlying each of the following words is one common **root:**

The **Aryan Root: bhar,** meaning *to bear*

English	brother
Anglo-Saxon	brothor
Gothic	brothar
Dutch	broeder
Swedish	broder
German	bruder
Irish	brathair
Russian	brat
Sanskrit	bhratr

A study of **root words** can lead to mastery of new or unfamiliar words. Note: **Root words** often change in spelling to accommodate the addition of suffixes or prefixes, as in *annual / perennial; dear / darling; one / only.*

Root	Meaning	Example
act, ag	do, move	active, agency
aero	air	aeronautics, aerodynamics
ama, amat, ami, amor	love, like	amiable, amatory, Amy, amorous
antho	flower	anthology, anther
anthropo	human	anthropology, anthropoid
aqua	water	aquarium, aquamarine
arch	chief, principal	archangel, archbishop
astro	star	astral, astrophysics
bio	life	biology, bioscope
cad, cas	fall	cadence, casualty
cap, capt, ceive, cept	take	capture, captive, receive, concept
capit	head	capital, decapitate
cent	hundred	century, centennial
chloro	green	chlorophyll, chlorine
chromo	colored, tinted	chromosome, chromium
chrono	time	chronology, chronometer
chrys	gold, yellow	chrysanthemum, chrysalis
civ	people, citizens	civic, civilian
clos, clud, clus	shut, close out	closet, conclusive, preclude
cracy, crat	people, citizens	democracy, theocratic
cred	believe	credence, incredibly
curr, curs	run	currency, concursive
dic, dict	say, tell	indicate, predictive
duc, duct	lead	conductive, induction

equ	• equal	equation, equidistant
	• horse	equine, equestrian
eth	belief, values	ethical, ethology
ethno	of a race or nation	ethnocentric, ethnic
fac, fact, fec, fect, fy	make, do	factory, confection, magnify
fem	woman	feminine, female
fer	carry	refer, conference
fid	faith	fidelity, fido
flect, flex	bend	reflective, flexible
grad, gress	step, advance	gradual, regress
graph	write	graphic, phonograph
gyn	woman	misogynist, gynecology
helio	sun	helium, heliotrope
hemato, hemo	blood	hematoma, hemoglobin
homo, homin	human	homo sapiens, hominid
hypno	sleep	hypnopedic, hypnotize
jec, ject	throw	conjecture, injection
judic, jur	right, justice, law	judicial, perjury
lact, lax	milk	lactate, galaxy
lat	• side	lateral
	• wide	latitude
	• carry	translate
	• hidden	latency
leg, lect	• choose	college, selective, collective
	• read	legible, legend, lectern
loc, loqu	speak	eloquent, elocution
manu	hand	manually, manumission
mis, mit	send	missive, manumit
mod	style, form	model, moderation
morph	shape	morphology, metamorphosis
mors, mort	dead, death	mortuary, immortality
nov	new, strange	novel, novice
path	• feeling	sympathetic, apathy
	• disease	pathogen, pathology
patri	country, nation	expatriate, repatriation
ped	• child	pediatrician, pediatrics
	• foot	pedestrian, impede
pend, pens	hang	pendulum, dispense
phil	love	philosopher, philanderer
phobi	fear	phobic, agoraphobia
phon	sound	phonograph, phonetic
phot	light	photosynthesis, photographic
phras	word	phrasing, periphrasis
phys	body	physical, physician
polis	city, government	metropolis, politician
pon, posit	place, position	postpone, positive
prim	first	primarily, primogeniture
psyche	mind, spirit	psychic, psychometry
rect, reg	rule, guide	correct, regal
scrib, script	write	transcribe, inscription
secu, sequ	follow	consecutive, sequential
spec, spect	look	spectator, respective
sta, stas, stat, sti	position	statue, stasis, static, constitution
tain, ten, tent	hold	contain, retentive
temp	• time	tempo, contemporary
	• weather	temperate, temperature
tend, tent, tens	stretch	intend, contention, tension
terra	earth, land	terrarium, inter
theo	god	theology, pantheism

thermo	heat	thermos, thermodynamics
thes, thet	belief	antithesis, hypothetical
tim	fear	timidity, intimidation
vent	• wind, air	ventilation, vent
	• come, move	advent, venture
verb	word	verbose, verbal
vers, vert	turn	vertigo, conversion
vid, vis	see, vision	provide, visually
voc, vok	words, sound	vocabulary, invoke
volv, volu	roll	involve, revolution

A Great Communicator

When Langston Hughes began publishing his poetry in the early 1920s, his work was rejected by many black literary figures. Yet when he died in 1967, he was regarded as the dean of African-American literature. Hughes was a major figure in the Harlem Renaissance — a period of artistic growth during the 1920s when black art and entertainment suddenly became popular among whites. His poetry melded jazz and blues music with black speech patterns. He wrote about racism, poverty, and violence and quickly became known as a militant. Hughes later toned down his political radicalism, but he remained a fierce critic of racism and social injustice. He also wrote plays, essays, novels, and short stories. Langston Hughes, considered by many to be *the* poet of the Harlem Renaissance, is not only a major figure in African-American literature but of twentieth century literature as well.

7.4 **Suffixes** are word endings that often alter the use of a word in a sentence.

For example:

minimum	an adjective or a noun
minimal	an adjective
minimally	an adverb
minimize	a verb
minute	an adjective or a noun
minutely	an adverb
minutia	a noun
minuscule	an adjective

The four charts of **suffixes** are divided into endings that form adjectives, endings that form nouns, endings that form verbs, and endings that form adverbs.

Suffixes That Form Adjectives

Suffix	Meaning	Example
able, ible	capable of, fit to be	breakable, inflatible
ac, ic	of, pertaining to	cardiac, comic
acious, aceous	inclined toward, given to, abounding in	veracious, vivacious, curvaceous
al	of, belonging to	autumnal, natural
an, ian	belonging to	sectarian, Italian
ar	relating to, like	angular, polar, lumbar
ate	forming, shaped like	pennate, desolate
ed	state, quality	learned, dogged, wicked
en	made of, resembling	ashen, leaden
eous, ious	full of, characterized by	beauteous, invidious
er	more, comparative	brighter, greener
ern	in, belonging to	northern, postern
escent	being, becoming	luminescent, pubescent
esque	in the manner of	picturesque, arabesque
est	most, highest	plainest, sharpest
ferous	bearing, producing	auriferous, coniferous
fold	times, multiplied by	threefold, manifold
ful	full of, characterized by	careful, doleful
headed	state of mind	bullheaded, hardheaded
hearted	state of emotion	hardhearted, gladhearted
ial	of, pertaining to	radial, celestial
ic, ical	of, pertaining to, like	angelic, titanic, conical
il, ile	of, pertaining to	civil, puerile
ine	tending toward	crystalline, feminine
ish	characteristic of	selfish, boyish, Turkish
ive	having the nature of	abusive, restive, festive
lent	full of	fraudulent, redolent
less	without, lacking	windless, timeless
like	resembling	childlike
most	to the highest degree	southernmost, foremost
ory	pertaining to, tending to	exploratory, explanatory
ous	full of	bulbous, ferrous
ple	multiplied by	multiple, quadruple

some	apt to	winsome, handsome
teen	ten	thirteen
vorous	feeding on, eating	omnivorous, carnivorous
ward	toward	backward, eastward
y	pertaining to	creamy, lemony

Suffixes That Form Nouns

Suffix	*Meaning*	*Example*
acy	state, quality	democracy, conspiracy
age	collection, sum of	carnage, mileage
al	action	survival, refusal
an	one of, a member of	Anglican, Republican
ana	a collection	Americana, Frostiana
ance, ence	of the quality of	endurance, existence
ant, ent	agent	claimant, emollient
ar	pertaining to	altar, solar, plantar
arch	ruler, chief	monarch, patriarch
archy	rule, government	anarchy, matriarchy
ary	person who belongs to or engages in	actuary, notary
ate	office, body of officers	consulate, senate
ation	action, state, result	stagnation, domination
dom	rank, domain, condition	kingdom, freedom wisdom
ee	receiver	payee, addressee
eer	one who	auctioneer, seer
er, or	one who	hatter, lawyer, collector
ery	art or occupation	surgery, bakery
ess	feminine agent	poetess, countess, duchess
ful	amount	cupful, eyeful
gram	drawing or writing	anagram, telegram
graph	something written	autograph, paragraph
hood	state, quality	boyhood, womanhood
ice	quality, state	service, justice
ine	• forming an abstract	discipline, doctrine
	• having the quality of	leonine, vulpine, porcine
ing	forming a verbal noun	casing, learning
ion	action, result, state	union, fusion
isk	a diminutive	asterisk
ism	system	cannibalism, symbolism
ist	one who does or is skilled at	moralist, artist
ite	one connected with	Jerseyite, cosmopolite
ition	action, result, state	definition, addition
itis	inflammation of	appendicitis, tinnitis
ity	state, quality	maturity, divinity
ix	feminine agent	aviatrix, executrix
let	diminutive	wiglet, owlet, piglet
ling	one connected with	hireling, changeling, yearling
man	agent, doer	postman, fireman
ment	act of, process of	atonement, enslavement
monger	dealer, trader	fishmonger, warmonger
ness	state, quality	grossness, happiness
ology	a belief or science	theology, ornithology
person	agent	spokesperson, chairperson
ry	• people as a whole	citizenry
	• study of	telemetry, carpentry
scopy	examination by	spectroscopy, microscopy
ship	state, quality, skill	fellowship, craftsmanship
tude	state, quality	amplitude, pulchritude
ure	act, result, means	disclosure, pleasure
us	formation of, member	prospectus, alumnus
woman	female agent	chairwoman, charwoman

wright	worker, maker	playwright, shipwright
y	• a diminutive	baby, doggy, piggy
	• result	secrecy, accuracy
	• study of, skill in	photography, competency

Suffixes That Form Verbs

Suffix	*Meaning*	*Example*
ate	become, cause, form	collate, orchestrate
en	make, cause	lengthen, broaden, enliven
fy, ify	make, cause	liquefy, falsify, amplify
ize	make, cause	aggrandize, terrorize

Suffixes That Form Adverbs

Suffix	*Meaning*	*Example*
er	more	sooner, earlier
est	most	fastest, oftenest
long	in the direction of, in the condition of	endlong, headlong
ly	in the manner, place, time, degree, or number	badly, hourly, centrally
meal	a portion at a time	piecemeal
ther	movement	hither, whether
ward, wards	in the direction of	backward, inwards
ways	in the manner of, toward	always, sideways
wise	in the manner of	clockwise

"It's not easy to know what is true for you or me
at twenty-two, my age. But I guess I'm what
I feel and see and hear, Harlem, I hear you:
  talk on this page.
(I hear New York, too.) Me. — who?
Well, I like to sleep, drink, and be in love.
I like to work, read, learn, and understand life.
I like a pipe for a Christmas present,
or records — Bessie, bop, or Bach.
I guess being colored doesn't make me *not* like
the same things other folks like who are
  other races."

— From "Theme for English B"
by Langston Hughes

7.5   A clear understanding of the parts of a word sometimes enables a person to make a more specific **definition.** There are several informal methods of defining a word. For example:

An appositive:	Near the exit stood the *concierge*, the hotel manager. *The fulcrum*, the wedge on which the lever rests, needs additional support.
A linking verb:	An *arachnid* is a member of the spider family. *Succulents* are plants with fleshy stems and leaves.
An example:	Unusual plurals *(phenomenon/ phenomena*, for example) occur more often in scientific writing. Rance was studying marsupials (for instance, *kangaroos* and *opossums.)*

A **formal definition,** however, must contain two specific parts:
- it names the class to which the term belongs
- it states how the term is different from other members of the same class

A *liaison* is an agent who establishes a closer relationship or understanding between two parties.

Jai alai is a game played on a court by two or four players using a ball and a long curved basket strapped to the wrist.

WRITING

8.1 The **writing process** is an orderly and creative approach to the complex, highly personal task of putting thoughts on paper. This process structures ideas from rough beginnings to the final polished form:

1. Prewriting:
- *Generate* an array of ideas to draw on with these methods:

using models	using diagrams	webbing
brainstorming	reading	skimming
interviewing	viewing	analyzing
listening	discussing	researching
outlining	listing	dramatizing
logging	fantasizing	making notes

For instance, before writing a paragraph about an ideal vacation spot, list aspects of your most enjoyable holidays and vacations, including foods, activities, companions, weather conditions, and geographical locale.
- *Sort through the data* to find the most useful ideas. For example, in your list of details about Custer's Last Stand, cross out any information that takes place too far in advance of the actual event, such as facts about General Custer's enrollment at West Point.
- *Cluster or classify ideas that share a central idea.* As you sort through details about learning to drive, cluster information that pertains to learning the parts of a car. Then group details which pertain to operating a car, learning safety precautions, maintaining a car, or studying for a road test.

2. Drafting:
- *Make a rough outline* to indicate the order in which main ideas will appear. (See Section 8.7 for more information about outlines.) Decide whether ideas should be arranged chronologically, least-to-greatest, greatest-to-least, left-to-right, right-to-left, or cause and effect. (See Section 8.3 for more information about arrangement.)
- *Generalize* from details that seem to lead to a single conclusion. For instance, the many military images in President George Washington's speeches may indicate that warfare was of major importance to him.
- *Support conclusions* by adding ideas, reasons, incidents, and examples. After statements concerning Huck Finn's loyalty, quote lines or cite

examples which prove that Huck was a dependable, trustworthy friend to Jim and Tom Sawyer.
• *Emphasize cause and effect.* For example, in a theme about quarrels between family members, describe situations that develop into feuds, such as jealousy over preference shown to the oldest child.

3. Composing:
• *Write a first draft,* concentrating on the flow of ideas rather than on handwriting, spelling, or neatness.
• *Leave plenty of space* for rewriting, adding, or rearranging.
• *Focus on a voice and an audience* which are appropriate to the situation. For example, a diary entry should be personal, intimate, and written in first person; a research paper, on the other hand, should be impersonal, objective, and written in third person; an essay could be either one, depending on the subject matter and tone.
• *Choose specific, concrete images and words* so that the reader can experience the same feelings and ideas that you see in your mind. For example, a way of describing the lengthening shadows of pine trunks is to compare them to long, thin legs.
• *Vary sentences* by length and type. For comparisons, use balanced sentences, as in:

> Phileas Fogg's journey encircled the globe; Miss Dove's travels, however, were anchored in her imagination.
>
> Note that the balanced sentence is always compound to offset one equal on one side of the connector with another equal on the other side.

For strong, demonstrative statements, choose a periodic sentence in which the key word falls last. For example: The greatest stronghold of learning during the Dark Ages was the Church.
• *Use transition words and phrases* to indicate the flow of ideas. For instance:
Without this first attempt at scaling Mt. McKinley, Ranson might never have organized his successful second assault.

4. Revising:
• *Analyze the material for logic and coherence.* For instance, be wary of trying to prove too many points at once or of loosely relating information that strays from the central idea. If your paper focuses on the celebration of Bastille Day, omit references to other French holidays.
• Make changes and additions that will *improve the arrangement of ideas.* For instance, insert a definition of personal computers before launching into how to select the p.c. that suits your needs.

- *Provide support for weak paragraphs.* If your explanation of how to make pomanders seems too thin, beef up the description with more physical details about shaping, preserving, spicing, wrapping, and tying.
- *Clarify portions of your work that raise additional questions.* If a history paper on the development of African languages indicates great changes during the nineteenth century, add commentary about the burst of travel and exploration by Europeans to justify these abrupt and unexplained alterations.
- *Share your work* with another student and follow your partner's advice about improvements.
- As you read the other person's writing, *ask appropriate questions:*

> Who is speaking?
> For whom is this work written?
> Why is this person writing?
> What is the main idea of the work?
> What details prove the main idea?
> Why are the supporting details placed in this
>   particular order?
> What further information do I need to understand
>   this work?
> What words or images seem weak or inappropriate?
> Which sentences should be reworded?
> Where do conclusions appear?
> Do transitional words and phrases help me follow the
>   flow of ideas?

5. Proofreading:
- *Edit* final copy for the four most common errors —

> grammatical structure
> capitalization
> punctuation
> spelling

Rely on a partner for a second opinion.

- *Read each sentence aloud* to test for complete thought and to avoid sentence fragments and run-on sentences.
- *Replace* nonspecific terms with more exact language.
Compare these:

soon	on May 23
by a friend	by Andy Mayhew
a local source	the *Evening Clarion*
went	ambled
in a few places	on three successive blocks

- *Capitalize proper nouns and adjectives.* Refer to your handbook as well as a dictionary and thesaurus.
- *Examine punctuation* of clauses and phrases as well as the ends of sentences. Pay special attention to introductory terms. For instance: Before he can get used to living in luxury, Pip is drawn into a circle of snobbish, materialistic friends.
- *Read through once from end to beginning* to check for spelling errors.

6. Publishing:
- *Publish your writing.* Read your work aloud to your family.
- *Exchange papers* with other students. Offer critical comments to strengthen their writing.
- *Accept criticism* as a means of improving your own work. Pay particular attention to errors that recur in your work, for instance, confusion of troublesome homonyms, such as principle/principal.
- *Enter your writing in essay contests,* student forums, and school publications.
- *Post your prize work* on your bulletin board.
- *Make a decorative copy* of a short poem or essay and display it in a frame.
- *Mail a copy* or a taped reading to a friend or relative.

A Great Communicator

Ask people to name the greatest writer in the English language and they might very well say William Shakespeare. Born in 1564, Shakespeare went to London as a young man. He became a successful actor, but when he died in 1616 he was far better known as a playwright and poet. He wrote over three dozen plays and a great deal of poetry. Shakespeare was widely respected in his lifetime, but in the years following his death his reputation soared, dwarfing such contemporary playwrights as Christopher Marlowe. By the nineteenth century he was held up as the greatest figure in English literature. Full of anachronisms and errors, his work nonetheless contains some of the most beautiful phrases ever written. Expressions such as "all that glitters is not gold" and "all the world's a stage" have become permanent fixtures in the English language. Characters such as Hamlet, Lady Macbeth, and Othello are some of the most vivid and memorable ever created.

8.2 Both written and spoken English is composed of thought units called paragraphs. A **paragraph** is a group of sentences arranged in a particular order to express a single whole idea.

Each paragraph has three identifiable parts: a **topic sentence,** the **development** or **body,** and a **conclusion** or **clincher sentence.** Each of these aspects is essential to the sense, direction, and purpose of the paragraph.

1. **The topic sentence,** which states the limits of the paragraph, makes clear what idea is being discussed and suggests the order in which the development will take place. The topic sentence usually begins the paragraph, but it may appear later.

Consider this example from a reflective essay:

Winter nights usually find the Colsons in their den. There the family shares a mutual love — making birdhouses. Long before the birds return in the spring, the Colsons have readied a variety of boxes, shelves, gourds, and martin houses to supply the needs of Indiana's numerous bird families. In addition, they collect and clean older birdhouses and ready them for future use. As a family project, the building of birdhouses unites the Colson clan in support of local wildlife.

2. The *development* or *body* of the paragraph presents an orderly group of sentences justifying or explaining the concept found in the topic sentence.

Consider this model, which describes a process:

Ridding a dog of fleas can be a formidable task, depending on the size of the animal and the length of its coat. First, soak the dog in warm, sudsy water. Then, after the hair has absorbed some of the soap, lather carefully around the ears, neck, and chest. Pay special attention to the underside and continue scrubbing to the tip of the tail, down each leg, and between the toes. After the preliminary wash, rinse and lather again, this time using flea soap and leaving the suds on the skin for 10-20 minutes.

Finish with a thorough rinse in clean, warm water. Continue rinsing until all traces of fleas and soap are gone. To prevent recurrence of fleas, dry the dog completely before dusting with a natural flea powder containing pyrethrins.

3. The *conclusion* or *clincher sentence* sums up the progression of ideas and makes clear to the reader that the author has completed the specified intent of the paragraph. The concluding sentence not only restates the main idea of the topic sentence, but also summarizes the information which serves as support. Consider this example from a children's book about holidays:

The weeks before Christmas are a busy time as Santa's elves form a diligent assembly line. One group molds doll bodies and sends them on to painters, hairdressers, and dressmakers for the final touches. Another group constructs the frames of planes, trains, cars, and trucks; then the assembly crew adds wheels, windshields, propellers, and mechanisms to operate each vehicle before the touch-up specialist sprays on paint. A special detail of workers cuts and sews furry pelts for stuffed animals. Assistants then stuff the animals, stitch on faces, and glue on bows and hats. The packing crew, after checking for flaws and omissions, places each toy in a box. By Christmas week, the shelves of the North Pole are neatly stocked with well-made toys to fill Santa's bag.

Note:

- The *topic sentence* limits the idea to the coordinated efforts of Santa's elves. Other ideas about Christmas, such as reindeer, Santa's toy sack, letters from children, and delivery to individual stockings, would not belong in this paragraph.

- The *body* of the paragraph is a step-by-step development of the notion of an assembly line: each toy has an initial stage of construction and a completion.

- The *concluding* or *clincher sentence* summarizes the point of the paragraph. After the elves follow a careful plan of attack, the task of making toys is completed, and carefully built toys await Santa's selection from the shelves at the North Pole.

Because the *topic sentence* leads the way to a satisfactory paragraph, it must include a workable idea, one that is neither too narrow nor too broad. For example, the following topic sentences are not suitable:

- Santa's elves have much to do to build toys, ready the sleigh, and make a list for Santa to fill. (too broad)

- The cutting of leather for doll shoes is an important job for Santa's elves. (too narrow)

- Santa's staff works harder than anyone! (can't be proved)

The *development* of the paragraph is a body of supporting information that offers examples, details, models, or reasons as proof of the opening statement. There must be an adequate amount of information to make the central idea understandable and readable. It is usually helpful to make a rough outline of key points in the development, for example:

1. dolls
2. wheel toys
3. stuffed animals

8.3   There are many ways in which **supporting data** can be arranged. For example, in a paragraph about

camping in Yellowstone Park	•a *chronological* approach would give the details in day-by-day order.
an historic lighthouse	•a *bottom-to-top* approach would order details from the ground up to the beacon.
business methods of a perfume manufacturer	•a *top-to-bottom* approach would show the basic set-up from the president down to the grower who gathers delicate blossoms and herbs.

a museum display of rocks and geodes	• a *left-to-right* or *right-to-left* approach would arrange items in the order in which the viewer encounters them.
a winner of an Olympic gold medal for skiing	• a *least-to-greatest* arrangement would compile statistics which show the athlete's development to Olympic status

Note: **Newspaper articles** are usually written in the **inverted pyramid** or **greatest-to-least** style so that the most important facts — who, what, where, when, why, and how — will appear in the first sentence. The purpose of this arrangement is speed: a reader of the newspaper can learn the major facts without going too far into the article. Thus, the reader can skip from item to item, completing only the articles which are of interest.

8.4   The test of a good paragraph lies in the answers to the following questions:

- Does the paragraph stress only one idea?
- Are the sentences arranged according to a coherent, logical plan?
- Does the paragraph reach a conclusion about the main idea?
- Is there enough support to justify the topic sentence?
- Do examples appear only in the body of the paragraph?

8.5   There are three basic styles of paragraphs: **narrative, descriptive,** and **expository.**

- A narrative paragraph explains a series of events in story form. For example, here is a paragraph from a friendly letter:

    Lon and his sisters helped us move from the farm into town. Lon drove the van. Sharma and Miriam packed boxes and marked on them the areas in which they belonged. Patty and I waited at the new place and pointed out locations for each item. In no time the five of us had emptied the old house and furnished the apartment.

- A descriptive paragraph relates sense impressions — how something tastes, smells, sounds, looks, or feels. Here is an example from a descriptive theme:

  The inviting strains of Strauss's *Liebeslieder* are truly dance music at its most elegant. The notes bubble and frolic, taunt and tease, drawing even the most reluctant wallflower onto the dance floor. The soothing flow of three/four rhythms coax feet into the familiar sway of the waltz, nineteenth-century Europe's favorite dance. Within a few bars, the simple but lovely dance tunes erase inhibitions and spark smiles on dancers' faces. Strauss was truly a master at making every listener feel welcome on the dance floor.

- An expository paragraph explains an opinion or seeks to persuade by defining, comparing and contrasting, analyzing, stating cause and effect, or classifying. Consider this example:

  Ancient philosophers were right. Friendship is the most rewarding of all human relationships. Different from the blood ties that ally family members, friendship brings together two kindred souls who admire each other for a host of reasons. Whether for the joys of a shared interest, such as sports or travel, or the pleasures of stimulating and entertaining conversation, friendship reassures each participant that there is at least one other human being on the planet with a similar outlook and temperament. When such relationships stand the test of time, they attest to the height of a truly civilized life wherein negative feelings, bloodlust, and pride are overwhelmed by an urge to commune with a fellow human being.

Here are some examples of topics which might be developed by each type:

• **narrative**	the final moments in a World Series game a concert violinist's preparations for a performance a Cherokee ceremonial dance a candidate's campaign for a county commission seat
• **descriptive**	an unusual method of folding table napkins having teeth cleaned a storm at sea making pita sandwiches
• **expository**	choosing a suitable songbird for a pet rewarding children for good behavior how to select seeds for a vegetable garden a plea for safer exercise programs

8.6 THE ESSAY

In comparison with the paragraph, an **essay** or **theme** is a longer, more thorough examination of a subject or idea. The composition of the essay is a process of assembling single paragraphs, each of which introduces a subtopic, develops it, and reaches a conclusion. The completed essay, which is begun by an **introductory paragraph** and ended with a **concluding paragraph,** should follow guidelines that are similar to those governing the paragraph, with each element contributing to a coherent discussion of a single theme or idea.

In contrast to the paragraph, the essay makes a more complex statement about a subject through the development of key points which follow an orderly arrangement. Each point is linked to the preceding material by **transition words** or **phrases** which relate the reader to the flow of ideas and maintain a sense of unity throughout. The **conclusion** enumerates the list of points covered in the body, reassuring the reader that the topic has been satisfactorily examined.

Consider this example of a formal theme about gardening:

The planting of seeds and seedlings is a restful hobby, whether done in greenhouse, landscape, or vegetable bed. The greenhouse, where unpromising trays of brown soil yield frail green tendrils set in artificially straight rows, makes an agreeable workshop on wintry days. Later, planting the yard provides a pleasant diversion from indoors. After the last frost of the season, the vegetable bed demands attention. In each phase, the gardener finds pleasure in the encouragement of green growing things, which soon flower into appealing vegetation, colorful blossoms, or tasty fruits and vegetables.

During the wet, gray days of winter, the housebound gardener can work off energies by preparing seeds and seed trays for planting. After the initial soaking and marking of each variety, the seeds are ready to be poked into peat pots or sprinkled over expanses of potting soil. A gentle allotment of moisture works small magic. Within a few days, some seedlings are bursting from their coats and pushing their way into the light. Within weeks, the greenhouse is filled with sturdy plants and vines.

By early spring, the doughty gardener can brave chill mornings and begin tilling beds for the first yard plantings. The toughest of plants, such as pansies, nasturtiums, daisies, and sweet peas, can survive even a brief winter setback and acclimate themselves to the outdoors. Tucked within the foliage of bulb plants, the first plantings draw strength from the soil and supplant the wilting leaves of tulips and daffodils. By May, weather conditions encourage the first blossoms, which brighten the neighborhood and ready the way to a full-fledged annual garden.

Because many food plants are tender, the cultivation of a vegetable bed must wait for frost-free weather. When nights warm to the mid-forties, it is time to set pepper and tomato plants, cucumber vines, squash, and melons. These plants require the most intense care. The gardener must not only outwit aphids, Japanese beetles, and cutworms but also juggle weeding, cultivation, and irrigation to maintain a suitable atmosphere for the propagation of vegetables.

The garden calendar fills a full twelve months. At the end of summer, beds are cleared, mulch is heaped and turned, and tools readied for indoor use. Winter finds the gardener again preparing trays for the planting of tender seeds. Early spring offers the first warm days for the preparation of outdoor beds. The end of frost marks the best time to set out vegetable plants. By summer, the culmination of these days of preparation offer the gardener's true reward — a bounty of wholesome vegetables and armloads of flowers to enjoy and share.

8.7 OUTLINING

The **outline** provides a skeleton of basic ideas upon which the writer adds flesh. The careful listing of **subtopics** under main topic headings focuses the writer's attention and identifies any areas which need more development.

There are two types of outlines — **topic** and **sentence.** The first type, which consists of phrases, requires fewer words and is easier to construct. The second type is constructed out of whole sentences which can be lifted in their entirety and placed in the body of the essay. Either style has its merits.

Example 1: Sample Essay Outline

I. Introduction
  A. Topic sentence
  B. Thesis statement
  C. Forecasting
    1. Point 1
    2. Point 2
    3. Point 3
    4. Transitional sentence

II. Body
  A. Point 1
    1. Defending statement
    2. Defending statement
    3. Defending statement
    4. Summary

  B. Point 2
    1. Defending statement
    2. Defending statement
    3. Defending statement
    4. Summary

  C. Point 3
    1. Defending statement
    2. Defending statement
    3. Defending statement
    4. Summary

III. Conclusion
  A. Restatement of thesis
    1. Point 1 restatement
    2. Point 2 restatement
    3. Point 3 restatement
  B. Concluding statement

"Fortune brings in some boats that are not steer'd."

— From *Cymbeline*
by William Shakespeare

Simple Topic Outline

The Roman House
I. Arrangement of rooms
  A. Atrium or main room
  B. Other inner rooms
    1. Tablinum or den
    2. Alae or bedrooms
  C. Hortus or garden
II. Outside of house
  A. Walls
  B. Culina or kitchen
  C. Roof
III. Furnishings
  A. Braziers
  B. Oil lamps
  C. Curtains
  D. Couches and chairs
  E. Tables

"The quality of mercy is not strained,
It droppeth as the gentle rain from heaven
Upon the place beneath: it is twice blessed;
It blesseth him that gives and him that takes:
'Tis mightiest in the mightiest; it becomes
The throned monarch better than his crown. . ."

— From *The Merchant of Venice*
by William Shakespeare

Sentence Outline

Security in a Medieval Castle

I. The external construction of the medieval castle was designed for security.
  A. A moat encircled the building to limit access to the external walls.
  B. A single drawbridge could be raised and lowered from within.
  C. Crenellated walls contained loops through which archers aimed their weapons.

II. The inner walls enclosed a courtyard and living quarters.
  A. Apartments and barracks were surrounded by fireproof walls.
  B. An inner gate prevented sudden takeover if the outer fortification was breached by invaders.
  C. Guard towers at each corner provided a vantage point for constant surveillance and protection.

III. Special features protected castle dwellers during attacks.
  A. A portcullis or grille sealed off the passage to each gatehouse.
  B. The hoarding or projection allowed defenders to drop boulders and hot liquids on invaders who approached too near the outer walls.
  C. Murder holes in the floor of the upper story enabled inhabitants to aim weapons or drop hot liquids on invaders who entered the ground floor.

Note: The **complexity** of the assignment will determine the amount of detail your outline should contain.

"Love looks not with the eyes, but with the mind.
And therefore is winged Cupid painted blind."
— From *A Midsummer-Night's Dream*
by William Shakespeare

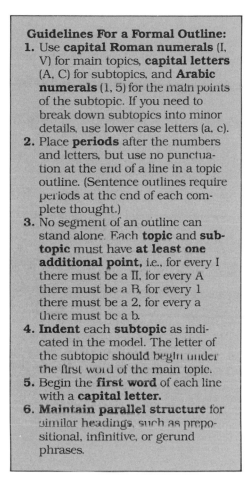

Guidelines For a Formal Outline:

1. Use **capital Roman numerals** (I, V) for main topics, **capital letters** (A, C) for subtopics, and **Arabic numerals** (1, 5) for the main points of the subtopic. If you need to break down subtopics into minor details, use lower case letters (a, c).

2. Place **periods** after the numbers and letters, but use no punctuation at the end of a line in a topic outline. (Sentence outlines require periods at the end of each complete thought.)

3. No segment of an outline can stand alone. Each **topic** and **subtopic** must have **at least one additional point,** i.e., for every I there must be a II, for every A there must be a B, for every 1 there must be a 2, for every a there must be a b.

4. **Indent** each **subtopic** as indicated in the model. The letter of the subtopic should begin under the first word of the main topic.

5. Begin the **first word** of each line with a **capital letter.**

6. **Maintain parallel structure** for similar headings, such as prepositional, infinitive, or gerund phrases.

"Glory is like a circle in the water,
Which never ceaseth to enlarge itself
Till by broad spreading it disperses to nought."
— From *King Henry the Sixth, Part I*
by William Shakespeare

CHAPTER 8

8.8 There are **six key issues** to consider when you begin writing your essay.

- **the audience**
  Will this paper be read by a specialized or general audience? A knowledge of the experience and education level of the audience determines the selection of appropriate facts, vocabulary, and tone.

- **the purpose**
  Will this paper persuade the reader to adopt a certain viewpoint? to learn a new procedure? to see a cause-and-effect relationship? A clear idea of the purpose will suggest a style and tone appropriate to the subject matter.

- **attitude or tone**
  Does this paper prove or disprove an idea? Is it clear what choice you want to portray? An essay that attempts to answer both sides of a question is impossible from the start.

- **narrowing the focus**
  Does this paper attempt too great or too small an idea for its size? An altered statement of purpose can benefit both writer and audience, such as the narrowing of "The Whaling Industry" to "Japanese Whaling Techniques."

- **order of ideas**
  Would the essay profit from a more dramatic arrangement, with the weakest ideas followed by progressively stronger ideas? The placement of the strongest argument or statement just before the conclusion leaves a lasting, more convincing impression in the reader's mind.

- **unity**
  Do all the sentences reflect the main idea? Does the evidence lead to an irrefutable conclusion? Do transitional devices reveal the relationships between ideas? In order for an essay to leave a firm impression, it must function as a single unit.

Like the paragraph, the **essay** or **theme** contains the same progression of ideas:
- introduction or statement of thesis
- body of evidence proving the thesis
- summary or conclusion

8.9   The **thesis statement** has a special function. As the straightforward statement of intent, it reveals to the reader an idea which requires demonstration, justification, or proof, as shown by this example.

The railroad once served as the backbone of American economic development by stimulating industrial growth, developing remote areas of the country, and providing work for laborers.

The writer uses the thesis statement to introduce or establish the **main idea,** assert an attitude toward it, and **forecast** the method by which the idea will be proved.

Note: The example above contains a simple overview or outline of the body:
- the stimulation of industrial growth
- the development of remote areas of the country
- the provision of work for laborers

Each **body paragraph** is a segment of proof. When all the paragraphs in the body are complete, they should comprise a solid structure which leaves no doubt that the topic sentence is a true and worthy statement. Some possibilities for development include:

- illustrations
- facts
- statistics
- examples
- specific details
- reasons
- analogies
- quotations from experts
- hypothetical cases
- models

The **concluding paragraph** should restate the original theme topic, highlight the main points that support the topic, and draw conclusions from the development of details in the body of the theme. No new points are introduced at this stage. The point of a concluding paragraph is the **summarization** of all that has gone before.

8.10 DICTION

Diction or appropriate word choice is crucial to accurate and effective expression. Terms or expressions that are appropriate to conversation, friendly exchange, or formal occasions are out of place in theme writing.

For example, avoid the following types of language:

• **slang**	colorful street language, such as *O.K.*, swear words or vulgar or suggestive terms
• **colloquial**	everyday spoken language and contractions, such as *don't, can't, home ec.*, and *p.e.*
• **formal**	erudite or overly impressive language, such as *visual acuity, temporary hiatus,* or *straitened financial means*
• **jargon**	words which only a specialist will understand, such as *RAM* or *DOS* from computer lingo
• **archaic**	expressions that belong to an earlier era, such as *methinks* or *forsooth*
• **cliché**	overused, unoriginal phrases, such as *each and every one, last but not least, as clear as crystal, at this point in time.*

The audience for which essays and themes are written is an educated and intelligent readership. **Standard English,** like the language used by most television newscasters and newspaper reporters, is the best choice of language for your purpose.

8.11 TRANSITIONAL DEVICES

Transitional devices assist the reader in understanding how the writer moves from one idea to another. In choosing a transitional device, ask yourself what relationship the second idea has to the first. Then select a term that expresses that relationship.

in similar style or direction

and	both . . . and	not only . . . but also
also	besides	moreover
furthermore	indeed	likewise
especially		

comparison

moreover	indeed	in fact
than	as . . . as	so . . . as
accordingly	similarly	such

contrast

but	yet	not only . . . but also
however	nevertheless	still
although	on the other hand	on the contrary
instead	in spite of	conversely

indication of results

therefore	thus	consequently
as a result	hence	obviously
for	so	inasmuch as
because	since	as
why	so that	in order that

introduction of examples

for example	for instance	a case in point
namely	indeed	in particular
such as	especially	

positive choice

or	either . . . or	still
moreover	whether	whereas
accordingly	likewise	also

negative choice

nor	neither	neither . . . nor
however	nevertheless	otherwise
only	except that	conversely

condition

if	providing	unless
as if	though	although
as though	provided	in the case of

concession

unless	insofar as	the fact that
though	although	while
yet	admittedly	

time

then	meanwhile	when
whenever	since	while
till	until	finally
before	as soon as	second
first	at the outset	now
to begin with	before	last
next	during	earlier
soon	at that moment	eventually
later	from then on	not long after
afterwards	in future	
at length	as long as	

place

where	wherever	here
thence	ahead	behind
overhead	nearby	beneath
near	inside	above
beyond	outside	

8.12   When the **first draft** of a theme is complete, the writer should be able to answer the following questions:

- Is the **wording** simple, clear, and exact?
- Are **sentences** a reasonable length, neither choppy nor run-on?
- Is there a **variety of sentence types,** including simple, complex, and compound sentences?
- Do **beginnings of sentences** include a variety of phrasing, such as prepositional phrases, introductory words and phrases, adverb clauses, and infinitive and participial phrases?
- Is there an overuse of **passive verbs?**
- Are **transitional terms** spaced throughout the writing rather than perched at the beginning of lines?
- Do **transitional devices** clarify logic?
- Is there too great a dependence on **state of being verbs** such as **am, is, are, was,** or **were?**
- Are **grammar, capitalization, punctuation,** and **spelling** correct?
- Is the **level of language** suitable for the intended audience?

8.13 PREPARING THE MANUSCRIPT

The **final draft** of your essay should be the best work that you are capable of producing. Follow these suggestions for a neat, readable manuscript:

- Write on good quality white **paper** that is 8 1/2 x 11 inches. Use unlined paper for both handwritten and typewritten or printed manuscripts. If you are writing your paper in longhand, prepare a liner sheet by darkening the lines on a standard piece of notebook paper. Clip this sheet to the back of your unlined page and use the darkened lines as a guide.
- Choose black or blue-black **ink.**
- Avoid decorative or unusual **fasteners,** such as brads. A single staple in the upper lefthand corner is sufficient.
- Leave a two-inch **margin** at the top and a one-inch at the bottom and on both sides. Keep your lefthand margin straight.
- **Indent** each paragraph one-half inch or five typewriter spaces.
- **Number** the pages in the upper righthand corner. Use no punctuation after the number.
- Prepare a **title page** according to your teacher's directions. Usually the title is centered vertically and horizontally. The student's name, class, and the date are centered two inches from the bottom of the page.
- If you are using a word processor, select a simple, undecorated font and ten- or twelve-point type. Activate the spell-check if you have doubts about the spelling of some words.
- If you are using tractor-feed paper, clear away perforated strips to leave a clean edge.

8.14 OTHER TYPES OF WRITING

A common task for the student or businessperson is the **summary** or **precis.** The purpose of this assignment is a condensation or narrowing of detail to the most important facts of an article, chapter, book, proposal, or lecture. Here are several steps that will help you:

- Locate and summarize the **main ideas** of the original.
- **Restate** the main ideas in your own words.
- Maintain the **tone, purpose,** and **order** of the original.
- Evaluate your version for **clarity** and **accuracy.**

Example: Here is a four-paragraph **biographical sketch** of Charles Dickens. A student **summary** of the article follows.

A champion of the poor and underprivileged, Charles Dickens pleased audiences on both sides of the Atlantic with his many novels. His more memorable characters, such as Ebenezer Scrooge and Oliver Twist, became household names to readers who devoured his works, which were often published in serialized form. In his lifetime, Dickens achieved the fame that few authors earn before their deaths.

Charles Dickens was a voracious reader and a scholarly child. He was born in 1812 at Portsea, England, to an unpretentious lower middle class family. His father showed little ability to manage money and subsequently served a sentence at Marshalsea prison for his debts. Charles's life changed at this point. He left school at the age of twelve and labored in a shoe polish factory pasting labels on bottles. His suffering and humiliation marked his life and writing, in which vivid portrayals of poverty and degradation characterize the lives of Oliver Twist, Pip, David Copperfield, Tiny Tim, and other hard-pressed or deprived children.

Dickens worked as an office boy in a law firm before establishing himself in journalism. His first novel, *Pickwick Papers* (1837), led to his lasting fame as an entertaining novelist. Subsequent emphasis on social issues earned him the reputation of reformer. In 1842, a tour of the United States brought him in contact with his American supporters, although the American press criticized him for some of his beliefs, such as his disdain for slavery.

At the height of his career Dickens produced his major classics — *David Copperfield* (1850), *A Tale of Two Cities* (1859), and *Great Expectations* (1861). His health suffered in his last years from the punishment of too many public readings and lectures and from the mental anguish he experienced when his marriage crumbled. He died in 1870, leaving the manuscript of *Edwin Drood* unfinished.

Model Summary:

Charles Dickens was a popular author who wrote about poor people. He was born at Portsea, England, in 1812. His family suffered from poverty, and his father went to jail for owing money. Dickens described some of his family's experiences in his novels. He worked as a law clerk and later as a journalist before writing his first novel, Pickwick Papers, in 1837. His most important works are David Copperfield, A Tale of Two Cities and Great Expectations. Dickens died in 1870.

Note: Underline quoted words which are italicized in the original.

8.15 A **business letter** is one of the most frequent forms of adult composition. Unlike electronic communication, such as telephone or FAX, the letter provides the recipient with a copy of the sender's message, which may be used as a reminder or confirmation of the information as well as legal proof that the information has been both transmitted and received. The following examples illustrate the style, purpose, and tone of three types of business letters.

Semi-Block Style

```
                                    Soames Research Center
                                    12 Dayton Place                    ——— Heading
                                    Madison, Vermont 23834
                                    February 4, 1991                   ——— Date
                                                                       —— 4-6 Spaces

   Dr. James L. Roberts
   Technical Director ————— Official Title
   C & M Industrial Exchange
   P.O. Box 87028 ——————— Inside Address
   Lincoln, Nebraska 68501
```

Salutation ——— Dear Dr. Roberts:　　　⟩ **Double Space**

Indention ——————— I have located information concerning the Adams 45 engine which
I think you will find beneficial in the preparation of your proposal.
Enclosed are photocopies of the plans, implementations, and costs of ——— **Body**
both the A-6 and C-2 models.

Double Space
Indention ——————— When you have had sufficient time to consider these facts, please
submit your opinion of the Adams product. My company is eager to have
your advice on the feasibility of this project.

Double Space

　　　　　　　　　　Sincerely, —— **Complimentary Close**
　　　　3-4 Spaces ———
　　　　　　　　　　Angela McNair —— **Signature**
　　　　　　　　　　Angela McNair ——————— **Full Name**
Double Space　　　Products Supervisor —— **Official Title**

```
   AM/mes
   encl. ——————————— Enclosure
   CC: Business Manager ————— Person(s) Receiving a Copy
       Chairman of the Board
```

**Reference Initials
of Sender and Typist**

Note the following facts about a business letter:

- It begins with the **heading** or address of the sender and the current date. (If the stationery has a printed **letterhead,** the address is not necessary. The date is centered beneath the letterhead.)
- The sender's address is repeated on the upper left corner of the **envelope.**
- The **inside address** contains the same information as the recipient's address on the envelope.
- The **body** of the letter is preceded by a **salutation,** which is punctuated by a colon.
- The **body** ends with a **complimentary close,** which is punctuated by a comma.
- Paragraphs are short and to the point.
- The sender mentions specific details and states clearly the purpose and the response expected from the receiver.
- The **signature** is handwritten above the typed name of the sender.
- If the typist signs the sender's name, the signature will be initialed.
- The **reference initials** at the bottom indicate that someone other than the sender typed the letter.
- The abbreviation **encl.** indicates that something besides the letter is enclosed in the envelope.
- The abbreviation **CC** indicates that other people will receive carbon copies or photocopies of the letter. A list of recipients follows the colon after CC.
- The business letter may be either typed single-spaced or neatly written in longhand.

Note: Writers of business letters are encouraged to use a variety of complimentary closings, such as these:

Respectfully yours,	With regards,
Yours truly,	With much appreciation,
With deep concern,	Gratefully yours,

Block Style

800 Graham Street
Atlanta, Georgia 30365
April 26, 1991

Elisabeth Anne Healey
Assistant Manager, Senior Division
Crown Optical Company
83 Lincolnshire Way
Dublin 2, Ireland

Dear Ms. Healey:

I read your ad in the *New York Times* in which you mention openings
in your New York office.   With seventeen years' experience polishing
industrial lenses, I feel that I am qualified for the job and am
interested in hearing more about the current needs of Crown Optical
Company.

Although my present job offers good working conditions and adequate
benefits, I would like to make a change in my employment in the near
future that will incorporate new challenges as well as opportunities
for advancement.   I request an interview at your earliest convenience.
My résumé is enclosed.

Yours sincerely,

Estelle Waters

Estelle Waters

EAW/encl.

Note that **block style** is similar to a semi-block with the exception of paragraph indentions, which are omitted. Also note that if the marital status of a female recipient is not known, the abbreviation **Ms.** is appropriate.

Full Block Style

8-B Lakeland Park Heights
Topeka, Kansas 66608
December 16, 1991

Kenneth Bailey, President
Foremost Tool Company
712 Donovan Road
Baldwin, New York 11510

Dear Mr. Bailey:

After four years of doing business with Foremost Tool Company, I feel I must complain about a change in your accounting procedure. In the past I have charged purchases to my account without incident. Since January of this year, however, my account has been closed without my knowledge. All recent order forms have been returned with no explanation.

I request that Foremost Tool Company reinstate my charge account so that I may continue purchasing your quality line of repair tools.

Yours truly,

Rodney M. Staunton

Rodney M. Staunton

RMS

Note that **full block style** omits paragraph indentions and aligns the heading, inside address, complimentary close, signature, and sender's name along the lefthand margin.

Envelope Style

Example 1:

Angela McNair
Soames Research Center
12 Dayton Place
Madison, VT 23834

ATTN: Dr. James L. Roberts
C & M Industrial Exchange
P.O. Box 87028
Lincoln, NE 68501

Note that the abbreviation **ATTN** directs the letter to the attention of a particular person at the company.

Example 2:

Mrs. Estelle Waters
800 Graham Street
Atlanta, GA 30365

Elisabeth Anne Healey
Assistant Manager, Senior Division
Crown Optical Company
83 Lincolnshire Way
Dublin 2, Ireland

Example 3:

Rodney M. Staunton
8-B Lakeland Park Heights
Topeka, KS 66608

Kenneth Bailey, President
Foremost Tool Company
712 Donovan Road
Baldwin, NY 11510

Note that envelope addresses contain **postal codes** in place of state names or other abbreviations. For a complete list of postal codes and abbreviations, consult Chapter **6.**

8.16 There are two proper methods of folding a business letter for insertion into an envelope:

> A. If you are using a standard business envelope (4 1/2" x 9 1/2").
> 1. Fold and crease the bottom third of the letter.
> 2. Fold the letter from the top edge down.
> 3. The last folded edge of the letter should enter the envelope first.
>
>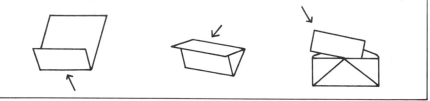

> B. If you are using a small envelope.
> 1. Fold and crease the bottom half of the letter.
> 2. Fold the letter into thirds.
> 3. The last folded edge of the letter should enter the envelope first.
>
>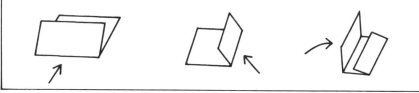

8.17 The **résumé** is an essential document for most people. It lists a person's qualifications and background and accompanies job applications and other requests for admittance or acceptance. There are five categories of data included in a résumé:

- **Personal information,** such as full name, mailing address, telephone number. (Note: By federal law you are under no obligation to mention either age, race, sex, marital status, or religious preference.)
- **Education and training,** including the schools from which you received your high school diploma, college degree, or certification in special skills, such as CPR or chauffeur's license.

- **Work history,** starting with your most recent job and including the address of the company, beginning and ending dates of employment, responsibilities, and major accomplishments while you held the position, such as salesperson of the year.
- **Memberships, interests, and hobbies,** including volunteer work, civic clubs, scout awards, military experience, and useful interests and skills, such as piano, art work, computer skills, public speaking, or physical fitness.
- **References,** which list the names, titles, addresses, and telephone numbers of several people who know you well and can attest to your character, work habits, and ambitions.

(Note: These names should not include relatives. Also, ask permission before naming anyone as a reference.)

Example:

	Résumé of Geneva Bennett 448 Steiner Street River Forest, Illinois 60305 (708) 575-1212
Education:	Barker Business College, Montford, Iowa Associate Degree in Secretarial Science December, 1979
	Montford High School, graduated with honors June, 1977
Past Jobs:	River Forest City Office, River Forest, Illinois 60305 1980 to present Receptionist and general file clerk for a staff of six
	Dennison's Department Store, Montford, Iowa 1975-1980 Sales clerk and window dresser; promoted to assistant cashier in 1978, responsible for all night deposits
Hobbies:	Swimming and diving, Red Cross certified swimming instructor, tole painting, calligraphy
Memberships:	United Methodist Church bell choir, Business Women's League
References:	Upon request

A **cover letter** should precede the résumé when it is used for a job application or as a statement of credentials. Here is an example:

---

448 Steiner Street
River Forest, IL 60305
January 28, 1991

Marta Edwards, Personnel Manager
Chamber of Commerce
Lahaina, HI 96761

Dear Ms. Edwards:

I am eager to interview for the post of Director of Local Promotions, which was advertised in the *Chicago Tribune*. As you can see from the enclosed resume, I have secretarial training and substantial office experience. Most important, I am enthusiastic about the opportunities for advancement through a change of jobs.

If the vacancy has not been filled, please advise so that I can book a flight to Lahaina and meet with you. I look forward to your response.

Yours respectfully,

Geneva Bennett
Geneva Bennett

GB/encl.

"If I could write the beauty of your eyes
And in fresh numbers number all your graces,
The age to come would say, 'This poet lies;
Such heavenly touches ne'er touch'd earthly
    faces.'"

— From Sonnet 17
by William Shakespeare

8.18 The **thank-you letter** is a common practice among well-mannered people as a means of expressing appreciation. A thank-you letter should follow promptly after every job interview, as well as for gifts, parties and dinners, awards, recommendations, and personal services. Usually letters of thanks are handwritten on personal note paper or blank greeting cards.

Example:

1101 Kentucky Avenue
Mobile, Alabama 21304
April 18, 1991

Dear Mrs. Hoffman,

   Thank you so much for recommending me for the American Field Service student exchange program. You have been a good friend and supporter for many years. I appreciate this recent expression of kindness more than I can say. Maybe with your help, I will be spending my summer in Ecuador.

                    With warm regards,

                    Amy Tallent

                    Amy Tallent

Note that a thank-you letter always mentions the gift or service for which you are showing your appreciation. Although the inside address is omitted in personal correspondence, both the recipient's address and a return address are included on the **envelope.**

Amy Tallent
1101 Kentucky Avenue
Mobile, AL 21304

                    Mrs. E. Reginald Hoffman
                    22-B Fieldstone Acres
                    Siddonsville, AL 36738

8.19 The **biographical essay** is a frequent request on college admission forms as well as scholarship applications and requests for special jobs and opportunities, such as camp counselor, summer intern, or overseas exchange student. Usually the writer is limited to a set length and must answer a specific question, for example: Why have you chosen this career as your life's work? The answer should contain as much factual, pertinent data as possible and a minimum of subjective or emotional responses. You may refer to correct essay form (Section 8.6) as a guide to the composition of a biograpical essay.

Example:

Since I was ten years old, I have wanted to learn more about raising farm animals so that I might devote my life to some area of agricultural work. I grew up on my family's 200-acre dairy farm outside Mason City, Iowa. During summers and after school, I have involved myself in numerous 4-H and community projects. Since entering Landry High School, I have chosen a concentration of science courses, including advanced biology, chemistry, earth science, and physics. With this background, I feel amply prepared for the challenge of a biology major at the University of Nebraska.

Our land has been in my family for three generations and will some day pass to me. My parents' belief in farm family traditions has been important in my early training. I would like to educate myself in modern biological theory and practice so that I may continue that tradition and establish a career in some agricultural support field, such as animal husbandry or genetic research. This knowledge, in combination with practical experience, will enable me to assist my father and uncle in the family dairy business after I graduate.

I have found many opportunities to learn on my own. When I was twelve, my father entrusted me with a small herd of heifers, which I groomed, fed, and tended until they were able to join the main herd. Last year, I won a 4-H competition for the state in herd management. My most recent project, computerized herd maintenance, was written up in the local newspapers. I intend to enter the results in the county fair this September. In past years I have taken three first prizes for best-in-show in my age division. These awards have given me confidence in my ability to produce quality dairy animals.

My work at Landry High School is consistent with your requirements for admission. I have maintained a B average in all subjects; my teachers have urged me to continue studying, particularly in the sciences. This spring I competed in the eastern division Science Fair. My slide program on the prevention of diseases in dairy cows won a second place ribbon and $200. Also, I received honorable mention in an essay contest sponsored by the Department of Agriculture for my paper on brucellosis. I feel that these independent research projects have been excellent preparation for the demands of a course of study at the university level.

I want to make farming my life's work because I believe that farmers have helped maintain our nation's greatness. Current challenges to farm families have caused many people to leave the land because they have not kept up with modern methods. To avoid the failure that often accompanies the trial and error method of farming, I want to begin my career in agriculture with the best technology for the job. A bachelor's degree in biology from the University of Nebraska is my best bet for a successful career in dairy management.

8.20 PREPARING A SPEECH

Composition, whether written or oral, demands similar skills, including research, organization, and a clear focus. However, delivering a speech puts the writer in closer contact with an audience than does writing on paper. For this reason, the speech-maker must consider the following points:

- *Assess the needs and educational level of the audience.*
  A good speaker suits the vocabulary and tone of a speech to the expectations of the audience. It is much harder to listen to complicated language than to read it from a written page. If the subject matter is technical, graphic presentations may be necessary to assure maximum comprehension. For example:

charts	audiotapes	overhead projections
chalkboards	diagrams	slides
photographs	models	videotapes
posters	demonstrations	dramatizations
films	filmstrips	

This method works well if the speaker is selling a product or demonstrating a three-dimensional object, such as proper use of a FAX machine or modem.

- *Evaluate physical limitations, particularly stage, lectern, microphone, seating, and acoustics.*
  Speaking from a seated position into a shared microphone limits a speaker. In contrast, a podium before a large assembly can be terrifyingly open to an inexperienced speaker, particularly at speaking contests. If possible, both situations should be practiced in advance to assure the most favorable intonation, posture, and delivery.

- *Select an appropriate topic.*
  A speaker needs to select a topic that fits the time allotted so that there is no feeling of urgency to cover large amounts of material in a short span of time. If the topic is controversial or emotionally stirring, the speaker should pause at appropriate moments so that the audience can react

with applause or laughter, for example at pre-election rallies or a fashion show.

- *Focus the composition on a single purpose.*
  A speaker should differentiate between passing along information, entertaining, and persuading. An informative speech, such as a travelogue, requires less emphasis than a speech designed to change people's minds, for example at a civic gathering. An entertaining speech, such as an after-dinner talk, stresses incongruities that cause the audience to chuckle. Whatever the focus, the speaker should be prepared to respond to the audience's reaction.

- *Organize facts*
  Speeches resemble other forms of composition in that they require clear statement of intent and logical arrangement of supporting data. It is wise to conclude with a memorable point, since the closing words of a speech are most likely to remain in the hearers' minds, for example at serious gatherings such as graduation ceremonies, club inductions, or dedications.

- *Rehearse the speech*
  Unlike writing, oral composition allows a speaker many opportunities to stress the organization of facts through manipulation of voice tone, hand gestures, nods of the head, and other physical demonstrations. After the speaker determines whether the task calls for impromptu or unprepared speech, extemporaneous speaking from an outline of ideas, recitation of a memorized text, or reading the composition aloud, the degree of formality determines how the speech is delivered.

- *Deliver with confidence*
  The primary instrument of the speaker is the voice. It allows a wide range of variations in volume, speed, pitch, and pronunciation. Combined with an upright, but flexible posture, sweeping eye contact, thorough preparation, and confidence, the speaker is assured a responsive audience.

"Friendship is constant in all other things
Save in the office and affairs of love:
Therefore all hearts in love use their own tongues;
Let every eye negotiate for itself
And trust no agent. . ."
— from *Much Ado About Nothing*
by William Shakespeare

LITERARY TERMS

9.1 **L**_iterary terms form a necessary body of descriptive language which enables us to label, define, examine, and discuss the style, function, and effect of literature._

A **genre** is the main classification of a work. The five major genres are **drama, poetry, fiction, nonfiction,** and **essay.** Each type has a set of characteristics that sets it apart from other literary works.

9.2 **Drama** consists of three elements:

- a story
- action that tells the story
- actors who impersonate the characters in the story.

The sequence of events in a drama is described by the following terms:
- **introduction** or **exposition** — in which the characters and the status quo are revealed to the audience.
- **rising action** or **complication** — the beginning of a conflict or entanglement.
- **climax** or **crisis** — the turning point, after which the characters' lives can never return to their original state.
- **falling action** or **denouement** — the unraveling of the suspenseful elements in the plot, such as the revelation of hidden facts or misconceptions, or the resolution of a problem.
- **catastrophe** — the conclusion of the conflict in which a tragic hero suffers punishment.

Note: Both comedy and tragedy follow the same pattern of action up to the last stage. In contrast to tragedy, a comedy ends in a **resolution** of the conflict to the good of all parties.

"It is brave to be involved,
To be not fearful to be unresolved."
— from "Notes from the Childhood
and the Girlhood,"
by Gwendolyn Brooks

Drama originated in religious ceremonies. Greek **comedies** and **tragedies,** the earliest dramas in the Western world, grew out of the worship of Dionysus, the Greek god of wine who roamed the earth and interacted with human beings. Plays marked the festivals which honored the planting, harvesting, and pruning of grapevines and attained religious and state importance.

Prizes were awarded for the best play: for the winning comedy, a laurel wreath, and the best tragedy, a goat. Originating on threshing floors, dramas were acted on circular, open-air spaces; the audience sat in rows carved out of a hillside. To enhance the projection of sound, actors wore **masks** which exaggerated facial expression and channeled sound through devices similar to megaphones.

Similarly, **medieval drama** began in the British Isles as a part of Christian worship. Members of early churches, who felt alienated by services held in Latin, pantomimed important stories of Christ's birth, death, and resurrection as a means of taking part in worship and learning more about religious faith.

The success of these Bible dramas or **mystery plays** led to the production of nonbiblical dramas called **miracle plays,** which dealt with saints' lives and **allegorical** or **symbolic** characters, such as Good Deeds, Sloth, Pride, and Envy. Because of their secular nature, miracle plays were banned from the church and performed in the streets or on portable stages called **pageant wagons.**

9.3   **Comedy,** based on the Greek word *komos* or merrymaking, is a light form of drama which entertains and amuses and always ends happily. Utilizing both **wit** and **humor,** the humor of comic situations arises from **incongruity** or unlikelihood in language, plot, or character. There are several classifications of comedy:

- **High comedy,** a subtle, often **satiric** drama which appeals to the intellect and reminds the audience of humorous situations that have serious overtones, such as greedy politicians or selfish parents. Shaw's *Androcles and the Lion* and *Pygmalion* are examples from the modern theater.

- **Low comedy** is a coarse, raucous performance which features drinking, singing, deception, posturing, dirty jokes, mockery, and fighting. The object of low comedy is the opposite of high comedy: to entertain by distracting the audience from more serious matters.

  The Greeks used **satyr plays** — short, absurdly comic scenes — to contrast the intensity of the tragedies. Shakespeare often interposed scenes of low comedy to relieve the tensions of more serious comedy as well as tragedy, such as the opening scene of *Julius Caesar*, the gatekeeper's scene in *Macbeth*, and the grave diggers' scene in *Hamlet*.

- **Romantic comedy,** in which love meets with obstacles, was a great favorite during the Elizabethan era. Some common elements include woodsy locales, idealized love matches, disapproving parents, mix-ups in identity, and disguises, particularly women dressed as men. Romantic comedies usually end in a general reconciliation, as in Shakespeare's *As You Like It* and *The Merchant of Venice.*

- **Tragicomedy** utilizes a serious plot in which situations could end disastrously but reach a happy conclusion by the intervention of a savior or by an unforeseen or improbable turn of events. Shakespeare's *Cymbeline* and *The Winter's Tale* are examples.

- **Comedy of manners** describes a drama which mocks or satirizes the artificiality and shallowness of sophisticated society. Major elements involve pretentious, jealous, or discontented characters who struggle against the conventions of polite society. The eighteenth century works of Goldsmith, Sheridan, and Congreve and twentieth century works by Noel Coward and Neil Simon are examples.

- **Court comedy or masque,** which maintains a light tone, was popular during the English Renaissance and was originally written to entertain and sometimes include members of a royal court. The emphasis on pageantry, music, dancing, costumes, masks, and intricate settings makes these plays difficult and expensive to perform. Examples can be found in pre-Easter festivities of the New Orleans Mardi Gras or similar celebrations in South America and the Caribbean.

Terms that refer to **comedy:**

- **humor** — a gentle emphasis on human faults and idiosyncrasies, such as talkativeness, gluttony, or curiosity.

- **wit** — an intellectual reaction to incongruity, usually displayed by a sharp, artful, or sophisticated arrangement of words.

- **satire** — mockery that attempts to correct human weaknesses, as in a satiric sketch of the boastful soldier or wily politician.

- **invective** — cruel, sarcastic abuse of a person or cause. This style of satiric comment usually has a particular individual, belief, or practice as its source, such as a powerful ruler or infamous person.

- **pun** — a witty play on similar meanings or sounds of words, such as the cobbler in Shakespeare's *Julius Caesar,* who insists that he is a "mender of bad soles."

- **burlesque** — absurdly exaggerated actions or costumes which poke fun at people and situations, such as a comedy routine in which grotesquely costumed surgeons use carpentry tools to perform mock surgery on an unwilling patient.

- **parody** — a composition that imitates another work in a ridiculous or absurd fashion, for example Alexander Pope's *The Rape of the Lock*, which uses eloquent epic language and mock seriousness to describe how a suitor steals a lock of hair from a young girl.

- **incongruity** — an unlikely or unseemly contrast of situations or language, such as a jealous husband who dresses as a ladies' maid in order to spy on his deceptive wife.

9.4   **Tragedy,** which is derived from *tragos,* the Greek word for the bleating cry of the goat, features the doomed struggle of a noble, but flawed human character against damaging or deadly forces. Each literary age has produced its own interpretation of this classic encounter:

- **The Greeks** emphasize a human being's struggle with fate or destiny.
- **The Romans** feature the struggle between individuals.
- **The Elizabethans** view tragedy in terms of an individual's struggle with his or her own nature.
- **Modern** playwrights stress the struggle between an individual and society.

Tragedy has the following identifiable elements:

- the **protagonist** (the **hero** or **heroine**) — the principal character.

- an **object** or **goal,** such as freedom, knowledge, power, or revenge.

- an **obstacle, person,** or **situation** which hinders the protagonist from attaining a goal, such as a corrupt law, poverty, or natural human weakness. Note: If the obstacle is human, the character is referred to as the **antagonist.**

- **complicating forces,** which further separate the protagonist from the goal, such as the objections of a family member, war, separation, or lack of opportunity.

- **resolving forces,** which assist the protagonist in removing the obstacle, such as the arrival of reinforcements, a change in weather, an inheritance, or a character's change of heart.

9.5 **Poetry** refers to the body of highly compressed, unified literary works which appeal to imagination, emotion, rhythm, the five senses, and theme for the purpose of expressing a significant or esthetic truth or giving pleasure.

Types of Poetry:

- **didactic** — conveying moral guidance, religious dogma, or instruction

- **satiric** — exposing human frailty or evil by means of irony and wit

- **lyric** — originally referring to lines sung to the accompaniment of the lyre, it features flowing, melodic verse such as in hymns, psalms, songs, odes, and ballads, which focuses on an intense, emotional impression

- **pastoral** — idealizing rustic or country life by means of overly simple characters and an artificial form or style

- **narrative** — telling a long, involved story in chronological order

- **epic** — recounting the great deeds performed by a hero who is involved in a struggle against national or cosmic forces

- **dramatic** — revealing emotional involvement of characters so as to resemble a scene from drama

- **elegaic** — meditating upon death or a serious theme

9.6 The **rhythm** of poetry is divided into **metrical feet** and described by a set of descriptive terms which relate the number of feet in each line and the arrangement of **stressed** and **unstressed** syllables in each **foot,** the standard unit of poetic measurement. The five major types of metrical feet include:

- **trochiac** — two syllables in the pattern of stressed/unstressed (´ -), as illustrated by *singer, tunnel*, and *basket.*

- **iambic** — two syllables in the pattern of unstressed/stressed (- ´), as illustrated by *bouquet, convey*, and *relax.*

- **spondaic** — two syllables, both stressed (´ ´), as illustrated by *Let go!, Come back!*, and *Not now!*

- **dactylic** — three syllables in the pattern of stressed/unstressed/ unstressed (´- -), as illustrated by *cheerily, cantering,* and *marketed.*

- **anapestic** — three syllables in the pattern of unstressed/ unstressed/stressed (- -´), as illustrated by *contradict, evermore,* and *interfere.*

The **classification** of a line of verse includes a description of the **pattern of stress** as well as a count of the **number of stresses in a line.** The count is described with Greek terms of measurement.

monometer — one foot per line
dimeter — two feet per line
trimeter — three feet per line
tetrameter — four feet per line
pentameter — five feet per line
hexameter — six feet per line
heptameter — seven feet per line
octameter — eight feet per line

Examples:

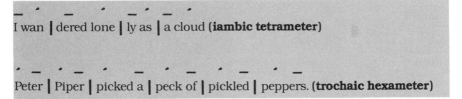

I wan | dered lone | ly as | a cloud **(iambic tetrameter)**

Peter | Piper | picked a | peck of | pickled | peppers. **(trochaic hexameter)**

The marking of the pattern of stresses is called **scansion.** To **scan** a line of poetry, place marks where they would naturally fall in words of two or more syllables. For one-syllable words, stress the noun in a noun/adjective pair. Follow the **normal stress** of your own voice as you read the line aloud. A pattern will form, even in lines of prose, for all language has a natural rhythm. Poets vary their verse in order to emphasize words or ideas. Therefore, few poems exhibit a perfect pattern of stresses.

Note: Every language has a standard pattern which characterizes its rhythm. The language of the classical Greek period falls naturally into **dactylic hexameter,** which is the meter used by Homer. English tends toward **iambic pentameter,** which was the verse pattern Shakespeare used.

9.7 POETIC DEVICES

This list of terms describes methods by which a poet emphasizes words or the relationship between words and sounds or between words and ideas.

Term	Meaning	Example
alliteration	repetition of consonant sounds	So I was once myself a swinger of birches.
apostrophe	address to a person, quality, or object	Death, be not proud.
assonance	repetition of a vowel sound	Ah, but a man's reach should exceed his grasp.
cacophony	harsh, discordant sounds	finger of birth-strangled babe
caesura	a natural pause or break	England — how I long for thee!
connotation	an implied meaning of a word	Good night, sweet prince, and flights of angels sing thee to thy rest. (burial)
consonance	the repetition of consonant sounds, but not of vowels	lake/lark; bad/bend
denotation	the literal meaning of a word	Good night, sweet prince, and flights of angels sing thee to thy rest. (sleep)
enjambment	a continuation of thought in several lines of poetry	My little horse must think it queer To stop without a farmhouse near . . .
euphony	soothing, pleasant sounds	O star (the fairest one in sight)
hyperbole	exaggeration	an eye of noblest fire
image	language that evokes one or all of the five senses (seeing, hearing, tasting, smelling, touching)	Wrap him for shroud in a petal (visual image) Soothed by music of a placid sea (aural image) That juice was wormwood (oral image) Stung by nettles; lashed by a storm (tactile image) Essence of winter sleep is on the night (olfactory image)
internal rhyme	rhyming within a line	I awoke to black flak

irony	an implied discrepancy between what is said and what is meant	"A fine thing indeed!" he muttered to himself.
metaphor	comparison of unlike things	Thou art sunshine
metonymy	substituting a word for another word closely associated with it	bowing to the sceptered isle (Great Britain)
onomatopoeia	a word that imitates the sound it represents	whistles far and *whee*
personification	giving human qualities to animals or objects	a smiling moon, a jovial sun
rhyme	a pattern of words that contains similiar sounds	know/though/snow
rhyme scheme	rhymed words at the ends of lines (labeled a, b, etc.)	Roses are red, **(a)** Violets are blue, **(b)** Sugar is sweet **(c)** And so are you. **(b)**
simile	a comparison using *like* or *as*	Vines *like* golden prisons
stanza	a unified group of lines	A penny for a spool of thread. A penny for a needle; That's the way the money goes. Pop goes the weasel!
symbol	an object or action that means something more than its literal meaning	the bird of night (*owl* — a symbol of death)
synecdoche	a part that represents the whole	lend me your ears (give me your attention)
verse	a line of poetry	Tyger! Tyger! burning bright

(For Frank Shepherd)

"Wonders do not confuse. We call them that
And close the matter there. But common things
Surprise us. They accept the names we give
With calm, and keep them. Easy-breathing then
We brave our next small business. Well, behind
Our backs they alter. How were we to know."

— From "The Artists' and Models' Ball"
by Gwendolyn Brooks

9.8 **Fiction** refers to imaginative or narrative prose in the form of **fables, fairy tales, myths, legends, folklore, short stories, novelettes,** or **novels.**

The standard **elements of fiction** include:

- **plot** — a series of events and their outcome.

- **character** — the people, animals, or fantastic creatures that perform the actions. These may be revealed by the author's description, as a result of participation in the action, or from the description of other characters. **Character** may refer to any of the following:

  > **narrator** or speaker
  > the **central character** or **protagonist,** the one about whom the plot turns
  > a **round character,** one who possesses a complex array of individual traits
  > a **flat character** or **stereotype,** one who performs a single function, such as a gas station attendant, and who reveals no depth of feeling, involvement, or intent
  > a **static character** remains unchanged by the action
  > a **dynamic character** alters in behavior as a consequence of the action. Protagonists are usually dynamic characters.

- **point of view** — the angle through which the reader perceives and interprets the action. There are several choices:

  > **omniscient** point of view, in which the author can move freely among all the characters
  > **first person** point of view, in which the author limits knowledge of the situation to the experience of a single character who describes the action using first person pronouns
  > **third person limited,** in which a single character speaks his or her experience using third person pronouns
  > **circular narrative,** which employs the individual testimony of several characters concerning a single event or issue.

- **tone** — the author's attitude toward the subject matter, such as humorous, serious, joking, ironic, mock serious, or doubtful.

- **setting** — the place of action at a particular time. Note that the setting can be imaginary, as in the dream landscape in *Alice in Wonderland.*

- **theme** — the main idea of a work, as summed up in such abstract terms as love, faith, parenthood, patriotism, loss, or alienation.

- **mood** — the prevailing atmosphere of the story, for example brooding, expectant, forbidding, solemn, relaxed, joyous, or intense.

Note: Although the **mood** and **tone** are similar, the author can manipulate the mood of the piece to indicate humor or irony, as in a mock-serious battle or a parody of a brooding gothic mystery.

The novel is often classified according to its **style** or **purpose:**

- **psychological novel** — a work that explores the motives and mental functions of a character, such as Feodor Dostoevsky's *Crime and Punishment* and Joseph Conrad's *Heart of Darkness.*
- **gothic novel** — a mystery which dwells on romance, imagination, supernatural influences, terror, ominous settings, and danger, such as Charlotte Brontë's *Jane Eyre* and Daphne du Maurier's *Rebecca.*
- **historical novel** — a fictional representation of a historical era, such as Nathaniel Hawthorne's *The Scarlet Letter* and Margaret Mitchell's *Gone with the Wind.*
- **epistolary novel** — a novel told through letters, such as Samuel Richardson's *Pamela* and Alice Walker's *The Color Purple.*
- **stream-of-consciousness novel** — a work which reveals the plot by means of the disconnected flow of thoughts through one character's mind, such as William Faulkner's *The Sound and the Fury* and Daniel Keyes's *Flowers for Algernon.*
- **sociological novel** — a work of fiction which employs character and action to reveal a social problem, such as unemployment or discrimination. Notable examples include Upton Sinclair's *The Jungle* and John Steinbeck's *The Grapes of Wrath.*
- **novel of manners** — a novel that typifies the customs, lifestyle, and values of a particular social class, such as Jane Austen's *Pride and Prejudice* and Edith Wharton's *Age of Innocence.*
- **detective novel** — the solution to a crime, usually murder or theft, in which the main character uses observation and keen deductive logic to unravel a mysterious or baffling situation, as in the works of Ellery Queen, Dashiell Hammett, and Agatha Christie. An offshoot of this genre is the **spy thriller,** which adds the extra touch of national or international intrigue, reconnaissance, or deception to the complication, as found in the works of John Le Carré.

Note: Although the **short story** possesses the same qualities as the novel and the novelette, its shorter length requires a greater compression of action and tension.

"My last defense
Is the present tense.

It little hurts me now to know
I shall not go

Cathedral-hunting in Spain
Nor cherrying in Michigan
or Maine."

— "Old Mary,"
by Gwendolyn Brooks

9.9 **Nonfiction** is the body of literature made up of factual writing, including **biography, autobiography, articles, diaries,** and **journalistic reporting.** In contrast to the more imaginative detail that colors a work of fiction, the author of nonfiction stresses clear, accurate reporting of an event, life, era, or situation. The six essential aspects of nonfiction are as follows:

- **who**— the people involved
- **what** — the situation itself
- **where** — the background or physical location
- **when** — the time frame
- **why** — the motivation of the people
- **how** — the means by which the event or situation takes place

A Great Communicator

In 1950 Gwendolyn Brooks became the first black author to win a Pulitzer Prize. *Annie Allen,* the book of poetry which garnered the prize, dealt with the experiences of poor African-Americans dwelling in Northern cities. When Brooks began writing in the 1940s, her works reflected the literary period of the time: calm, restrained, unsentimental. She dealt with people, not issues or causes. Rather than address racism directly, she confronted it with the characters she created. As racial tensions in the United States grew during the 1960s, Brooks's poetry gained a new intensity and sharpness, but she retained the mixture of objectivity and compassion that made her one of the most respected poets in the United States. Gwendolyn Brooks, although she fills her poetry with the daily experiences of poor urban blacks, gives her works a universal appeal, full of respect for all human beings.

9.10 The **essay,** a brief prose composition, contains a unified theme and a methodical, tightly-constructed style of development. Essays may be **subjective,** as in accounts, opinions, or anecdotes from a personal point of view designed to entertain or inform; or **objective,** as in formal, logical statements on a single topic of interest delivered from an unbiased, unemotional point of view, such as editorials or pamphlets. (See Chapter 8 for information about writing an essay.)

Essay varieties include:

- **monograph** — a treatise or article on a serious subject, usually scientific
- **memoir** — a short recollection written from a biographical or autobiographical point of view
- **eulogy** — a tribute or commendation in praise of a person of worthy character, usually composed after the person's death
- **biography** — a life history which emphasizes the dignity, morality, habits, lifestyle, and motivations of a particular person
- **autobiography** — a personal account of an individual's own life which emphasizes introspection or reflection
- **journal** — a meticulous daily account of events which reveal personal impressions or reactions. Purpose can vary from **diary** descriptions of ordinary human endeavors to an objective, chronological observation of a scientific nature, such as a naturalist's **notebook,** an astronomer's telescopic **studies,** or a **chronicle,** such as Caesar's *Gallic Wars*
- **sermon** — a didactic speech which seeks to impart moral or religious teachings, such as an **exegesis,** which interprets a biblical passage; or an **exemplum** or **parable,** which teaches by means of illustrative example or allegory.

The Pool Players
Seven at the Golden Shovel

"We real cool. We
Left school. We

Lurk late. We
Strike straight. We

Sing sin. We
Thin gin. We

Jazz June. We
Die soon."

— "We Real Cool,"
by Gwendolyn Brooks

SOURCES OF INFORMATION

10.1 **S**ince the beginning of the "knowledge explosion," **information** has been growing at an ever-increasing rate. No longer can a single mind encompass all the useful and necessary facts that it will need in a lifetime. Consequently, the key to education is not the memorization of facts but the wise use of **reference materials.**

The **sources** mentioned in this chapter will enable you to locate tidbits of information with a minimum of work so that you can accomplish a wide array of tasks: make a speech, write a report, finish a carpentry project, compose a letter, plan a vacation, locate a favorite poem, enjoy stamp collecting, buy a car, enroll in a college, invest in stocks, learn to pronounce a new word. These reference tools are divided into the following categories:

- **almanacs and yearbooks**
- **atlases**
- **encyclopedias**
- **biographies**
- **dictionaries**
- **handbooks**
- **thesauruses**
- **indexes**
- **catalogs**
- **computerized listings**

10.2 ALMANACS AND YEARBOOKS

These works are generally **annual** publications and contain **statistical and general information** from a single twelve-month period in tabular form, i.e., they are arranged in columns in alphabetic or numeric order.

- *Congressional Quarterly Almanac* — an annual listing of statistics and issues from the key areas of American involvement: politics, national issues, economic policy, national security, energy, environment, health, education, welfare, housing, urban development, transportation, communication, law, justice, labor, agriculture, Congress, government, foreign policy, the Presidency, and election law and procedures.

- *Facts on File* — a loose-leaf arrangement of up-to-date facts, statistics, and world events.

- *Information Please Almanac* — an annual compendium of miscellaneous information written by specialists and arranged by general classifications: politics, sports, theater, fiction, movies, music, historical statistics, who's who, and world statistics.

- *The People's Almanac* — little-known or curious facts and trivia.

- **The Statesman's Year-Book** — a concise and reliable yearly compendium of historical, descriptive, governmental, and statistical information about countries of the world and the United Nations. Contains a useful bibliography.

- **Vital Statistics of the United States** — a three-volume annual covering three classifications of information: births, deaths, and marriage and divorce.

- **The World Almanac and Book of Facts** — the most comprehensive and useful book of miscellaneous information about such diverse subjects as sports, noted personalities and entertainers, astrological events, world history, current information about nations of the world, geography, colleges and universities, U.S. presidents, and zip and area codes. There is an alphabetical index at the front of each volume.

Example:

Underwater Vehicular Tunnels in North America
(3,000 feet in length or more)

Name	Location	Waterway	Lgth. Ft.
Detroit-Windsor	Detroit, Mich.	Detroit River	5,280
Callahan Tunnel	Boston, Mass.	Boston Harbor	5,046
Midtown Tunnel	Norfolk, Va.	Elizabeth River	4,194
Baytown Tunnel	Baytown, Tex.	Houston Ship Channel	4,111
Posey Tube	Oakland, Cal.	Oakland Estuary	3,500
Downtown Tunnel	Norfolk, Va.	Elizabeth River	3,350
Webster St.	Alameda, Cal.	Oakland Estuary	3,350
Bankhead Tunnel	Mobile, Ala.	Mobile River	3,109
I-10 Twin Tunnel	Mobile, Ala.	Mobile River	3,000

The World Almanac and Book of Facts

10.3 ATLASES

An **atlas** is a collection of maps, tables, and charts on a wide variety of subjects. **Maps** are made up of several parts — **scales, latitudes, longitudes, projections, symbols, legends,** and **illuminations.**
The **atlas** usually includes an introduction, a section explaining how to find places on those maps, and a guide to interpreting facts from the charts and tables. A **glossary** assists with definitions and pronunciations of unfamiliar terms.

- **Atlas of the Bible** — a series of maps, trade routes, conquests, archeological sites, and descriptions of the Mediterranean world during Old Testament and New Testament times.

- **Atlas of World History** — covers historical periods around the world, topography, conquests, and social and governmental growth.

- **Goode's World Atlas** — includes maps of the world and tables of world facts.

- **Hammond's New World Atlas** — a complete historical, economical, political, and physical view of the world with indexes, illustrations, and a gazetteer or index of geographical names.

- **Rand McNally Signature World Atlas** — detailed maps of the countries of the world along with tables of facts, abbreviations, and a comprehensive index.

Rand McNally World Atlas

10.4 ENCYCLOPEDIAS

The **encyclopedia** is a good beginning point for any type of research. It contains an **overview** of specific places, objects, events, movements, and people; in addition it lists a **bibliography, cross references,** and an **index** to point your research in other productive directions. The alphabetic arrangement of the essays speeds the process of finding information.

The **four major encyclopedias:**

- **Collier's Encyclopedia** — geared toward both adults and young people, it contains maps, drawings, and photography and focuses on the sciences, arts, and literature.

- **Encyclopedia Americana** — an up-to-date arrangement of articles written by specialists on a wide variety of topics with emphasis on America. Many articles are signed and contain a bibliography.

- **Encyclopaedia Britannica** — a comprehensive, scholarly view of information, international in scope, and divided into four parts: the Propaedia, an outline of knowledge; the Micropaedia, quick reference; the Macropaedia, in-depth knowledge; and the Index. This work is the most famous encyclopedia in English.

Example:

Table 27: Vowel Shifts in London English

Chaucer's spelling	Chaucer's pronunciation*	Shakespeare's pronunciation	Present pronunciation*	Present spelling
lyf	li:f	leif	laif	life
deed	de:d	di:d	di:d	deed
deel	de:l	de:l	di:l	deal
name	na:mə	ne:m	neim	name
hoom	ho:m	ho:m	houm	home
mone	mo:n	mu:n	mu:n	moon
hous	hu:s	hous	haus	house

*Expressed in the International Phonetic Alphabet.

ENCYCLOPEDIAS ON SPECIFIC SUBJECTS:

* **Encyclopedia of the Animal World** — an alphabetized arrangement of facts about species of animals, their behavior, and habitats.

* **Encyclopedia of Associations** — a three-volume listing of clubs and organizations grouped together under specific headings: social, health, medical, public affairs, fraternal, foreign, ethnic, religious, veterans, hobby, athletics, labor, commerce, Greek letter, agriculture, trade, legal, military, science, education, and culture.

* **Encyclopedia of Philosophy** — a compendium of abstract topics, research, periods of influence, and philosophical development.

* **Encyclopedia of Religion and Ethics** — a multi-volume compendium with index of ethical and religious topics.

* **Encyclopedia of Science and Technology** — a scholarly source of information about pure science and technology.

* **Encyclopedia of Space** — a detailed listing of information about the universe.

* **Encyclopedia of Sports** — facts, details, rules, and records from a wide array of sports.

* **Encyclopedia of World Art** — an alphabetized listing of facts, illustrations, and drawings that concern artists, artistic works, and the philosophy of fine arts.

* **How It Works** — a twenty-volume set of information about practical applications of science and technology to everyday problems.

* **The Illustrated Family Health Encyclopedia** — a simple, pertinent listing of facts concerning health and hygiene for family use, including childhood diseases, first aid, symptoms of disease, standard treatment, and preventative measures.

* **The International Encyclopedia of the Social Sciences** — a multi-volume set with index featuring anthropology, economics, geography, history, law, political science, psychiatry, psychology, sociology, and statistics.

* **Man, Myth, and Magic** — an alphabetized compendium of facts about the occult, superstition, religion, parapsychology, legends, and myths. Heavily illustrated with drawings and photographs.

- **The New Lincoln Library Encyclopedia** — a manual of daily reference for self-instruction and general culture.

- **The New Book of Popular Science** — a six-volume compendium of data on science, machines, and technological applications complete with drawings.

- **The Universal Jewish Encyclopedia** — a multi-volume work with index which covers ideas, philosophy, events, and issues dealing with Judaism, including data from the Torah and Talmud.

10.5 BIOGRAPHIES

Collected **biographies** are multi-volume listings of the lives of people who fit under specific headings.

- **American Men and Women of Science** — includes people in the physical, biological, social, and behavioral sciences.

- **Current Biography** — an annual listing in alphabetic order of famous and influential people throughout the world.

- **Dictionary of American Biography** — a collection of biographical data about people who have achieved notoriety or greatness in American history. Does not include the living.

- **Dictionary of National Biography** — focuses on famous people from British history.

- **Twentieth Century Authors** — details works by and about twentieth-century authors.

- **Webster's Biographical Dictionary** — covers thousands of people, living and dead, in all periods of history.

- **Who's Who Among Black Americans** — focuses on the lives and accomplishments of prominent black Americans.

"Once in a long while, four times so far for me, my mother brings out the metal tube that holds her medical diploma. . . . When I open it, the smell of China flies out, a thousand-year-old bat flying heavy-headed out of the Chinese caverns where bats are white as dust, a smell that comes from long ago, far back in the brain."

— from *The Woman Warrior*
by Maxine Hong Kingston

- **Who's Who in America** — lists names of prominent Americans, their positions, and their accomplishments.

Example:

[1] GIBSON, OSCAR JULIUS, [2] physician, medical educator; [3] b. Syracuse, N.Y., Aug. 31, 1937; [4] s. Paul Oliver and Elizabeth H. (Thrun) G.; [5] m. Judith S. Gonzalez, Apr. 28, 1968; [6] children: Richard Gary, Matthew Cary, Samuel Perry. [7] BA magna cum laude, U. Pa., 1960; MD, Harvard U., 1964. [8] Diplomate Am. Bd. Internal Medicine, Am. Bd. Preventive Medicine. [9] Intern Barnes Hosp., St. Louis, 1964-65, resident, 1965-66; clin. assoc. Nat. Heart Inst., NIH, Bethesda, Md., 1966-68; chief resident medicine U. Okla. Hosps., 1968-69; asst. prof. community health Okla. Med. Ctr., 1969-70, assoc. prof., 1970-74, prof., chmn. dept., 1974-80; dean U. Okla. Coll. Medicine, 1978-82; v.p. med. staff affairs Bapt. Med. Ctr., Oklahoma City, 1982-86, exec. v.p., 1986-88, chmn., 1988—; [10] mem. governing bd. Ambulatory Health Care Consortium, Inc., 1979-80; mem. Okla. Bd. Medicolegal Examiners, 1985—. [11] Contbr. articles to profl. jours. [12] Bd. dirs., v.p. Okla. Arthritis Found., 1982—; trustee North Central Mental Health Ctr., 1985—. [13] Served with U.S. Army, 1955-56. [14] Recipient R.T. Chadwick award NIH, 1968, Am. Heart Assn. grantee, 1985-86, 88. [15] Fellow Assn. Tchrs. Preventive Medicine; mem. Am. Fedn. Clin. Research, Assn. Med. Colls., AAAS, AMA, Sigma Xi. [16] Republican. [17] Roman Catholic. [18] Clubs: Harvard (Oklahoma City); Miami Country. [19] Lodge: KC. [20] Avocations: swimming, weight lifting, numismatics. [21] Home: 6060 N Ridge Ave Oklahoma City OK 73126 [22] Office: Bapt Med Ctr 1986 Cuba Hwy Oklahoma City OK 73120	**KEY** [1] Name [2] Occupation [3] Vital Statistics [4] Parents [5] Marriage [6] Children [7] Education [8] Professional certifications [9] Career [10] Career Related [11] Writings and creative works [12] Civic and political activities [13] Military [14] Awards and fellowships [15] Professional and association memberships [16] Political affiliation [17] Religion [18] Clubs [19] Lodges [20] Avocations [21] Home address [22] Office address

Who's Who in America

10.6 DICTIONARIES

Dictionaries offer detailed information about a particular subject. The traditional dictionary covers **spelling, definition, pronunciation, usage, syllabification,** and **etymology** of English words.

A thorough coverage of the subject is called an **unabridged** version; a shortened coverage is an **abridged** edition. In addition to English dictionaries, there is a wide array of dictionaries on special interests and limited topics.

A. UNABRIDGED DICTIONARIES

- *Oxford English Dictionary* — a thorough treatment of the scope and development of the English language from its beginning.
- *New Standard Dictionary of the English Language*
- *Random House Dictionary of the English Language*
- *Webster's New International Dictionary of the English Language*

Example:

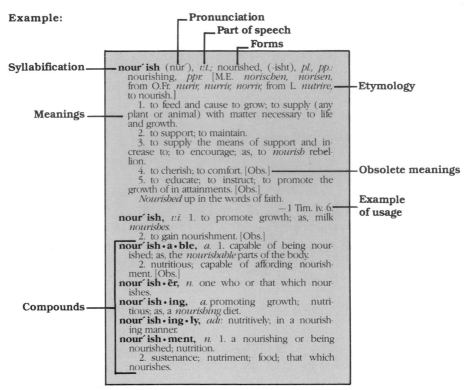

Pronunciation
Part of speech
Forms

Syllabification —

nour´ish (nŭr´), *v.t.;* nourished, (-isht), *pl., pp.:* nourishing, *ppr.* [M.E. *norischen, norisen,* from O.Fr. *nurir, nurrir, norrir,* from L. *nutrire,* to nourish.] — Etymology

Meanings —

1. to feed and cause to grow; to supply (any plant or animal) with matter necessary to life and growth.
2. to support; to maintain.
3. to supply the means of support and increase to; to encourage; as, to *nourish* rebellion.
4. to cherish; to comfort. [Obs.] — Obsolete meanings
5. to educate; to instruct; to promote the growth of in attainments. [Obs.]
   Nourished up in the words of faith.
   —1 Tim. iv. 6. — Example of usage

nour´ish, *v.i.* 1. to promote growth; as, milk *nourishes.*
2. to gain nourishment. [Obs.]

nour´ish•a•ble, *a.* 1. capable of being nourished; as, the *nourishable* parts of the body.
2. nutritious; capable of affording nourishment. [Obs.]

nour´ish•ĕr, *n.* one who or that which nourishes.

nour´ish•ing, *a.* promoting growth; nutritious; as, a *nourishing* diet.

nour´ish•ing•ly, *adv.* nutritively; in a nourishing manner.

nour´ish•ment, *n.* 1. a nourishing or being nourished; nutrition.
2. sustenance; nutriment; food; that which nourishes.

Compounds —

Webster's New International Dictionary of the English Language

B. ABRIDGED DICTIONARIES

- *The American Heritage Dictionary of the English Language*
- *The Oxford American Dictionary*
- *Webster's New World Dictionary of the American Language*
- *Webster's New Collegiate Dictionary*

Example:

Syllabification
Pronunciation (preferred and alternate)
Part of speech

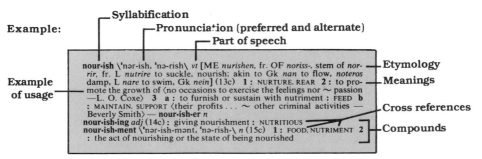

nour·ish \'nər-ish, 'nə-rish\ *vt* [ME *nurishen,* fr. OF *noriss-,* stem of *norrir,* fr. L *nutrire* to suckle, nourish; akin to Gk *nan* to flow, *noteros* damp, L *nare* to swim, Gk *nein*] (13c) **1 :** NURTURE, REAR **2 :** to promote the growth of ⟨no occasions to exercise the feelings nor ∼ passion —L. O. Coxe⟩ **3 a :** to furnish or sustain with nutriment **:** FEED **b :** MAINTAIN, SUPPORT ⟨their profits . . . ∼ other criminal activities —Beverly Smith⟩ — **nour·ish·er** *n* — Cross references

nour·ish·ing *adj* (14c) **:** giving nourishment **:** NUTRITIOUS — Compounds
nour·ish·ment \'nər-ish-mənt, 'nə-rish-\ *n* (15c) **1 :** FOOD, NUTRIMENT **2 :** the act of nourishing or the state of being nourished

Example of usage — Etymology — Meanings

Webster's New Collegiate Dictionary

- *World Book Dictionary* — serves as a complement to the *World Book Encyclopedia*

C. SPECIAL DICTIONARIES

- *Cassell's French Dictionary* (also German, Italian, Latin, Spanish, and other languages)
- *Dictionary of American Slang*
- *Dictionary of Contemporary Usage*
- *Dictionary of Foreign Terms*
- *Dictionary of Modern English Usage*
- *Dictionary of Mythology, Folklore, and Symbols*
- *Dictionary of Quotations*
- *Dictionary of Word and Phrase Origins*
- *Grove Dictionary of Music and Musicians*
- *Illustrated Dictionary of Mankind*
- *Interpreter's Dictionary of the Bible*
- *Webster's Dictionary of Proper Names*
- *Webster's New Dictionary of Synonyms*

10.7 HANDBOOKS

A handbook or guidebook is a compact reference manual containing facts or instructions on a particular subject. For example,

- *The American Book of Days* — a thorough listing and explanation of religious, national, and regional holidays and celebrations.

- *The Bicentennial Almanac* — a chronological listing of events in American history with emphasis on the Presidents.

- *Crowell's Handbook of Classical Mythology* — an alphabetical listing of gods and goddesses, characters from mythology and Greek and Roman drama, and major authors of classical literature.

- *Gray's Anatomy* — the most famous and most widely used handbook of facts concerning human anatomy, systems, and body functions.

- *Gray's Manual of Botany* — the most famous and most widely used handbook of plant classification.

- *Lovejoy's College Guide* — an index of all 2- and 4-year colleges, including majors, matching of curricula and fields of endeavor, financial aid, sports scholarships, admissions procedures, required test scores, student life, special programs, transfer requirements, and graduate degrees.

Example:

Subject → **■[1] HAWAII, UNIVERSITY OF, AT MANOA**
Address → 2530 Dole Street, Honolulu 96822 (808) 948-8111
Resource Person → Director of Admissions: Donald R. Fukuda

Telephone Number
Essential Information →
- Full Time Undergraduates: 7,093m, 7,750w
- Tuition per academic year (1984/85): $450 (in-state), $1,125 (out-of-state)
- Room & Board per academic year: $1,830-$2,268
- Fees: $31
- Degrees offered: BA, BS, BBA, BFA, BSW, BArch, BEd, BMus, AS
- Student-faculty ratio: 9 to 1

A public university established in 1907. 300-acre campus in Oahu Island's residential Manoa Valley, between downtown Honolulu and Waikiki.
Academic Character WASC and professional accreditation. Semester system, 2 6-week summer terms. Over 110 majors offered by the Colleges of Arts & Sciences, Business Administration, Education, Engineering, Health Sciences & Social Welfare, Tropical Agriculture & Human Resources, and the Schools of Architecture, Law, Library Studies. College of Health Sciences & Social Welfare includes Schools of Medicine, Nursing, Public Health, Social Work. Courses in ethnic and women's studies. Graduate and professional degrees granted. Independent study. Phi Beta Kappa. Credit by exam possible; some credit/no credit options. Numerous research and science centers, including marine biological, astronomical, geophysical, biomedical centers. Population genetics lab. Environmental, Water Resources Research, and Cancer Research centers. Urban & Regional Planning Program. Language lab. Computer center. ROTC, AFROTC. 1,750,000-volume library.
Details → **Financial** CEEB CSS. University, state, medical, AFROTC scholarships; short-term, state, and health professions loans; PELL, SEOG, NSS, NDSL, NSL, GSL, CWS, university work program.
Admissions High school graduation with 15 units required. Admission standards higher for out-of-state applicants. SAT or ACT required. $10 fee for out-of-state applicants. Rolling admissions. Application deadline May 1; later applications considered if space available. Partial tuition deposit required with acceptance of offer of admission. Early Admission for local students. Transfers accepted. Credit possible for CEEB AP and CLEP exams. Trio Project for disadvantaged students.
Student Life Student government. Newspaper, literary magazine, yearbook. Debate. Drama & music groups. Numerous special interest, academic, and honorary groups. Fraternities and sororities. Limited campus housing; state residents receive priority. Some off-campus university housing. 28% of students live on campus. 10 intercollegiate sports for men, 8 for women; intramurals. Student body composition: 73.1% Asian, 0.4% Black, 1.3% Hispanic, 0.1% Native American, 20.4% White, 4.7% Other. 17% from out of state.

Lovejoy's College Guide

- ***Peterson's Guide to Four-Year Colleges*** — profiles over 1900 four-year schools, their admissions requirements, financial aid, student body, athletics, 446 majors, cost list, advice on selection, required scores, career planning, and photographs of campuses.

- ***The Timetables of History*** — a useful desk reference to the entire span of history, arranged by single years and divided into seven categories: history, politics, literature, theater; religion, philosophy, learning; visual arts; music; science, technology, growth; daily life.

- ***Twenty Thousand Years of Fashion*** — a chronological picture book of styles of dress around the world throughout history complete with drawings and commentary.

- ***Weapons and Warfare*** — a compendium of weaponry, strategy, and methods used in warfare from early times.

10.8 THESAURUSES

A **thesaurus** is a word book which offers detailed lists of **synonyms, antonyms, usage, spelling,** and **shades of meaning.** Used in conjunction with a dictionary, it is the second most important desk reference for writing and comprehension.

Example:

Numbered entry	**551. FIGURE OF SPEECH**
Noun usage	.1 NOUNS figure of speech, figure, image, trope. turn of expression, manner or way of speaking, ornament, device, flourish, flower; purple passage; imagery, nonliterality, nonliteralness, figurativeness, figurative language; figured or florid or flowery style, asiaticism, floridity, euphuism.
Verb usage	.2 VERBS metaphorize, figure [archaic]; similize; personify, personalize; symbolize
Paragraph number of cross reference	572.6.
	.3 ADJS figurative, tropological; **metaphorical**, trolatitious; allusive, referential; man-
Adjective usage	nered, figured, ornamented, **flowery** 601.11.
	.4 ADVS figuratively, tropologically; **meta-**
Adverb usage	**phorically;** symbolically; **figuratively speaking,** so to say or speak, in a manner of speaking, **as it were.**
	.5 figures of speech
Specific examples	agnomination catachresis
	alliteration chiasmus
	allusion circumlocution
	anacoluthon climax
	anadiplosis conversion
	analogy ecphonesis
	anaphora emphasis
	anastrophe enallage
	antiphrasis epanaphora
	antithesis epanodos
	antonomasia epanorthosis
	apophasis epidiplosis
	aporia epiphora
	aposiopesis eroteme
	apostrophe exclamation

10.9 INDEXES

An **index** is the first step in a multi-step process of gathering information. It locates **words, concepts,** or other **information** in books, periodicals, and reports so that you can find articles or books related to your research topic or locate specific quotations, articles, poems, plays, essays, or short stories in anthologies or bound volumes. Indexes may be limited to a small span of years.

- *Book Review Index*
- *Books in Print*
- *ERIC (Education Resources Information Center)*
- *Essay and General Literature Index*
- *Familiar Quotations*
- *Granger's Index to Poetry*
- *Index to Science Fiction*

- *Magazine Index*
- *Newspaper Index*
- *New York Times Index*
- *Paperbacks in Print*
- *Play Index*
- *Readers' Guide to Periodical Literature*
- *Short Stories Index*

Example:

Books In Print	Books In Print	Books In Print	Books In Print	Books In Print	Books In Print	Books In Print	Books In Print	Books In Print	Books In Print
1991-92	1991-92	1991-92	1991-92	1991-92	1991-92	1991-92	1991-92	1991-92	1991-92
AUTHORS	AUTHORS	AUTHORS	TITLES	TITLES	TITLES	SUBJECTS	SUBJECTS	SUBJECTS	SUBJECTS
Vol. 1 A-G	Vol. 2 H-P	Vol. 3 Q-Z	Vol. 4 A-G	Vol. 5 H-P	Vol. 6 Q-Z	Vol. 1 A-C	Vol. 2 D-I	Vol. 3 J-P	Vol. 4 Q-Z
Bowker	Bowker	Bowker	Bowker	Bowker	Bowker	Bowker	Bowker	Bowker	Bowker

Books in Print

Note: The spine of each volume indicates the year(s) covered and the span of the alphabet included in that volume. Individual volumes are organized by author, or title, or subject.

Examples of a book as listed in the subject and title guides of **Books in Print:**

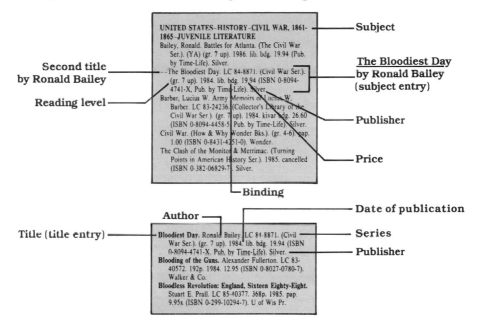

Subject

UNITED STATES–HISTORY–CIVIL WAR, 1861–
1865–JUVENILE LITERATURE
Bailey, Ronald. Battles for Atlanta. (The Civil War
Ser.). (YA) (gr. 7 up). 1986. lib. bdg. 19.94 (Pub.
by Time-Life). Silver.
--The Bloodiest Day. LC 84-8871. (Civil War Ser.).
(gr. 7 up). 1984. lib. bdg. 19.94 (ISBN 0-8094-
4741-X, Pub. by Time-Life). Silver.
Barber, Lucius W. Army Memoirs of Lucius W.
Barber. LC 83-24236. (Collector's Library of the
Civil War Ser.). (gr. 7 up). 1984. kivar bdg. 26.60
(ISBN 0-8094-4458-5 Pub. by Time-Life). Silver.
Civil War. (How & Why Wonder Bks.). (gr. 4-6). pap.
1.00 (ISBN 0-8431-4251-0). Wonder.
The Clash of the Monitor & Merrimac. (Turning
Points in American History Ser.). 1985. cancelled
(ISBN 0-382-06829-7). Silver.

Second title
by Ronald Bailey

Reading level

**The Bloodiest Day
by Ronald Bailey
(subject entry)**

Publisher

Price

└─Binding

Author ─

Bloodiest Day. Ronald Bailey. LC 84-8871. (Civil
War Ser.). (gr. 7 up). 1984. lib. bdg. 19.94 (ISBN
0-8094-4741-X, Pub. by Time-Life). Silver.
Blooding of the Guns. Alexander Fullerton. LC 83-
40572. 192p. 1984. 12.95 (ISBN 0-8027-0780-7).
Walker & Co.
Bloodless Revolution: England, Sixteen Eighty-Eight.
Stuart E. Prall. LC 85-40377. 368p. 1985. pap.
9.95x (ISBN 0-299-10294-7). U of Wis Pr.

Title (title entry) ─

Date of publication

Series

Publisher

A Great Communicator

Maxine Hong Kingston was born in 1940 in Stockton, California, the daughter of Chinese immigrants who worked in a laundry and as field hands. Her mother, who had come from China less than a year before, wanted Maxine to have the up-bringing commonly given to girls in China. The traditional status of women in China was quite low; they were to be totally subservient to men and often were little better than slaves. *Woman Warrior,* Kingston's first book, showed the clash between the traditional role awarded Chinese women and the totally different opportunities available in the United States. Another book. *China Men,* discusses the experiences of Kingston's male ancestors and other Chinese men as laborers in the Gold Mountain — the United States. Throughout her books Kingston weaves autobiography and history with Chinese myths and legends. Her work has provided a link between modern Chinese-Americans and their heritage.

Example:

Key Word: LIBERTY   Page & paragraph number

Liberty a beloved discipline, 877 : 14
  abstract l. not found, 372 : 18
  Americans love l., 351 : 3
  and glory of his country, 450 : 5
  and justice for all, 677 : 10
  and tyranny, 523 : 7
  and Union, 450 : 16
  arduous struggle for l., 383 : 1
  as end and means, 677 : 12
  assert and maintain l. and
    virtue, 380 : 6
  basis of democratic state is l., 88 : 12
  bulwark of continuing l., 780 : 6
  bulwark of our l., 520 : 7
  bulwarks of l., 367 : 6
  by accident got its l., 154 : 8
  cannot be preserved without
    knowledge, 380 : 9
  captivity is consciousness so's
    l., 605 : 9
  change from l. to force, 418 : 2
  condition on which given l., 397 : 21
  contending for l., 379 : 1
  corruption symptom of l., 383 : 11
  cost of l., 724 : 18
  courage secret of l., 677 : 12
  cradle of l., 451 : 15
  crust of bread and l., 339 : 11
  definition of word l., 523 : 7
  degradation of idea of l., 882 : 10
  democracy seeks equality in
    l., 506 : 12
  deprived of life l. or
    property, 391 : 17, 392 : 4
  divinest l., 435 : 13
  doing what laws permit, 341 : 8
  doing what one desires, 508 : 15
  enjoy delight with l., 174 : 12
  enjoy such l., 296 : 4
  enjoyment of life and l., 367 : 4
  equality fraternity, 928 : 2
  establish our real l., 164 : 17
  extremism in defense of l., 385 : n 2
  freedom enfranchisement, 216 : 6
  from despotism to l. in
    featherbed, 388 : 9
  give me l. or death, 383 : 5
  God who gave life gave l., 387 : 8
  greatest dangers to l., 677 : 15

Author

Paragraph 5

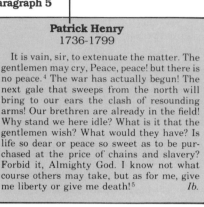

Patrick Henry
1736-1799

5 It is vain, sir, to extenuate the matter. The gentlemen may cry, Peace, peace! but there is no peace.[4] The war has actually begun! The next gale that sweeps from the north will bring to our ears the clash of resounding arms! Our brethren are already in the field! Why stand we here idle? What is it that the gentlemen wish? What would they have? Is life so dear or peace so sweet as to be purchased at the price of chains and slavery? Forbid it, Almighty God. I know not what course others may take, but as for me, give me liberty or give me death![5]   *Ib.*

Page 383, paragraph 5

Whole
phrase

Familiar Quotations

Example:

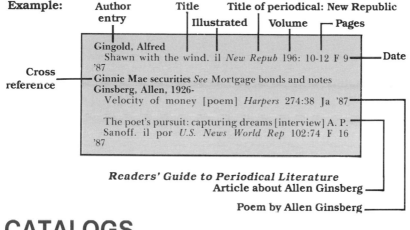

Readers' Guide to Periodical Literature
Article about Allen Ginsberg
Poem by Allen Ginsberg

10.10 CATALOGS

The **catalog** is the key to the library. It lists what materials are available, which are relevant to your subject, and where you can find them. There are several types: the **traditional catalog,** composed of file cards in small drawers, and the **online catalog,** housed in a computer.

Either type may be arranged by the **Dewey Decimal Classification system** or the **Library of Congress Classification System.** Both methods attempt to arrange materials in an orderly fashion to make retrieval of information easier and more productive.

Dewey Decimal Classification System

000-099	General Works
100-199	Philosophy, Related Disciplines
200-299	Religion
300-399	Social Sciences
400-499	Language
500-599	Pure Science
600-699	Technology or Applied Science
700-799	The Arts
800-899	Literature
900-999	General Geography and History

The decimal system allows librarians to achieve greater accuracy in pinpointing the subject and purpose of a work. For example, with the classification 591.525, the numbers indicate the following information:

500	science
590	zoological science
591	general zoology
591.5	ecology of animals
591.52	specific relationships and kinds of environments
591.525	migrations

Library of Congress Classification Key

A	General Works, Polygraphy
B	Philosophy, Religion
C	History, Auxiliary Sciences
D	History and Topography (except America)
E-F	America
G	Geography, Anthropology
H	Social Sciences
J	Political Science
K	Law
L	Education
M	Music
N	Fine Arts
P	Language and Literature
Q	Science
R	Medicine
S	Agriculture, Plant and Animal Industry
T	Technology
U	Military Science
V	Naval Science
Z	Bibliography and Library Science

10.11 Each book in the library is represented by at least three cards in the **card catalog,** a title card, an author card, and at least one subject card.

Example of title card:

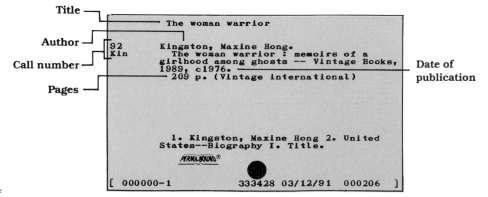

Example of author card:

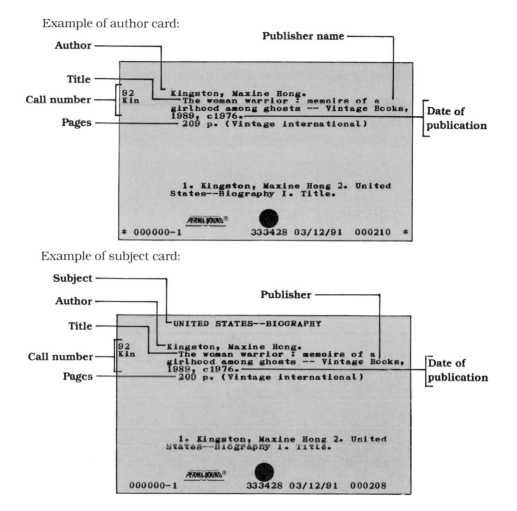

Example of subject card:

"Once in a while an adult said, 'Your grandfather built the railroad'. . . We children believed that it was that very railroad, those trains, those tracks running past our house; our own giant grandfather had set those very logs into the ground, poured the iron for those very spikes with the big heads and pounded them until the heads spread like that, mere nails to him."

— from *China Men*
by Maxine Hong Kingston

COMPUTERIZED CATALOGS

Many libraries now store their card catalog material on
computer. Users refer to the catalog computer terminals,
which display pertinent information onscreen.

Example of title search:

PUBLIC CATALOG

TITLE:	Mary Shelley/edited with an introduction by Harold Bloom.
PUBLISHER:	New York: Chelsea House, c1985.
PHYSICAL DESC:	205 p.; 24 cm.
NOTES:	Modern Critical Views
	Includes index.
	Bibliography p. 197-198.
	Contains eleven critical essays on her fictional works, arranged in chronological order of publication.
SUBJECTS:	Shelley, Mary Wollstonecraft, 1797-1851—Criticism and interpretation.
LOCATION	PR5398.M25 1985

Example of author search:

PUBLIC CATALOG   Searching

NAME: TWAIN, MARK 1835-1910
FOUND: 5

REF	DATE	TITLES	AUTHOR
R1	1983	Adventures of Huckleberry Finn	Twain, Mark
R2	1981	Pudd'nhead Wilson	Twain, Mark
R3	1970	Mark Twain's autobio	Twain, Mark
R4	1962	Letters from Earth	Twain, Mark
R5	1962	Life on the Mississippi	Twain, Mark

Example of subject search:

```
SEARCH TERM(S): SUBJECT =
NO. HEADINGS
   REFERENCES FOUND
```

1. Dinners and dining	10
2. Dinners and dining—History	3
3. Dinosauria	12
4. ALSO FOUND UNDER: Tyrannosaurus rex	
Dinosaurs	12
5. Diplomacy	11
6. Diplomacy—History	8
7. Diplomats	15

Press Line Number(s) to Select One or More Headings.
Then Press BRIEF to See the Matching References.

Or PRESS:
NEXT Page.
PREVious Page.   SEARCH HISTORY for Next Search.
HELP for Assistance   START OVER Completely.

"When she was about sixty-eight years old, Brave Orchid took a day off to wait at San Francisco International Airport for the plane that was bringing her sister to the United States. She had not seen Moon Orchid for thirty years. She had begun this waiting at home, getting up a half-hour before Moon Orchid's plane took off in Hong Kong. Brave Orchid would add her will power to the forces that keep an airplane up. Her head hurt with the concentration. The plane had to be light, so no matter how tired she felt, she dared not rest her spirit on a wing but continuously and gently pushed up on the plane's belly. She had already been waiting at the airport for nine hours. She was wakeful."

— From *The Woman Warrior*
by Maxine Hong Kingston

10.12 PARTS OF A BOOK:

A thorough knowledge of the **divisions of a book** will assist the reader in finding information. The following list names the parts of a book in the usual order in which they appear:

- **frontispiece** a photograph or sketch pertaining to the author, title, or subject

- **title page** complete title, author(s), editor(s), translator(s), publisher, and place of publication

- **copyright page** date of copyright and reprints, name of copyright holder, Library of Congress Catalog number

- **dedication** a personal remark from the author or a quotation about the subject matter

- **preface** also referred to as the *foreword* or *introduction*, an explanation of the scope and purpose of the book, often written by another author

- **acknowledgments** a list of persons who assisted or inspired the author or who allowed the author to use their work

- **table of contents** the contents of the book listed in order by sections with page numbers

- **illustrations** a list of maps, sketches, charts, diagrams, plates, figures, portraits, or photographs

- **text** the body of the book

- **appendix** additional diagrams, documents, charts, tables, and explanatory or helpful material

- **glossary** an alphabetical list of technical or unfamiliar terms including pronunciations and definitions

- **bibliography** a list of sources used by the author, sometimes including suggested readings for further research

- **index** an alphabetical list of topics and subtopics used in the book with page numbers for handy reference

THE RESEARCH PAPER

11.1 **A** *research paper* *is an intense study of a single topic. It requires:*

- **disciplined investigation**
- **reading**
- **notetaking**
- **analysis**
- **organization**
- **writing**

For most students, however, the most overwhelming part of the task is following the required **form.** *Once you have the assignment and have chosen a topic of investigation, these suggestions will help you complete your work.*

A Great Communicator

Maya Angelou has been, among other things, a singer, actress, playwright, poet, composer, director, and screenwriter. The first part of her autobiography, *I Know Why the Caged Bird Sings*, has been hailed as a coming-of-age classic. She has written several books of poetry and was the first African-American woman to have an original movie script produced. Born in 1928, she spent much of her childhood with her grandmother in the small town of Stamps, Arkansas. During the 1950s she was an actress and singer, and was active in the civil rights movement. During the 1960s she spent time in Africa, where she was a political activist and magazine editor. Angelou has also worked in television and appeared in Broadway plays, and has held positions at several universities. She is considered one of the major figures in contemporary African-American literature and is widely respected for overcoming many social and economic obstacles.

11.2 LIMITING THE TOPIC

- If possible, **choose a topic that interests you.** If you have no choice in the matter, focus your investigation on some aspect of that choice which interests you, such as the imaginary hobbit world of J.R.R. Tolkien's *The Hobbit* or the western work ethic depicted in Larry McMurtry's *Lonesome Dove.*

- **Jot down informal subtopics** pertaining to a topic, such as the Gettysburg Address, Lincoln's campaign speeches, addresses to Congress.

- Group your ideas into an **informal outline.** When you see a pattern forming, you are ready to begin.

- **Get an overview** of the subject by reading a general description of the topic, for example an encyclopedia article on space stations or a book about interplanetary travel.

- **Write a rough outline** of points you might include in your paper, such as

> 1. Prehistoric writing
> 2. The first alphabet
> 3. The Greek alphabet
> 4. The Roman alphabet
> 5. The beginning of modern writing

- **Narrow your topic** to a manageable one. Fit the topic to the required length of your assignment. For example, you cannot possibly cover the life of Shakespeare in a term paper, but you can cover one aspect, such as the flower images in Shakespeare's *A Midsummer Night's Dream.*

> - Shakespeare
>   - Shakespeare's plays
>   - Shakespeare's comedies
>   - Shakespeare's *A Midsummer Night's Dream*
>   - Poetic images in *A Midsummer Night's Dream*
>   - Flower images in *A Midsummer Night's Dream*

- As you read and analyze your topic, other ideas will come to you. Therefore, be prepared to **refine your topic** as you work. Having an open mind is a major benefit to research. If you already know what you will find, you are not really researching a topic.

11.3 STATING YOUR THESIS

- **Summarize in one sentence the scope of your research.** This controlling idea or **thesis statement** will focus your research and keep you from straying from the task at hand.

- Use a **declarative sentence** rather than a question. For example: In *The Chocolate War*, Robert Cormier creates an unsettling, sinister private school environment.

- **Alter your thesis** whenever you find that the bulk of your research is leading toward a particular conclusion.

- **Finalize your thesis** at the end of your note-taking so that you have a definite goal for your paper. For example:
Through careful description of the working poor in *The Grapes of Wrath*, John Steinbeck offers a stark, realistic picture of the sufferings of migrant workers during the 1930s.

11.4 GATHERING INFORMATION

- **Look through indexes** such as the *Readers' Guide to Periodical Literature, Books in Print, InfoTrac, Facts on File*, and the subject index in your library's card catalog for articles and books on the subject. (See Chapter 10 for information about library catalog systems.)

- **Begin reading,** referring to the table of contents or index of each book for specific references to your topic.

- **Summarize general information** on the topic, even though you may not need it for your paper.

- **Paraphrase** information by putting it into your own words. For example, consider this quotation from Brian Wilks's *The Brontës: An Illustrated Biography* and the student version that follows:

> Charlotte wrote to Southey, the poet laureate, confessing her lifelong wish to become a writer only to be admonished and warned that so unfeminine a career was hardly likely to be suitable:
>
> Literature cannot be the business of a woman's life, and it ought not to be. The more she is engaged in her proper duties, the less leisure she will have for it, even as an accomplishment and a recreation.
>
> Student's paraphrase:
> The poet laureate, Southey, wrote to Charlotte Brontë and urged her to give up writing so that she could tend to womanly duties.

A second example comes from the *Oxford Illustrated Literary Guide to Great Britain & Ireland:*

> **Dublin.** Capital of the Republic of Ireland, a cathedral and university city and port situated on the Liffey at the head of Dublin Bay. Its site as a human settlement dates from prehistoric times and it was a community of some consequence when the Vikings invaded and established themselves in the 9th and 10th centuries.

> Student's paraphrase:

> The city of Dublin was already established when the Vikings invaded in the 9th and 10th centuries.

Note: In the second model, by deleting other details, the student emphasizes the piece of information which relates to the subject of the paper, the extent of Viking invasions in the British Isles.

- **Use small note cards** for recording information about each work. Keep meticulous records of the title, author(s) and/or editor(s), publisher, and date and place of publication on each source.

- **Place the call number** of the book in the upper righthand corner for easy reference. Use these sample cards as models:

920.8
L68S

Sampson, S.E., ed. World Masterpieces. New York: American Book Publishers, Inc., 1967.

Periodical

Lafone, Bonnie, and L. Jay Robinson, "Oriental Philosophers of the Nineteenth Century," World Literary Review, 21 (June, 1990), 134, 285-87.

Note: The information after the title of the journal reads "Volume 21, June, 1990, pages 134 and 285-87."

- **Use large note cards** for taking notes.

- **Number** multiple cards from a single source. For example, Canaday 1, Canaday 2, etc. If there are several sources by Canaday, briefly identify the particular title, as in Canaday, Works, 1; Canaday, Literary, 1.

- **Summarize one topic per card.** Don't try to squeeze great quantities of information onto a single card.

Note: When you begin your rough draft, you will arrange these cards according to topics. Each stack of cards will comprise a **single paragraph.**

- State the **topic, source, and page numbers** at the top of each card, for example:

    "Scientific Method"   Gray's Handbook, pp. 45-61

- **Quote verbatim** any phrase or segment that rings true of your topic.

- If you choose to **delete parts of a quotation,** use three dots or ellipsis points to mark the absence of the author's exact words. For example,

Lincoln stated his intention to "extend the hand of brotherhood . . . to all people, whether they supported North or South, whether they owned slaves or not."

A second example demonstrates the use of three ellipsis points and a period at the end of a sentence:

In his dialogue dated January 13, 1944, Alfred North Whitehead states that "No period of history has ever been great or ever can be that does not act on some sort of high, idealistic motives . . . ."

Note: Quoted material that is interrupted too often by ellipsis loses its original meaning, flavor, rhythm, and purpose. If a passage seems useful, but requires extensive cutting, it should be paraphrased.

Sounds / Like pearls / Roll off your tongue / To grace this eager ebon ear.

Doubt and fear, / Ungainly things, / With blushings / Disappear.

— "Sounds Like Pearls"
by Maya Angelou   153

- Don't overlook other sources of information in a library, such as

special collections	vertical files	films
filmstrips	disc recordings	audio tapes
video tapes	maps	globes
drawings	framed art prints	microfische
microfilm	children's books	display
newspapers	unbound periodicals	charts

Also, you can get more information from live interviews with local experts, interlibrary loan, and special requests to the Library of Congress.

11.5 WRITING THE PAPER

- **Choose an organizational** style which suits the tone and scope of your paper, such as cause and effect, comparison or contrast, left to right, top to bottom, chronological order, or least to greatest (see Chapter 8).

- **Compose a formal outline,** using either topic or sentence style (see Chapter 8).

- **Separate your note cards** into stacks according to the subtopics of your outline. For example, in a paper on the early history of choral music, group together information under subtopics, such as chants, antiphonal arrangement, and the invention of harmony.

- Using individual stacks of cards for each paragraph and following the flow of your outline, **compose a rough draft** of the introduction, body, and conclusion.

Note: Use no quoted or paraphrased material in the introduction or conclusion of your paper. Instead, concentrate on a clear statement of your theory, objective, or problem in these sections and the points that support your thesis.

"If we were a people much given to revealing secrets, we might raise monuments and sacrifice to the memories of our poets, but slavery cured us of that weakness. It may be enough, however, to have it said that we survive in exact relationship to the dedication of our poets (include preachers, musicians and blues singers).

— from *I Know Why The Caged Bird Sings*
by Maya Angelou

- Incorporate quotations into your writing by introducing and concluding each with a statement of source or meaning. For example,

  a. In his biography of Queen Victoria, *Queen and Consort*, Steven Abrams insists that . . .
  b. At the conclusion of his remarks in *Business Review*, Karl Jamison, an authority on Latin American commerce, adds . . .
  c. After a detailed analysis of Dr. King's speech for the *Los Angeles Times*, Sandra O'Hare notes that . . .
  d. In her article on whaling vessels in the *American Journal of History*, Rita Martinez concludes . . .

> Note: If quoted material covers more than three lines, **center** the quotation by **indenting** ten spaces from the left margin and typing or writing the quotation **single spaced.** Use no quotation marks to set off a centered quotation.

- When citing **act, scene, or line numbers** from a play, or **book, canto, and line numbers** from a poem, use the following form:

> Play: *Hamlet,* II, iii, 16-19
> Poem: *The Iliad,* IX, 145-148

- **Maintain a normal tone and standard diction** in your composition. Avoid first person or casual language, such as slang, contractions, overly technical language, and personal remarks or opinions.

- **Stress what you have concluded** about the topic rather than what authors have said in books and journals.

11.6 TRADITIONAL FOOTNOTING

- If you are following traditional research paper style, follow the required form in **crediting the sources** you consulted.

- Include the author or editor, title, publisher, and place and date of publication. Where authorship is unknown, as is often the case with newspaper and encyclopedia articles, begin with the title. For example:

> **book with one author**
> [1] April Anderson, *Susan B. Anthony: A Leader for the Ages.* (Chicago: Allen Publishing Co., 1982), p. 126.

book with two authors
[2]William Longcrier and Carl Baker, *Presidential Facts.* (Bakersfield, California: University City Press, 1986), pp. 114-15.

book with multiple authors
[3]Donna Samson, *et al. The History of Drama from Sophocles to O'Neill.* (New York: Summerset Press, 1983), pp. 341-47.

edited work
[4]McKinley Summers, ed., *Great Speeches.* (London: British Universal Press, 1985), p. 449.

article from a periodical or journal (no author given)
[5]"The New England Heritage of Edith Wharton," *Biographical Notes and Sketches,* 17 (June, 1984), 319-321.

translation
[6]Aesop's *Fables,* trans. Avery Richardson Grahame (Oxford: Oxford Literary Press, 1952), pp. 77-80.

encyclopedia article
[7]"Industrial Revolution," *Encyclopedia Americana,* 1987.

multivolume work
[8]Connor Fambrough. *The Harlem Renaissance.* (Springfield, Illinois: American Press, 1943), VII, 771-774.

dramatic work or long poem
[9]Anita Ryan. *A Celtic Vision,* II, i, 34. (San Diego: Seven Muses Press, 1980), p. 28.

(Note: The three numbers after the title indicate Act II, Scene i, Line 34.)

- Subsequent references to articles can be shortened to the author's last name and the page:
  [10]Summers, p. 80.
  [11]Ibid., p. 86.

Note: Ibid. is an abbreviation of the Latin word *ibidem* meaning "in the same place." It refers to the work mentioned in the previous note. This and other **scholarly and technical terms** and **abbreviations** are listed and explained at the end of this chapter.

11.7 **BIBLIOGRAPHY**

- The **bibliography,** the last section of your paper, should compile the works you have used. There are two types of bibliographies:

> a list of works cited
> a list of works consulted

The first list mentions only works which you quote or paraphrase. The second list includes every work you used in your research.

- **Alphabetize your small note cards** and prepare your bibliography according to this form:

Andersen, Hans Christian. *Stories from Scandinavia,* trans. Lynn Small. Oxford: Oxford Library Press, 1969.

Anderson, Wilson E. *A Compendium of European Folklore.* Chicago: Damon Press, 1982.

Fensterwald, Jacob C. *World Authors.* Mobile, Alabama: Southern Press, 1983.

"Folklore," *Encyclopedia Americana,* 1990.

"The Importance of Story Hour," *Parenting,* 7 (Summer, 1989), 221-224.

Leighton, Simpson, and R. Annette Warden, "Reading Aloud," *Children's Literary Review,* 217 (April, 1977), 51, 199-203.

Lozier, Tamara, and Sydney Rampling *Simple Tales from Nature.* Denver, Colorado: Libraries Unlimited, 1986.

Rasmussen, J.D. *Naming the Stars.* San Francisco: Indigo Press, 1980.

Sievers, Walter, et al. *A Collection of the World's Best Stories.* New York: Ray Press, 1983.

Sievers, Walter, ed. *Where the Best Are Found.* New York: Central Publishers, Inc., 1967.

Winstead, Lola, ed., *Memorable Works of Fantasy.* London: Heathrow Press, 1985.

Note: Bibliographical entries are **indented** on the second and subsequent lines and are **alphabetized** by the first word. Authors' names are given last name first. Page numbers of books are omitted.

11.8 MLA TERM PAPER STYLE

Of the many styles of term paper format that are available today, perhaps the most influential is the one proposed by the Modern Language Assocation, which is used by scholars as well as serious high school and college students. Although similar to the traditional style, there are certain variations, particularly where sources are cited.

- **Title Page**
Omit a cover sheet and begin one inch from the top on page one with your name followed by your teacher's name, the title of the course, and the date. Then center your title, double space, and begin the first paragraph, as in:

Rhoda Laffon   Laffon 1
Mr. Jacob V. Samuelson
English 12
March 21, 1990
    Dream Landscapes in Katherine Anne Porter's Short Stories

    A key element in the notable short fiction of Katherine Anne Porter, the inclusion of extensive passage of memory, usually reported in

---

Notice that the title is not underlined or punctuated in any way.

- **Pagination**
Number each page consecutively using your last name and an unadorned arabic numeral in the upper righthand corner, one half inch from the top. Refer to the example above as a model.

- **Citing Sources**
The end of your term paper will contain a thorough listing of all sources from which you took information. Begin on a separate page one inch from the top and list the sources by author in alphabetical order. Type the first line flush with the left margin and indent all subsequent lines. For example,

---

                                            Laffon 12

Rippey, Joseph L. *Women Authors of American Literature.*
      Boston: A. L. Withrow, 1979.
Underwood, Joseph Parks, and David Miles, Jr., eds. *A Compendium*
      of Characters from Twentieth Century Fiction. Cambridge:
      Avon Press, 1982.

Notice that the author's name is written last name first and ends with a period. The title is underlined if written in longhand, and typed in italics or underlined on a typewriter or word processor. It is followed by a period. The last part of the notation includes city of publication and colon, name of publisher and comma, followed by the year of publication and a period.

The following are the most common sources you will be using:

Book with one author
Lattimore, James T. *In Pursuit of the Dream.* New York: Universal Press, 1988.

Book with two authors
Grandstaff, Susanna, and T.F. Epperson. *Themes in American Art.* Chicago: Tompkins Press, 1989.

Anthology
Richards, Norman J., ed. *The Best of African Short Fiction.* New York: Macomson and Job, 1980.

Books by the same author
Baker, Jane. *The Life of George Orwell.* Lincoln, Nebraska: University of Nebraska Press, 1978.

---, *The Utopian World Picture.* San Francisco: Alverson, Trask, Inc., 1988.

Anonymous works
A Photographic Exploration of America's Heartland. London: Crown Press, 1987.

A section of an anthology
Porter, Katherine Anne. "The Jilting of Granny Weatherall." *Cavalcade of Short Fiction.* Ed. Louis Rafferty and Edna Spears. Chapel Hill: University of North Carolina Press, 1976.

An introduction
Downs, Dr. Margaret Blanche. Introduction. *Letters from Soldiers.* New York: Waterston and Lee, 1990.

A multivolume set
Landry, Charles D., and Ralph McGraw, eds. *Notable Inventions of the Twentieth Century.* 8 vols. Chicago: Collins and Thompson Press, 1966.

A translation
Seri, Romano. *Women in Fiction.* Trans. M.E. Robinson, Jr. London: Worldwide Press, 1983.

An encyclopedia article
"Photography." *Graham's Student Encyclopedia.* 1986 ed.

A magazine or journal article
Whitcomb, Doris. "Handicrafts of the Appalachians." *Mountain Crier.* 23 Aug. 1971: 8-14.

Note that the day, month, and year are followed by a colon and the page numbers of the article. Abbreviate all months except May, June, or July.

A newspaper article
Suttler, Rachel V. "Florida Revisited." *Atlanta Tribune.* 30 Mar. 1967: C10, 13-14.

[Note that articles continued on nonconsecutive pages are indicated with a comma separating sets of page numbers.]

An article from a computer service
Daves, Patricia. "On the Upheaval in Central Europe." *Princeton International Bulletin.* Summer 1987, 87-89, 91. CompuLoad file G-105, item 70086-2.

• **Documenting Your Sources**
As you draw on notes that you have taken from your list of sources, refer to each reference with the author's last name and the page number. For example,

Commentary dating from a later period indicates that Heinrich Schliemann established his credibility as an archeologist after only a single discovery. (Suttler, 13)

Note: If you mention the author's name in the body of the paper, omit a repeated reference in the parenthetical material and give only the page number.

"When spring came to St. Louis, I took out my first library card, and . . . spent most of my Saturdays at the library (no interruptions) breathing in the world of penniless shoeshine boys who, with goodness and perseverance, became rich, rich men, and gave baskets of goodies to the poor on holidays. The little princesses who were mistaken for maids, and the long-lost children mistaken for waifs, became more real to me than our house, our mother, our school or Mr. Freeman.
— from *I Know Why The Caged Bird Sings*
by Maya Angelou

11.9 **PREPARING A PAPER FOR SUBMISSION**

- **Check the paper for sense, accuracy, and form.** Be sure that you have used quotation marks around original sentences and phrases of an author. Be certain that you have included a footnote for each quotation or paraphrase.

Note: The reader will assume that unfootnoted material is your original work. (Passing off someone else's work as your own is **plagiarism,** which is another word for *stealing.*)

- Include **transition words and phrases** to explain how ideas are related (see Chapter 8).

- **Limit quotations and footnotes** to an average of three per page.

- **Follow your teacher's instructions** concerning placement of footnotes, thesis statement, outline form, and type of bibliography.

- **If a title page is assigned,** compose one that centers the title vertically and horizontally. Center your name three inches from the bottom. Center the name of the course, the instructor's name, and the date beginning two inches from the bottom. Don't number the title page.

- **Number the outline page(s)** with small Roman numerals centered at the bottom of the page, beginning with ii. Don't add underlining, parentheses, brackets, periods, or other notation to the page number.

- **Number the body of your paper** with Arabic numerals, beginning on page two with 2. Place the number in the upper righthand corner, one inch from the top and one inch from the side. Don't number page one. Don't add underlining, parentheses, brackets, periods, or other notation to the page number.

- **Assemble your work in order:**

    title page
    outline with thesis statement at the top
    body
    footnotes (if separated from the body)
    bibliography

- **Staple** in the upper lefthand corner. Don't decorate or fasten your work in any other fashion.

11.10 STANDARD REFERENCE ABBREVIATIONS

These abbreviated terms appear frequently in scholarly source material. Terms in italics are Latin words. To write them in longhand, underline to indicate that they would be italicized in print.

anon.	anonymous
art./arts.	article(s)
bk./bks.	book(s)
c	copyright
c. or ca.	*circa* or about, as in Chaucer was born *ca.* 1340.
cf.	*confer*, compare
ch./chs.	chapter(s)
col./cols.	column(s)
ed./eds.	editor(s), edition, edited by
e.g.	*exempli gratia*, for example
esp.	especially
et al.	*et alii* or *et alia*, and others
et seq.	*et sequentia*, and the following
f./ff.	and the following page(s)
fl.	*floruit*, flourished
facsim.	facsimile
ibid.	*ibidem*, in the same place
i.e.	*id est*, that is
illus.	illustrated by, illustration, illustrator
infra	below
intro.	introduction
l./ll.	line(s)
loc. cit.	*loco citato*, in the place cited
ms./mss.	manuscript(s)
n./nn.	note(s)
n.d.	no date
no./nos.	number(s)
n.p.	no place (of publication)
op. cit.	*opere citato*, in the work cited
p./pp.	page(s)
passim	here and there
pseud.	pseudonym
pt./pts.	part(s)
q.v.	*qui vide*, which see
rev.	revised, revision, review, reviewed by
rpt.	reprint(ed)
sec./secs.	section(s)
sic	thus, as in "at the tailor's shoppe *(sic)* outside Boston"
st./sts.	stanza(s)
sup., supra	above
s.v.	*sub verbo*, under the heading
tr./trans.	translator, translated, translation
vide	see
vol./vols.	volume(s)

PREPARING FOR TESTS

12.1 **T**ests *are a necessary means of* **assessing aptitude, progress, competency, and skills** *in a variety of careers: piloting an airplane or driving a car, practicing law or medicine, operating business machines or firefighting equipment, becoming a teacher, barber, police officer, or hairdresser.*

Examples of career tests include the following:
- **GMAT** *Graduate Management Admission Test*
- **GRE** *Graduate Record Examination*
- **LSAT** *Law School Admission Test*
- **NTE** *National Teacher Examinations*
- **MAT** *Miller's Analogy Test*

Students also face different types of assessment in their school careers, such as daily **quizzes,** *chapter* **reviews,** *semester and final* **exams, aptitude tests, intelligence tests,** *and college performance predictors, such as these:*
- **PSAT** *Preliminary Scholastic Aptitude Test*
- **SAT** *Scholastic Aptitude Test*
- **ACT** *American College Test*
- **GED** *General Educational Development*
- **CLEP** *College Level Examination Program*
- **TOEFL** *Test of English as a Foreign Language*

There are many **strategies** *which will enhance test performance, although no method will replace* **intense daily study and concentration.** *Here are some suggestions for improving* **test-taking skills.**

12.2 DAILY QUIZZES, CHAPTER REVIEWS, AND SEMESTER EXAMS

- Keep a notebook of lectures and labs. **Date** each entry. Keep a daily **calendar of assignments,** noting dates of tests, projects, and exams.

- **Summarize** the theme or focus of each day's work.

- **Fill in information** from at least three sources (summary sheets, teacher notes, handouts, student notes, lab manuals, chapter summaries) when you are **absent.** If you know ahead of time that you must miss class, have someone make an **audio tape.**

- **Review** records, filmstrips, or tapes on your own time. If possible, check them out of the resource center and study them at home.

- Maintain a **steady pace** of reading and studying. Post a written schedule in a prominent place above your desk to remind you of each day's requirements.

- Work in a **quiet place** which is well supplied (dictionary, paper, pencils, ruler, typewriter, reference books), well lighted, and always available.

- Before each class, **mentally review** the information (rules, facts, examples, demonstrations) from the preceding week.

- **Reread notes,** underlining or highlighting with yellow marking pen.

- Keep a **separate list** of difficult information (spelling and vocabulary lists, formulas, dates, rules, idiomatic expressions). **Review** each list.

- **Read aloud** difficult passages or phrases, particularly if they are in a foreign language.

- **Divide** passages, problems, lists, charts, or sentences into manageable sections for intense study or memorization.

- Take **frequent breaks.** Vary your activities to include quiet study, exercise, conversation, high-energy snacks, and outdoor walks.

- **Readjust** the lighting or seating arrangements when you find yourself straining to read or shifting in your chair.

- **Study with other students** before a large test.

- **Vary your study** to include oral summary, drill, written outlines, question and answer, conversation, and practice problems.

- **Review old work,** notes, graded tests, and text material, such as chapter headings, information in bold-face, rules, captions, charts, graphs, appendices, study questions, and summaries.

- **Plan your study** so that you allow time for adequate rest, nutrition, hobbies, family activities, and sleep.

- Divide outside reading assignments into **workable segments.** Divide the total number of pages to be read by the number of days you plan to spend on the task. Try to accomplish the same number of pages at each sitting rather than save great portions for last minute reading.

- **Keep a list** of important characters and events and the page numbers where they first appear. Refer to the list for later assignments, such as rereading, theme-writing, research, outlining, discussion, and testing.

- **Ask your teacher** for tips on how to organize and study, types of questions to expect, and areas to be stressed on the test.

- **Begin study for a test in plenty of time** to allow for frequent breaks, meals, and sleep.

On test day, follow these strategies to improve your score:

- **Read through the test** before beginning work.

- Allot **major portions of time** to questions which receive the most points.

- **Circle problems** that may require more thought or calculation.

- **Check off sections** as they are complete, particularly answers used in matching and questions which allow student choice.

- **Look around the room** for charts, displays, models, and posters that may refresh your memory. (Note: Do not jeopardize your test grade by giving the appearance of looking at someone else's paper.)

- If time permits, **return** to problems or essay questions which present the most challenge.

- **Apply thoughts and ideas** that you may have learned from other sections of the test.

- **Proofread** for accuracy, careless errors, omissions, blurred figures or handwriting, continuity, misunderstanding of instructions, misspelling, misstatement of rules, and inadequate support for ideas.

- Remember that some tests are hard for everyone. **Reward yourself** for doing a good job of preparation.

12.3 STANDARD TESTS OF APTITUDE AND ACHIEVEMENT

Most **standardized tests** share the following characteristics:

a verbal and a math section	**specific instructions for each test section**
a multiple-choice format	
	answer sheets that are read by machine
rigid time requirements	

You will need to devise **strategies** to solve **four major problems:**

unfamiliar questions	**guessing**
time management	**emotional response to pressure**

Unfamiliar questions
Most items on standardized tests are based on **common, predictable academic experience** rather than tricky or little-known facts or rules. Math problems usually require knowledge of only the basic elements of arithmetic, algebra, and geometry. Problems occur because test questions are often, by design, phrased in unfamiliar, non-traditional ways.

> **Strategy:** Purchase or check out of the library or guidance department books that contain **sample tests.** Familiarize yourself with the types of questions you will encounter.

Time Management
An unprepared student may mismanage **time** on standardized exams by spending an inordinate proportion of allotted time on the more difficult questions, thereby missing the easier ones.

> **Strategy:** Recognize a problem which you have very little chance of answering and move on to the next question without hesitation. If a question requires complex computation, move on to the next question and return to the harder one if time permits. Many tests are designed in the order of **increasing difficulty.**

Guessing

To guess or not to guess? When is guessing not guessing? When is it to your advantage to guess? What is the difference between an educated guess and a wild guess?

To answer these questions in a way that will increase your score, remember that, on many tests, points are deducted for wrong answers. Before you take the test, **determine how this particular test is graded** by reading descriptions of the test, studying pamphlets or manuals that accompany the test, or asking teachers, librarians, or guidance counselors for advice.

On many tests, the following rules affect your **score:**

- You get credit for each **correct answer.**

- You do not damage your score by **omitting a question.**

- **You receive a penalty for incorrect answers,** usually a fraction of a correct answer credit (1/4 or 1/5 penalty).

> **Strategy:** If the above situation is true, you may hesitate to guess. However, if you can **narrow the possibilities to two choices,** you have a 50% chance of being correct. If you guess in six situations, the most likely outcome will be three correct answers (+ 3 points) and three incorrect answers (– 3/4 points) for a net gain of 2 1/4 points.

A Great Communicator

You have probably never heard of Edward Stratemeyer, but there is a very good chance you have read a book he created. If not, you are most likely familiar with at least some of his creations. During his lifetime he turned out some 800 books. He wrote under dozens of different names — and created dozens of heroes that have been favorites of young readers for generations. The Hardy Boys, Nancy Drew, the Bobbsey Twins, Tom Swift, and the Rover Boys are some of his most famous creations. At first, Stratemeyer wrote all of the books by himself, but his books grew so popular that in 1906 he formed a syndicate to do much of the writing. Until he died in 1930, he personally outlined and edited each book. His two daughters continued the syndicate after his death. No one would ever argue that any of the Stratemeyer books are great literature, but these books have introduced millions to the unique pleasures that can be found in books.

Emotional Response to Pressure

Before you take any test, understand that **nervous reactions** (worry, shortness of breath, dry mouth, sweaty palms, trembling) are not unusual.

Strategy: Concentrate your energies on your own answer sheet. Avoid concerning yourself over students who turn pages before you do. Remember that your pace is right for you and may produce better results than the hasty approach of others.

Congratulate yourself on the number of problems or questions that are easy for you. Keep an eye on the time limit so that you can return to more difficult questions when you complete the easier ones. Tests are designed to **challenge** everyone, so no one ever feels confident about knowing all the answers.

Here are a few **suggestions** that benefit your performance on any standardized test.

- **Listen to the verbal instructions** of the test administrator.

- **Read carefully the instructions** for each section.

- **Check the answer sheet** to be certain you record answers in the proper section.

- Carefully **fill in gridded answers** with your name and other pertinent information.

- If you have questions, **ask a proctor** before the test begins.

- **Use a soft-lead pencil** for easy erasure.

- Avoid bending or defacing the **answer sheet.**

- **Erase stray marks** at the end of the test.

GRAPHS, MAPS, AND CHARTS

13.1 **M**uch information, particularly **graphs, maps,** and **charts,** is written in highly compressed **symbolic** form to clarify the relationships between ideas or to give dramatic representation to facts that are difficult to put into words. These visual statements encourage the reader to employ spatial evaluations, i.e., lines, rectangles, circles, as well as verbal skills in **interpreting data.**

13.2 **Graphs** are **diagrams** in the form of **curves, wedges, lines,** or other **visual representations** which demonstrate the changes in the numeric value of a variable quantity. There are three basic types of graphs: **bar, circle** or **pie,** and **line.** In order to interpret graphs, the reader must understand how much each unit is worth under what circumstances.

A Great Communicator

The great American poet Emily Dickinson (1830-1886) was not like any other poet of her time. She could be called the first modern American poet. Dickinson was a quiet person who spent much of her life as a recluse in the home she was born in. During her lifetime, only seven of her poems were published. She wrote more than 1,000 poems, in words which show that beauty of language and accuracy are the same thing. Dickinson describes the fear experienced at unexpectedly seeing a snake as "zero at the bone." In another poem, which begins with the startling line, "I heard a fly buzz when I died," she writes of the fly's "blue, uncertain, stumbling buzz." Nobody ever wrote with such jolting clarity. She helped us to continue inventing our language, which is the job of poets.

Bar graphs utilize either **vertical** or **horizontal** lines in parallel arrangement to show proportions. Information must be read along the vertical axis and the horizontal axis and interpreted according to the **key** or **legend,** which explains the relationship between the two planes. For example,

Vertical form

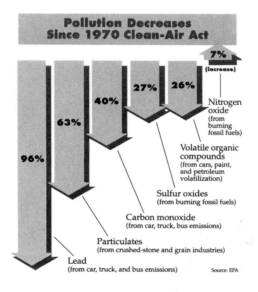

Illustration 1: Vertical Bar Graph

This vertical bar graph notes changes in levels of six types of pollutants since the 1970 Clean-Air Act. This visual form gives the information more impact because of the obvious differences in the length of each bar.

• **One conclusion:**	A quick glance at the graph reveals that nitrogen oxide is the only pollutant that has increased.
• **Another conclusion:**	Lead from vehicle emissions has all but vanished from the air.
• **Another conclusion:**	About the same amount of sulfur oxides and volatile organic compounds have been removed from the air.

Horizontal Bar Graph

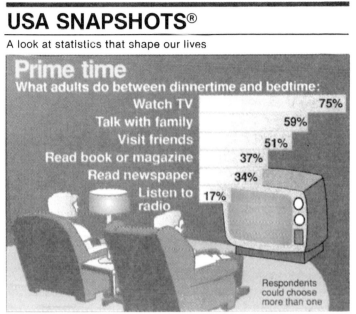

USA SNAPSHOTS®

A look at statistics that shape our lives

Prime time
What adults do between dinnertime and bedtime:

Watch TV	75%
Talk with family	59%
Visit friends	51%
Read book or magazine	37%
Read newspaper	34%
Listen to radio	17%

Respondents could choose more than one

Source: Roper Report poll of 2,000 adults   By Web Bryant, USA TODAY

Illustration 2: Horizontal Bar Graph

This graph consists of parallel rectangles or lines drawn on a horizontal plane. Like the vertical bar graph, the horizontal bar graph makes a numerical comparison, such as the comparison of after dinner activities.

• **One conclusion:**	Over half the respondents watch television, talk with family, and visit friends between dinnertime and bedtime.
• **Another conclusion:**	Twice as many people read the newspaper than listen to radio.
• **Another conclusion:**	Some people apparently engage in more than one activity at a time.

Note: Information in a bar graph is recorded along both the **X axis** and the **Y axis.**

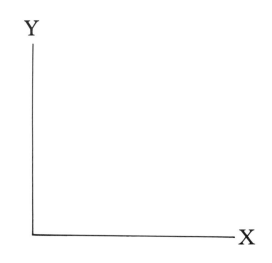

Illustration 3: Model of X and Y Axes

For example, in the graph labeled Prime Time, the different types of activities are listed vertically along the **Y axis.** The percentage of people engaging in each is indicated by the length of the bar that is parallel to the **X axis.**

In order to interpret bar graphs, look for the following information:

- The **title** of the graph
- Information listed along the **X axis**
- Information listed along the **Y axis**
- Any **keys** or **legends** which explain the symbols
- **Interpretations or explanations of values**

"As we pass Houses musing slow / If they be occupied / So minds pass minds / If they be occupied."

—Emily Dickinson

Illustration 4: Vertical Bar Graph

The preceding **vertical bar graph** contains the following information:

- The **title,** which explains that the graph compares types of U.S. Defense Recruiting.
- The **key,** which shows that the dark bars represent 1989 while the lighter bars project figures for 1990.
- The **X axis,** which illustrates the four different branches of the military — Air Force, Army, Marine Corps, and Navy.
- The **Y axis,** which gives the number of recruits in thousands.

One conclusion:	The graph shows that, even with a drop in recruitment, the Army still outstrips the other three branches in soldiers recruited for service.
Another conclusion:	The Marine Corps is the only military branch that anticipates an increase in recruitment.
Another conclusion:	The Air Force may drop to half its previous level of recruitment.
Another conclusion:	Navy recruitment will fall from around 97,000 to around 88,000.

Circle graphs or pie graphs illustrate the relationship of segments or wedges to each other and to the whole circle.

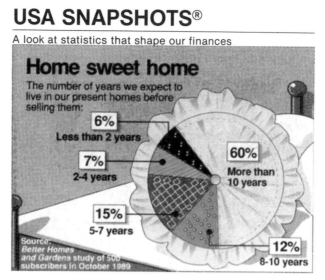

By Suzy Parker, USA TODAY

Illustration 5: Circle or Pie Graph

From the preceding **pie graph,** the reader gains the following information:

- The title is "Home sweet home."

- The total pie represents overall home ownership.

- Each section or slice represents a different span of time an owner will live in a home before selling it.

- 60% will keep their homes ten years or longer. 12% will remain 8-10 years. 15% will stay 5-7 years. 7% will keep their homes 2-4 years. 6% will remain less than two years. The total adds up to 100%.

One conclusion:	The fewest number of people move in two years or less.
Another conclusion:	The majority of homeowners stay ten years or longer.
Another conclusion:	72% of homeowners remain in their homes eight years or longer.

A **line graph,** a third type of visual representation of data, is designed to show the **movement** of a numerical entity along an X axis, a Y axis, or both.

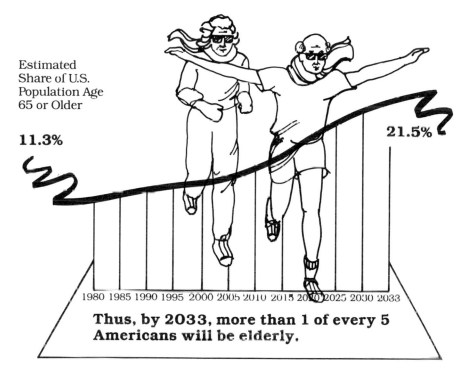

Estimated Share of U.S. Population Age 65 or Older

11.3%

21.5%

1980 1985 1990 1995 2000 2005 2010 2015 2020 2025 2030 2033

Thus, by 2033, more than 1 of every 5 Americans will be elderly.

Illustration 6: Line Graph

The **increase** in the number of elderly Americans is evident in the rising line from 11.3% in 1980 to a projected 21.5% by the year 2033. Note that the artist has made a **creative** connection between the horizontal line and the ribbon at a finish line, suggesting that older people are enjoying healthier, more active lives.

One conclusion:	The population of elderly Americans will continue to show a steady increase.
Another conclusion:	Within a fifty-year span, the percentage of elderly Americans will nearly double.

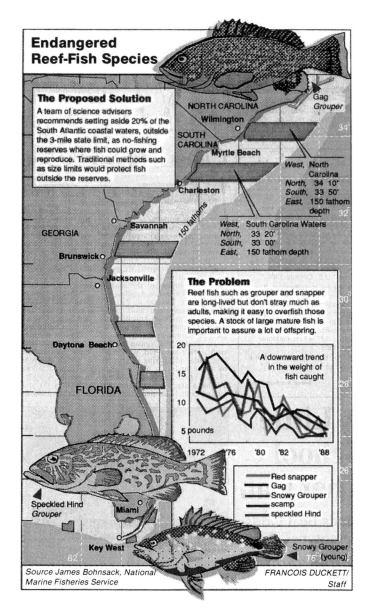

Endangered Reef-Fish Species

The Proposed Solution
A team of science advisers recommends setting aside 20% of the South Atlantic coastal waters, outside the 3-mile state limit, as no-fishing reserves where fish could grow and reproduce. Traditional methods such as size limits would protect fish outside the reserves.

Gag Grouper

NORTH CAROLINA
Wilmington

SOUTH CAROLINA
Myrtle Beach

Charleston

West, North Carolina
North, 34 10'
South, 33 50'
East, 150 fathom depth

GEORGIA
Savannah

West, South Carolina Waters
North, 33 20'
South, 33 00'
East, 150 fathom depth

Brunswick

Jacksonville

The Problem
Reef fish such as grouper and snapper are long-lived but don't stray much as adults, making it easy to overfish those species. A stock of large mature fish is important to assure a lot of offspring.

Daytona Beach

FLORIDA

20
15
10
5 pounds

A downward trend in the weight of fish caught

1972   '76   '80   '82   '88

Red snapper
Gag
Snowy Grouper
scamp
speckled Hind

Speckled Hind Grouper
Miami

Key West

Snowy Grouper (young)

Source James Bohnsack, National Marine Fisheries Service

FRANCOIS DUCKETT/ Staff

Illustration 7: Multiple Line Graph

The diagram above compares the weight of five kinds of fish: the green line shows red snapper, the blue line the gag, the brown line the snowy grouper, the purple line the scamp, and the red line the speckled hind.

One conclusion:	Two fish, the gag and the snowy grouper, experienced initial rises in weight between 1973 and 1974.
Another conclusion:	All five varieties have fallen to weights of seven pounds or lower.
Another conclusion:	The speckled hind has remained low in weight over a longer period of time than the other four species of fish.

"A narrow Fellow in the Grass
Occasionally rides —
You may have met Him — did you not
His notice sudden is —
The Grass divides as with a Comb —
A spotted shaft is seen —
And then it closes at your feet
And opens further on —"

. . .

"Several of Nature's People
I know, and they know me —
I feel for them a transport
Of cordiality —
But never met this Fellow
Attended, or alone
Without a tighter breathing
And Zero at the Bone —"

— Emily Dickinson

13.3 **Maps** are **detailed diagrams** of sections of the universe — land, sea, or sky. They are **drawn to scale** — that is, drawn in miniature — to suggest the **spatial relationships** between landmarks, such as cities, bodies of water, weather fronts, roadways, county and state lines, international boundaries, stars, planets, constellations, airline routes, population clusters, climates, or even product distribution, opinions, and lifestyles.

Note: Because maps are usually **two-dimensional,** they oversimplify distances by omitting mountains, valleys, and the natural curvature of the earth. A map drawn in **mercator projection** (commonly called an "orange peel map") rectifies that error and presents distances as they naturally occur on the globe.

Weather maps reveal contours of invisible, constantly moving air masses. **Isobars,** the contour lines which connect areas that have the same barometric pressure, show the type of weather each area is experiencing at a given moment. For example,

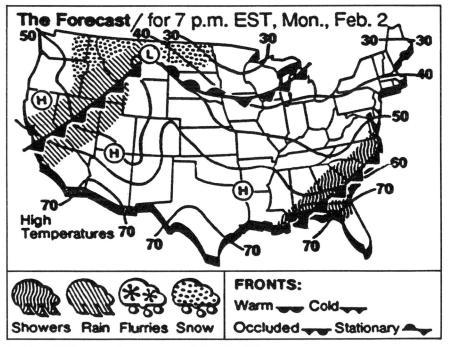

National Weather Service NOAA Dept. of Commerce

The **weather map** gives specific information about weather patterns in the continental United States, including:

- The **time and date** of the National Weather Service's observations

- **Temperatures** and **precipitation** in large, easy-to-read numbers and symbols

- **Circled letters** to pinpoint high and low pressure points

- A **legend** with graphic explanations of types of weather patterns

One conclusion:	It was snowing and 30 degrees in North Dakota at 7 p.m., February 2.
Another conclusion:	The time of the forecast is based on Eastern Standard Time.
Another conclusion:	Much of the central portion of the country experienced no precipitation.
Another conclusion:	Temperatures along the east coast varied over a forty-degree range.

"When Memory is full
Put on the perfect Lid —
This Morning's finest syllable
Presumptuous Evening said —"

— Emily Dickinson

A **road map,** the type of map that people use most often, contains a **pattern of roads** marked with route numbers, capitals, cities, towns, bridges, tunnels, airports, railroads, hospitals, points of interest, natural land formations, and other significant data.

The Legend

In addition to the **cartographer's** (map-maker's) drawing there will be a **legend** or **key** to the symbols and distances represented by the map. Here is a model legend:

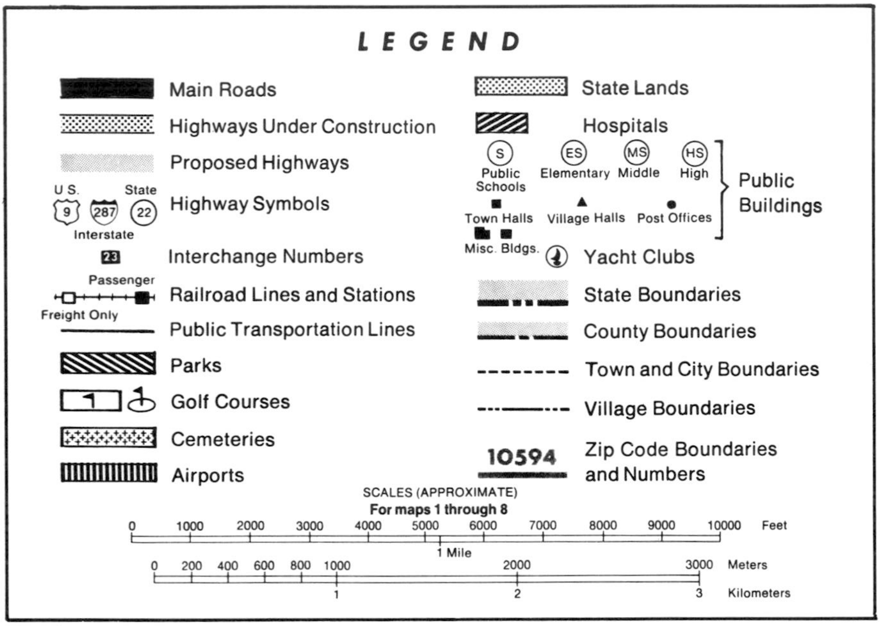

Illustration 9: A Legend

Note that the information contained in the legend is easily interpreted by means of the symbols, such as the types of boundaries, public buildings, transportation routes, and other landmarks featured on the map and the relative distances between them.

"Surprise is like a thrilling — pungent — /
Upon a tasteless meat / Alone — too acrid — but
combined / An edible Delight."

— Emily Dickinson

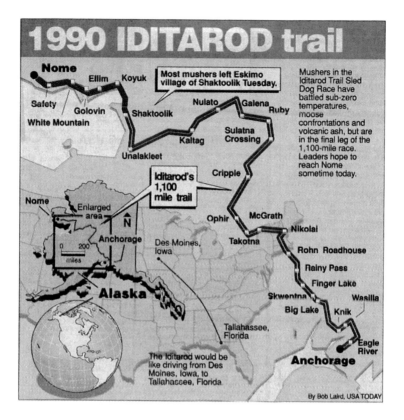

Illustration 10: Map

Note the **compass point** indicates which way is north. Also notice that the numerous insets help readers compare distances and locate the Iditarod trail on the globe. The scale of miles indicates a span of 200 miles. Commentary describes some of the hazards of the 1,100-mile trail.

Other Types of Maps

MAP OF THE UNITED STATES AREA CODES AND TIME ZONES

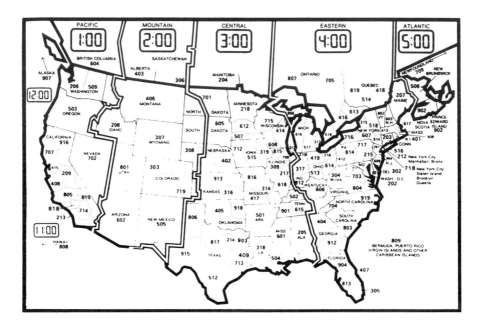

This map indicates the division of states in the continental United States into **time zones** and the **telephone area codes** that are used in each. Note: The times in Alaska and Hawaii are included on the lefthand side along with the area codes for each state.

One conclusion:	The continental United States is composed of four time zones.
Another conclusion:	Compared to the other states, California has the largest number of area codes.
Another conclusion:	The eastern time zone contains the largest number of states; the Pacific time zone contains the least number of states.

U.S. DEPARTMENT OF AGRICULTURE MAP OF HARDINESS ZONES

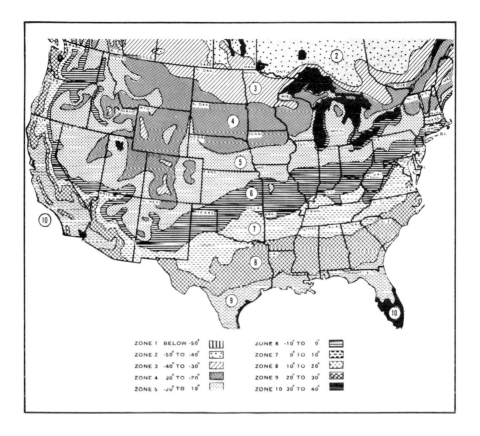

ZONE 1	BELOW -50°	ZONE 6	-10° TO 0°
ZONE 2	-50° TO -40°	ZONE 7	0° TO 10°
ZONE 3	-40° TO -30°	ZONE 8	10° TO 20°
ZONE 4	-30° TO -20°	ZONE 9	20° TO 30°
ZONE 5	-20° TO 10°	ZONE 10	30° TO 40°

This map indicates the average **low temperatures** in sections of the United States. The purpose of the information is to establish what plants will tolerate the extremes of cold. Most botanical specimens are keyed to this system, for example, "hardy in zones 6-9."

One conclusion:	Parts of Florida, Texas, and California are above freezing most of the time.
Another conclusion:	No part of the continental United States exists in the extreme cold of Zone 1.
Another conclusion:	Most states lie in more than one hardiness zone.

CHAPTER 13

**A DISPERSAL MAP SHOWING ETHNIC GROUPS
IN THE SOVIET UNION**

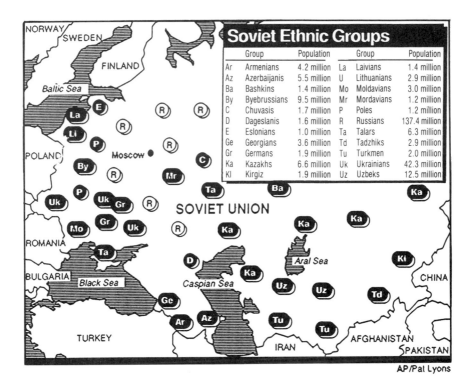

AP/Pat Lyons

This map depicts the twenty-two **ethnic groups** that make up the Soviet
Union. The enclosed chart indicates the size of each population group
and the abbreviation which identifies the location of each group.

One conclusion:	Nearly 55% of the Soviet population is composed of Russians.
Another conclusion:	Estonians, who live on the Baltic coast, comprise less than 4% of the Soviet population.
Another conclusion:	The western portion of the Soviet Union contains the greatest variety of ethnic groups.
Another conclusion:	Ukrainians are the second largest ethnic group in the Soviet Union.

13.4 A **chart** is a **tabular or columnar** arrangement of facts or figures, such as statistics, genealogy, or an alphabetic list. The advantage of a chart is that it **compresses** much information into small space and utilizes a handy arrangement for ready access of data. For example,

Multiplication Tables

1	2	3	4	5	6	7	8	9	10	11	12
2	4	6	8	10	12	14	16	18	20	22	24
3	6	9	12	15	18	21	24	27	30	33	36
4	8	12	16	20	24	28	32	36	40	44	48
5	10	15	20	25	30	35	40	45	50	55	60
6	12	18	24	30	36	42	48	54	60	66	72
7	14	21	28	35	42	49	56	63	70	77	84
8	16	24	32	40	48	56	64	72	80	88	96
9	18	27	36	45	54	63	72	81	90	99	108
10	20	30	40	50	60	70	80	90	100	110	120
11	22	33	44	55	66	77	88	99	110	121	132
12	24	36	48	60	72	84	96	108	120	132	144

Note: By placing one finger at a point on the top horizontal line and another finger on the far lefthand vertical line, you can draw your fingers together and stop on the number that is the **product of the first two numbers,** as in the example of 3 x 4 = 12 on the model.

"At eight I was brilliant with my body.
In July, that ring of heat
We all jumped through, I sat in the bleachers
Of Romain Playground, in the lengthening
Shade that rose from our dirty feet.
That game before us was more than baseball.
It was a figure — Hector Moreno
Quick and hard with turned muscles,
His crouch the one I assumed before an altar
Of worn baseball cards, in my room."

             — From "Black Hair"
             by Gary Soto

The following models show other types of information found in charts:

Baseball Standings of the American League

East Team	Won	Lost	Pct.	Last 10	Streak
Boston	44	31	.587	8-2	Won 1
Toronto	42	36	.538	3-7	Won 1
Cleveland	37	37	.500	6-4	Won 2
Detroit	37	41	.474	4-6	Won 2
Baltimore	34	41	.453	4-6	Won 2
Milwaukee	33	41	.446	3-7	Lost 4
New York	28	45	.384	5-5	Lost 1
West Team	**Won**	**Lost**	**Pct.**	**Last 10**	**Streak**
Chicago	46	26	.639	9-1	Won 1
Oakland	47	27	.635	5-5	Lost 1
Seattle	40	38	.513	8-2	Won 5
California	38	39	.494	4-6	Lost 2
Minnesota	35	40	.467	4-6	Lost 4
Texas	35	42	.455	5-5	Lost 1
Kansas City	31	42	.419	4-6	Lost 2

This chart contains detailed information which interprets major league baseball team standings. Abbreviated information in column four gives percentage of games won. Notice that the chart is divided into two sections — east coast teams and west coast teams.

One conclusion:	Cleveland has a percentage of .500 because its record of games won equals its record of games lost.
Another conclusion:	Out of all teams listed, Chicago has the best record for the last ten games. It has won nine out of ten.
Another conclusion:	Even though Toronto has a good percentage, the last ten games have proved less successful.

"What could I do but yell *vivas* / To baseball, milkshakes, and those sociologists /Who would clock me / As I jog into the next century / On the power of a great, silly grin."

— From "Mexicans Begin Jogging" by Gary Soto

Time Schedule

> **SUNDAY**
> **Auto Racing:** Formula One Grand Prix.
>   (ESPN, noon EST/9 a.m. PST)
> **College Basketball:** Southeast Regional Championship.
>   (CBS, 1:30 p.m. EST/10:30 a.m. PST)
>   West Regional championship
>   (CBS, 4 p.m. EST/1 p.m. PST)
> **Boxing:** 10-round junior featherweight.
>   (NBC 2:30 p.m. EST/11:30 a.m. PST)
> **Golf:** Nestle Invitational
>   (NBC, 4 p.m. EST/1 p.m. PST)
>   LPGA Standard Register Turquoise Classic
>   (ESPN, 2 p.m. EST/11 a.m. PST)
> **Hockey:** Pittsburgh Penguins at Hartford Whalers
>   (SCA, 7 p.m. EST/4 p.m. PST)
> **Horse Racing:** Johnnie Walker Black Classic
>   (SCA, 5 p.m. EST/2 p.m. PST)
> **Show Jumping:** Johnnie Walker Grandprix of Florida
>   (SCA, 1 p.m. EST/10 a.m. PST)
> **College Wrestling:** Division I Championships
>   (ESPN, 7:30 p.m. EST/4:30 a.m. PST)
> **Tennis:** Lipton International Players Championships
>   (ABC, 1 p.m. EST/10 a.m. PST)

This Sunday sports lineup gives broadcast time for both Eastern Standard and Pacific Standard zones.

One conclusion:	The network that offers the least choice of sporting events for Sunday is ABC.
Another conclusion:	The lapse in broadcast times for EST and PST indicates that there is a span of three hours' difference between zones.
Another conclusion:	A viewer will be unable to watch both show jumping and tennis because they are broadcast in the same time slot.

"When it was obvious that, for whatever reason, the poems I had been writing were bad, I began to consider finding a real job. Gas station attendant, car salesman, apprentice baker? The choices were endlessly sad..."

— From *Living Up The Street*
by Gary Soto

FACTS ABOUT GREAT BRITAIN (January 2, 1984)

COUNTRY	AREA (SQ. MI.)	POPULATION	POP./SQ. MI.
England	50,362	46,465,000	923
Ireland	27,136	3,555,000	131
Scotland	30,416	5,175,000	170
Wales	8,019	2,810,000	350

One conclusion:	Of the four parts of the British Isles, England has the largest area, population, and density (population per square mile).
Another conclusion:	Ireland has the lowest population density.
Another conclusion:	Wales has the smallest area and population.

A Great Communicator

Gary Soto grew up in Fresno, California, in a poor Chicano family. Much of his poetry has drawn upon this background, communicating to the reader all aspects of life for the migrant worker in California's San Joaquin Valley. Soto, who worked for a time as a field hand, uses his poetry to bring to life both the despair and dreams of these laborers. Besides his poetry, Soto has written several nonfiction collections. His vivid images and metaphors, often about suffering and hardship, have enlarged his reputation not just as an important ethnic writer but as a significant contemporary American poet.

KINGS AND QUEENS OF GREAT BRITAIN SINCE 1066

Normans
William I, 1066-1087
William II, 1087-1100
Henry I, 1100-1135
Stephen, 1135-1154

House of Plantagenet
Henry II, 1154-1189
Richard I, 1189-1199
John, 1199-1216
Henry III, 1216-1272
Edward I, 1272-1307
Edward II, 1307-1327
Edward III, 1327-1377
Richard II, 1377-1399

House of Lancaster
Henry IV, 1399-1413
Henry V, 1413-1422
Henry VI, 1422-1461

House of York
Edward IV, 1461-1483
Edward V, 1483
Richard III, 1483-1485

House of Tudor
Henry VII, 1485-1509
Henry VIII, 1509-1547
Edward VI, 1547-1558
Mary I, 1553-1558
Elizabeth I, 1558-1603

House of Stuart
James I, 1603-1625
Charles I, 1625-1649

**Interregnum
(1649-1659)**
Oliver Cromwell,
  1653-1658
Richard Cromwell,
  1658-1659

House of Stuart
Charles II, 1660-1685
James II, 1685-1688

House of Orange
William II & Mary II
  1689-1702

House of Stuart
Anne, 1702-1714

House of Hanover
George I, 1714-1727
George II, 1727-1760
George III, 1760-1820
George IV, 1820-1830
William IV, 1830-1837
Victoria, 1837-1901

**House of Saxe-
Coburg-Gotha
(after 1917, Windsor)**
Edward VII, 1901-1910
George V, 1910-1936
Edward VIII, 1936
  (abdicated)
George VI, 1936-1952
Elizabeth II, 1952-

This chart lists the **rulers of England** from the invasion of William the Conqueror in 1066 to the accession of Elizabeth II.

One conclusion:	The house of Plantagenet has had the longest reign, 245 years, as contrasted with the House of Orange, with a short reign of thirteen years.
Another conclusion:	There was no king or queen from 1649-1659.
Another conclusion:	There were three successive kings of England in the year 1483.
Another conclusion:	During World War I, the house of Saxe-Coburg-Gotha changed its name to Windsor.

Alphabet Comparisons

Greek			Gothic		Italic		Roman	
alpha	A	α	𝔄	a	A	a	A	a
beta	B	β ϐ	𝔅	b	B	b	B	b
gamma	Γ	γ	ℭ	c	C	c	C	c
delta	Δ	δ	𝔇	d	D	d	D	d
epsilon	E	ε	𝔈	e	E	e	E	e
zeta	Z	ζ	𝔉	f	F	f	F	f
eta	H	η	𝔊	g	G	g	G	g
theta	Θ	ϑ θ	𝔥	h	H	h	H	h
iota	I	ι	𝔍	i	I	i	I	i
kappa	K	κ	𝔍	j	J	j	J	j
lambda	Λ	λ	𝔎	k	K	k	K	k
mu	M	μ	𝔏	l	L	l	L	l
nu	N	ν	𝔐	m	M	m	M	m
xi	Ξ	ξ	𝔑	n	N	n	N	n
omicron	O	o	𝔒	o	O	o	O	o
pi	Π	π	𝔓	p	P	p	P	p
rho	P	ρ	𝔔	q	Q	q	Q	q
sigma	Σ	σ ς	𝔕	r	R	r	R	r
tau	T	τ	𝔖	s	S	s	S	s
upsilon	Y	υ	𝔗	t	T	t	T	t
phi	Φ	φ	𝔘	u	U	u	U	u
chi	X	χ	𝔙	v	V	v	V	v
psi	Ψ	ψ	𝔚	w	W	w	W	w
omega	Ω	ω	𝔛	x	X	x	X	x
			𝔜	y	Y	y	Y	y
			𝔷	ȝ	Z	z	Z	z

One conclusion:	Each of the alphabets has both upper and lower case letters.
Another conclusion:	The Greek alphabet contains only twenty-four characters whereas the other three have twenty-six.
Another conclusion:	Gothic letters are the most ornate of the four alphabets.

Stock Reports

Stock is the proportionate share an individual investor owns of a corporation. The **stock market report,** published every business day in most newspapers, is a listing of significant facts concerning companies whose stock is sold to the public. The report contains a record of the previous day's transactions.

1		2	3	4	5	6	7			8
52 Weeks				Yld	P-E	Sales				Net
High	Low	Stock	Div.	%	Ratio	100s	High	Low	Close	Chg.
16 3/8	8 1/8	BestPd		...	...	904	9 7/8	9 1/2	9 1/2	− 1/4
20 3/4	4 5/8	BethStl		...	...	9877	13 3/8	12 1/4	13 1/8	+ 3/4
52 3/8	12 3/4	BethSt pf		...	...	71	34 1/2	33 1/4	33 1/4	− 1/2
27 1/2	6 5/8	BethS pfB		...		549	17 1/2	16 3/4	16 7/8	− 1/8
22 1/2	14 1/8	Bevrly s	.20	1.3	21	4855	15 5/8	14 7/8	14 7/8	− 5/8
29	21 7/8	BevIP n	2.13e	9.9	13	307	22 1/8 d	21 1/4	21 1/2	− 1/2
24 3/8	11 7/8	Biocft		...	52	471	21 3/4	21 1/8	21 3/8	− 1/8
25 1/4	14 1/2	BlackD	.40	2.0	32	1712	20 1/4	19 7/8	19 7/8	− 3/8
28	19 1/2	BlkHC s	1.20	6.0	11	91	20 1/2	20	20 1/8	− 1/2
58	35 3/4	BlkHR	1.48	3.1	23	588	50	47	47	− 2 1/2
10 1/8	9 3/4	BluChp n		...	...	100	10 1/8	10	10 1/8	...
64 7/8	48 1/4	Boeing	1.40	2.9	11	6120	49 d	47 7/8	48	3/4
86 7/8	51 1/2	BoiseC	1.90	2.5	20	3372	76 1/4	74 3/8	75 3/8	− 1 3/8
68 1/2	48 1/4	Boise pfC	3.50	5.7	..	120	62	61 1/2	61 1/2	− 1
59 7/8	36 7/8	BoltBer	.10	.2	28	289	45 1/4	43	43	− 2 1/4
60 1/2	38 1/4	Borden s	1.28	2.3	19	1231	57 1/2	56	56 3/8	− 1 1/4
49 7/8	25 3/4	BorgWa	1.00	2.1	21	6018	49 5/8	48 5/8	48 3/4	...
25 3/4	14 1/4	Bormns	.20	.9	9	48	21 1/2	20 7/8	21 1/8	+ 1/8
18 3/8	13 1/4	BCelts n	.35e	2.5	...	32	14 1/4	14	14	− 1/8
28	20 3/4	BosEd s	1.78	7.8	9	239	23 1/4	22 5/8	22 7/8	− 1/4

The following definitions explain the numbered sections of the chart:

- **52 weeks** — High and Low columns indicate the **performance** of the stock during the preceding 52-week period.

- **Stock** — **Name of the company** issuing the stock, usually abbreviated.

- **Dividend** — **Annual dollar amount** paid by the company for each stock on a specified date. The company's board of directors decides whether a dividend will be paid or not. If this dividend is blank, the company has elected not to issue a dividend. **Example:** Bethlehem Steel offers no dividend: Bordon offers 1.28 or $1.28 per share.

- **Percent Yield** — The percentage, calculated by dividing the annual dividend (if any) by the stock's price, is a measurement of what percent of the current stock is paid in **dividends.**

- **Price Earnings**

  The **P-E ratio** is a percentage calculated by dividing the current market price of the stock by the company's annual earnings per share and is another measurement of a stock's **value.**

- **Day's Sales**

  Listed in hundreds, this column indicates the total number of **shares sold** and informs the investor of how actively the stock is traded. Numerous events, such as announcements of new products or an impending acquisition or takeover by another company, can cause unusual volume.

- **Daily Prices**

  The dollar amounts in the next three columns signify these prices:
  High — the highest dollar amount at which the stock traded during the day.
  (A **u** printed next to the amount indicates a new high for the year.)
  Low — the lowest dollar price paid for the stock during that day.
  (A **d** printed next to the amount means a new low for the year.) See Boeing.
  Close — the final price paid at the end of the day.

- **Net Change**

  Determined in fractional amounts, the net change is the difference between the day's closing price and the last session's closing price. **Example:** Bethlehem Steel was up 3/4 or 75¢ higher.

The Dow Jones Industrial Average

The **Dow Jones Industrial Average** is one useful and widely accepted measurement of the stock market's combined performance. Published every business day, the Dow, as it is commonly called, is a compilation of stock prices of **thirty major American industrial stocks** which account for approximately one quarter of the entire value of the stocks listed on the New York Stock Exchange. The stocks selected for inclusion in the average cover a broad range and offer a **general view** of market fluctuations.

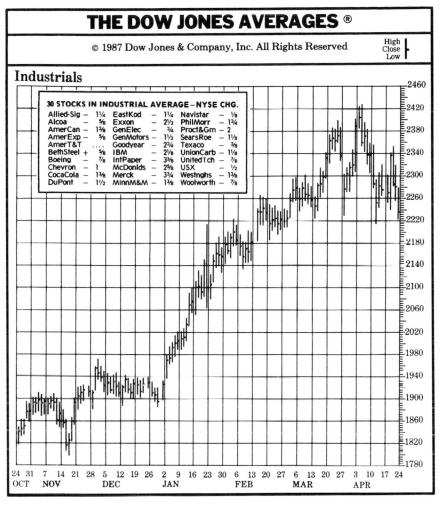

THE DOW JONES AVERAGES ®

High
Close
Low

Industrials

30 STOCKS IN INDUSTRIAL AVERAGE–NYSE CHG.

Allied-Sig	− 1¼	EastKod	− 1¼	Navistar	− ⅛
Alcoa	− ⅝	Exxon	− 2½	PhilMorr	− 1¾
AmerCan	− 1⅜	GenElec	− ¾	Proct&Gm	− 2
AmerExp	− ⅝	GenMotors	− 1½	SearsRoe	− 1⅛
AmerT&T	....	Goodyear	− 2¾	Texaco	− ⅜
BethSteel	+ ⅝	IBM	− 2⅛	UnionCarb	− 1⅛
Boeing	− ⅞	IntPaper	− 3⅜	UnitedTch	− ⅞
Chevron	− 1	McDonlds	− 2⅝	USX	− ½
CocaCola	− 1⅜	Merck	− 3¾	Westnghs	− 1⅜
DuPont	− 1½	MinnM&M	− 1⅜	Woolworth	− ⅞

2460
2420
2380
2340
2300
2260
2220
2180
2140
2100
2060
2020
1980
1940
1900
1860
1820
1780

24 31 7 14 21 28 5 12 19 26 2 9 16 23 30 6 13 20 27 6 13 20 27 3 10 17 24
OCT NOV DEC JAN FEB MAR APR

This line graph from the *Wall Street Journal* depicts a six-months'
performance. Note the **high, closing, and low averages** of the thirty
stocks, as indicated by this symbol:

High
Close
Low

One conclusion:	The market exhibited a steady rise after the first of the year.
Another conclusion:	The market showed some unsteadiness between March 27 and the end of April.
Another conclusion:	The overall performance ranged from BethSteel (+ 5/8) to Merck (-3 3/4).

THE INDO-EUROPEAN LANGUAGE TREE

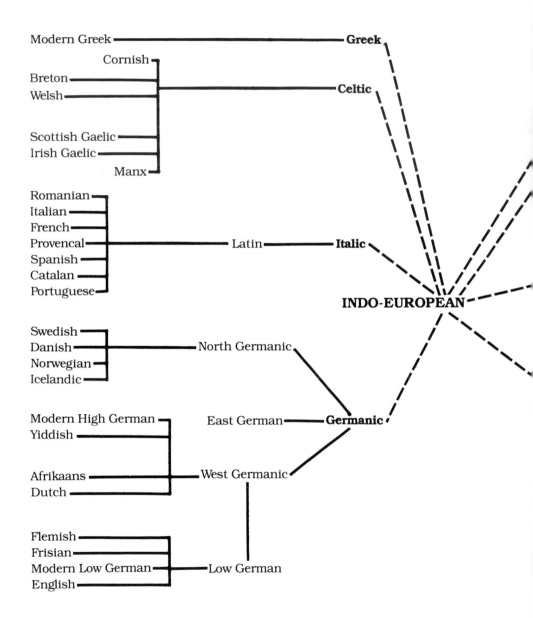

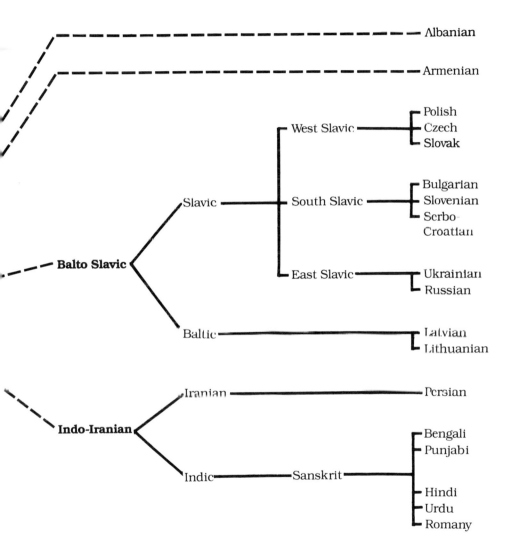

SEE - 7.3, Page 76

WORLD MAP

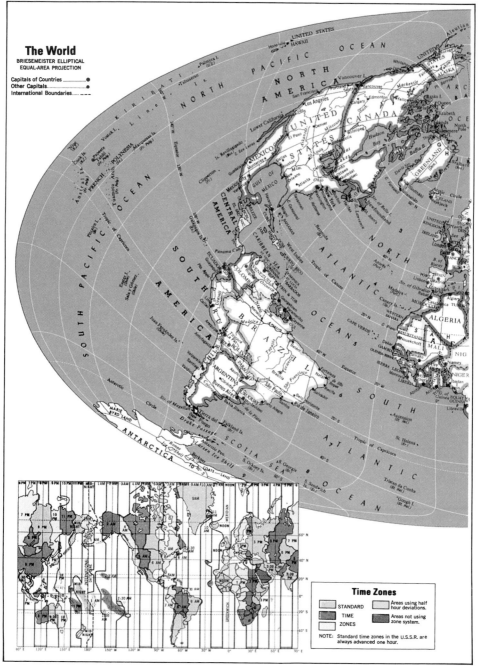

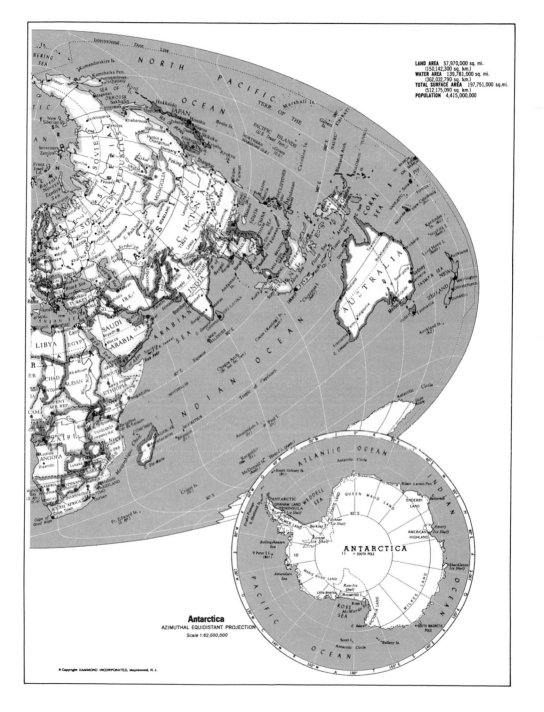

LAND AREA 57,970,000 sq. mi.
(150,142,300 sq. km.)
WATER AREA 139,781,000 sq. mi.
(362,032,790 sq. km.)
TOTAL SURFACE AREA 197,751,000 sq.mi.
(512,175,090 sq. km.)
POPULATION 4,415,000,000

Antarctica
AZIMUTHAL EQUIDISTANT PROJECTION
Scale 1:62,000,000

Copyright HAMMOND INCORPORATED, Maplewood, N. J.

FORMS OF ADDRESS

	SALUTATION	ENVELOPE ADDRESS
Professional		
attorney	Dear Mr. Clark:	Fielding E. Clark, Esq.
judge	Dear Judge Martinez:	The Honorable Edith Martinez
		Judge of the U.S. District Court
physician	Dear Dr. Wise:	Thomas Wise, M.D.
veterinarian	Dear Dr. Legrand:	Sarah Legrand, D.V.M.
dentist	Dear Dr. Peyton:	Lee Peyton, D.D.S.
Government		
President	Dear Mr. President:	The President
		The White House
		1600 Pennsylvania Avenue
Vice-President	Dear Madam Vice-President:	The Honorable Christine Lowe
		Vice-President of the U.S.
U.S. Senator	Dear Senator:	The Honorable Annette Greene
		United States Senator
U.S. Attorney General	Dear Mr. Attorney General:	The Honorable Samuel Thayer
		The Attorney General
Representative U.S. Congress	Dear Representative Hudson:	The Honorable Wm. T. Hudson
		U.S. House of Representatives
Supreme Court, Chief Justice	Dear Mr. Chief Justice:	The Chief Justice of the U.S.
		The Supreme Court of the U.S.
Governor	Dear Governor Tate:	The Honorable Charlotte Tate
Mayor	Dear Mayor Suarez:	The Honorable Robert M. Suarez
		Mayor of Edgerton, Virginia
Clerk of Court	Dear Mr. Yee:	Paul S. Yee, Esq.
Prime Minister	Excellency:	His Excellency Charles Winthrop
College & University Officials		
Professor	Dear Professor Lee:	Professor Edwina Lee
College President	Dear Dr. Andrews:	President Theodore Andrews
College Dean	Dear Dean Howell:	Dean Andrea Howell
Religious		
Pope	Your Holiness:	His Holiness the Pope
Priest	Dear Father:	The Reverend Father McNeil
Rabbi	Dear Rabbi Brown:	Rabbi Abraham Brown
Nun	Dear Sister Anne:	Sister Anne Carmichael, S.C.*
		(Sisters of Carmelite)
Brother	Dear Brother Daniel:	Brother Daniel, S.J.*
		(order of St. Joseph)
Clergyman	Dear Ms. Latham:	The Reverend Judith Latham
Bishop (Catholic)	Your Excellency:	The Most Reverend Thomas Taft

Bishop (Episcopal)	Right Reverend Sir:	The Right Reverend L.D. Cane
Cardinal	Your Eminence	His Eminence Louis Cardinal Lafferty
Private Individuals		
woman whose marital status is unknown	Dear Ms. Jones:	Ms. Gail Atchison Jones
unknown person	Dear Sir or Madam:	The Director of Admissions
company or organization	Dear Sir or Madam:	Board of Commissioners

PROOFREADER'S SYMBOLS

PROOFREADERS' MARKS AND SAMPLE COPY

Symbol	Meaning	Symbol	Meaning	Symbol	Meaning
ℓℰ	Delete	tr	Transpose	⌇	Superscript
◡	Close up	eq# or va	Equalize space	⌃	Subscript
ℰ	Delete and close up	⊐	Indent 1 em	?/	Question mark
◡	Push down lead that prints	ℓd	Insert lead between lines	!/	Exclamation point
⊗	Broken letter	ℓd	Take out lead	=/	Hyphen
#	Space or more space	stet	Let it stand	(/)	Parentheses
ꝰ	Reverse; turn over	sp	Spell out	[/]	Brackets
¶	Begin a paragraph	|⌐M⌐|	Em dash	or lig	Use ligature
⊐⊏	Center	|⌐N⌐|	En dash	wf	Wrong font
⊐	Move to right	⊙	Period	ℓf	Lightface type
⊏	Move to left	⌃	Comma	bf	Boldface type
⊔	Lower letters or words	;/	Semicolon	rom	Roman type
⊓	Raise letters or words	:/	Colon	ital	Italic type
||	Align type vertically	⌄	Apostrophe or 'single quote'	caps	CAPITALS
=	Straighten line	⌄/⌄	Quotation marks	sm.c.	SMALL CAPITALS
ʌ	Insert from margin	run on	No paragraph	ℓc	Lower case

DIAGRAMMING SENTENCES

The following models illustrate some basic sentence diagramming techniques.

1. Simple sentence: Aaron left home by boat.

2. Compound sentence: Aaron left, but I stayed behind.

3. Complex sentence: My brother, who left home, has returned.

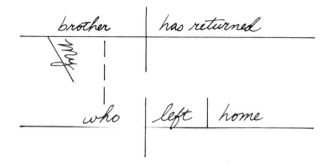

4. Compound-complex sentence: I know where Aaron went, but I didn't tell.

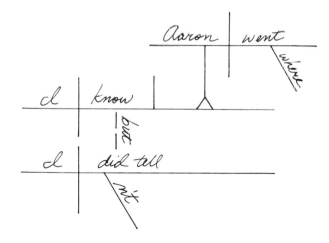

SIMPLIFIED PARLIAMENTARY PROCEDURE

F1 All organizations which hold formal meetings, including ruling bodies, civic, social, and religious clubs, and special interest groups, such as science clubs, honor societies, and fraternal organizations, need **a method of structuring meetings.** The purpose of **order** is obvious — more is accomplished when all participants know what to expect and when everyone has an equal part in the group's function.

(Note: For the most complete coverage of parliamentary procedure, consult *Robert's Rules of Order,* a handbook composed by General Henry Martin Robert in 1876 and accepted as standard procedure throughout the United States.)

Basic Rules

F2

1. The **chair,** president, or moderator presides over meetings, opens sessions, calls members to order, states the agenda or business to be acted upon, calls for votes when there are motions from the members, and announces the results of each vote. The chair also keeps order and casts the deciding vote when results are indecisive. In general, the chair strives to serve the will of the majority. If the chair desires to participate in the debate, a **chair pro tem.** is appointed for the duration of that session only.

(Note: The organization may designate a **vice president** to share the platform with the president and serve in place of the presiding officer when there is need.)

2. The **secretary** records the events of each meeting in the **minutes,** an official, signed document noting whether the session was a regular or called meeting as well as its date, place, and the name of the presiding officer, *i.e.* the president or president *pro tem.* The secretary leaves a margin in which corrections or additions can be made to the minutes. The secretary makes no personal comments about the proceedings, but concentrates upon what each participant says. In addition, the secretary announces the number of votes for and against each motion and the method by which the vote was determined, *e.g.* show of hands or secret ballot.

3. The **reading of the minutes** from the previous session is noted in the opening line of the current minutes. If the minutes are published, they are signed by both the secretary and the chair. After the minutes are read, a simple vote of adoption is taken; however, corrections may be made and approved at any time errors or deletions are discovered. The secretary is responsible for assembling and preserving all **committee reports,** which are briefly summarized in the minutes. All documents pertaining to the group are open for members to inspect at any time.

4. Before the session begins, the secretary provides the chair with an **agenda** or a list of business to come before the members in the order in which each item should be discussed.

5. Each **meeting** constitutes a separate session of business, although a meeting can be carried over from one day to the next or subsequent days. Business is conducted when a **quorum** is present. Usually, a quorum is a majority of the membership; however, some large groups select a pre-determined number for a quorum, sometimes only a fraction of the entire body of members.

6. Sessions follow a standard **order of business.** For example,
  A. Reading of the minutes of the previous meeting
  B. Approval of the minutes
  C. Committee reports
  D. Old or unfinished business
  E. New business
If members wish to change the order, a two-thirds vote is necessary to override the accepted order of business.

7. Members may propose an activity, change of order, rule, or suggestion by raising their hands, waiting to be identified by the chair, and saying, "I move that . . . ." The chair states the member's **motion** and asks for a second. If a second member replies, "I second the motion," the chair asks for discussion and calls for a vote. The vote, usually determined by the majority, is announced. If the motion carries, the spirit and intent of the motion becomes the will of the entire organization.

8. When the business of the agenda is completed, the chair asks for a **motion of adjournment.** If the majority vote for adjournment, the chair ends the meeting at that point and no further business may be conducted until a subsequent meeting begins.

9. When a group is holding an **organizational meeting** to establish a permanent society, members may propose the names of an **acting chair** and an **acting clerk** to preside over the selection of permanent officers. Committees are formed to study the needs of the organization and to formulate a **constitution, bylaws,** and **rules of order.** At the second meeting, members discuss and vote on each aspect of the constitution, decide rules for membership, and standards for orderly procedure.

10. The most important decisions faced by a newly-formed organization include the following:

  A. Name
  B. Purpose
  C. Officers and duties
  D. Committees
  E. Meeting time and place
  F. Voting procedures, as stated in the bylaws
Rules for governing the club should include methods by which members can **amend** the constitution and bylaws at any time.

11. The **treasurer** maintains and accounts for funds and pays them out at the secretary's request. (Note: Small organizations combine the task of secretary and treasurer, in which case expenditure of funds is ordered by the chair.) The treasurer is responsible for getting and preserving receipts for all transactions and for presenting a true and honest account of all expenditures. As a part of each meeting, the treasurer presents a brief **treasurer's report** of the following information:

    A. Balance on hand at the beginning of the year

    B. Money received during the year

    C. Expenses

    D. Balance on hand

12. The following are suggestions to guide officers in the smooth operation of club meetings:

    A. Learn the rules of parliamentary procedure and keep a list on hand for immediate reference.

    B. Provide each member with copies of the constitution and bylaws.

    C. Refrain from interrupting members or from inhibiting individuals from full participation in club activities.

    D. Resort to strict parliamentary procedure when order is threatened, but avoid tedious rules and unnecessary restrictions.

    E. Above all, allow only one motion to be discussed at a time by ruling out extraneous comments, personal remarks, or emotional arguments.

    F. Apply the rules of good manners by extending courtesy to everyone present at the meeting. Insist that other members do the same.

    G. Insist on democratic procedure by following majority rule.

PRESIDENTS OF THE UNITED STATES

Name	Years in Office	Vice President	Wife's Name	Party	State of Residence
George Washington	1789-1797	John Adams	Martha Dandridge Custis	Fed.	Virginia
John Adams	1797-1801	Thomas Jefferson	Abigail Smith	Fed.	Massachusetts
Thomas Jefferson	1801-1809	Aaron Burr George Clinton	Martha Wayles Skelton	Rep.	Virginia
James Madison	1809-1817	George Clinton Elbridge Gerry	Dolly Payne Todd	Rep.	Virginia
James Monroe	1817-1825	Daniel Tompkins	Elizabeth Kortwright	Rep.	Virginia
John Quincy Adams	1825-1829	John C. Calhoun	Louise Catherine Johnson	Rep.	Massachusetts
Andrew Jackson	1829-1837	John C. Calhoun Martin Van Buren	Rachel Donelson Robards	Dem.	Tennessee
Martin Van Buren	1837-1841	Richard M. Johnson	Hannah Hoes	Dem.	New York
William Henry Harrison	1841	John Tyler	Anna Symmes	Whig	Ohio

APPENDIX G

President	Years	Vice President	First Lady	Party	State
John Tyler	1841-1845	–	Letitia Christian Julia Gardiner	Whig	Virginia
James Knox Polk	1845-1849	George M. Dallas	Sarah Childress	Dem.	Tennessee
Zachary Taylor	1849-1850	Millard Fillmore	Margaret Smith	Whig	Louisiana
Millard Fillmore	1850-1853	–	Abigail Powers Caroline Carmichael McIntosh	Whig	New York
Franklin Pierce	1853-1857	William R. King	Jane Means Appleton	Dem.	New Hampshire
James Buchanan	1857-1861	John C. Breckinridge	None	Dem.	Pennsylvania
Abraham Lincoln	1861-1865	Hannibal Hamlin Andrew Johnson	Mary Todd	Rep.	Illinois
Andrew Johnson	1865-1869	–	Eliza McCardle	Dem.	Tennessee
Ulysses S. Grant	1869-1877	Schuyler Colfax Henry Wilson	Julia Dent	Rep.	Illinois
Rutherford B. Hayes	1877-1881	William A. Wheeler	Lucy Ward Webb	Rep.	Ohio

APPENDIX G

James A. Garfield	1881	Chester A. Arthur	Lucretia Rudolph	Rep.	Ohio
Chester A. Arthur	1881-1885	—	Ellen Lewis Herndon	Rep.	New York
Grover Cleveland	1885-1889	Thomas A. Hendricks	Frances Folsom	Dem.	New York
Benjamin Harrison	1889-1893	Levi P. Morton	Caroline Lavinia Scott Mary Scott Lord Dimmock	Rep.	Indiana
Grover Cleveland	1893-1897	Adlai E. Stevenson	Frances Folsom	Dem.	New York
William McKinley	1897-1901	Garret A. Hobart	Ida Saxton	Rep.	Ohio
Theodore Roosevelt	1901-1909	Charles W. Fairbanks	Alice Hathaway Lee Edith Kermit Carow	Rep.	New York
William H. Taft	1909-1913	James S. Sherman	Helen Herron	Rep.	Ohio
Woodrow Wilson	1913-1921	Thomas R. Marshall	Ellen Louise Axon Edith Bolling Galt	Dem.	New Jersey
Warren G. Harding	1921-1923	Calvin Coolidge	Florence Kling De Wolfe	Rep.	Ohio

APPENDIX G

President	Term	Vice President	First Lady	Party	State
Calvin Coolidge	1923-1929	Charles G. Dawes	Grace A. Goodhue	Rep.	Massachusetts
Herbert C. Hoover	1929-1933	Charles Curtis	Lou Henry	Rep.	California
Franklin D. Roosevelt	1933-1945	John N. Garner Henry A. Wallace Harry S. Truman	Anna Eleanor Roosevelt	Dem.	New York
Harry S. Truman	1945-1953	Alben W. Barkley	Elizabeth Virginia Wallace	Dem.	Missouri
Dwight D. Eisenhower	1953-1961	Richard M. Nixon	Mamie Geneva Dowd	Rep.	New York
John F. Kennedy	1961-1963	Lyndon B. Johnson	Jacqueline Bouvier	Dem.	Massachusetts
Lyndon B. Johnson	1963-1969	Hubert H. Humphrey	Claudia Alta Taylor	Dem.	Texas
Richard M. Nixon	1969-1974	Spiro T. Agnew Gerald R. Ford	Patricia Ryan	Rep.	New York
Gerald R. Ford	1974-1977	Nelson A. Rockefeller	Betty Anne Bloomer	Rep.	Michigan
James E. Carter	1977-1981	Walter Mondale	Rosalynn Smith	Dem.	Georgia
Ronald Reagan	1981-1989	George Bush	Nancy Davis	Rep.	California
George Bush	1989	J. Danforth Quayle	Barbara Pierce	Rep.	Texas

THE CONSTITUTION OF THE UNITED STATES

We, the People of the United States, in order to form a more perfect union, establish justice, insure domestic tranquility, provide for the common defence, promote the general welfare, and secure the blessings of liberty to ourselves and our posterity, do ordain and establish this Constitution for the United States of America.

ARTICLE I.

Sect. 1. ALL legislative powers herein granted shall be vested in a Congress of the United States, which shall consist of a Senate and House of Representatives.

Sect. 2. The House of Representatives shall be composed of members chosen every second year by the people of the several states, and the electors in each state shall have the qualifications requisite for electors of the most numerous branch of the state legislature.

No person shall be a representative who shall not have attained to the age of twenty-five years, and been seven years a citizen of the United States, and who shall not, when elected, be an inhabitant of that state in which he shall be chosen.

(Representatives and direct taxes shall be apportioned among the several states which may be included within this Union, according to their respective numbers, which shall be determined by adding to the whole number of free persons, including those bound to service for a term of years, and excluding Indians not taxed, three-fifths of all other persons.) The actual enumeration shall be made within three years after the first meeting of the Congress of the United States, and within every subsequent term of ten years, in such manner as they shall by law direct. The number of representatives shall not exceed one for every thirty thousand, but each state shall have at least one representative; and until such enumeration shall be made, the state of New-Hampshire shall be entitled to chuse three, Massachusetts eight, Rhode-Island and Providence Plantations one, Connecticut five, New-York six, New-Jersey four, Pennsylvania eight, Delaware one, Maryland six, Virginia ten, North-Carolina five, South-Carolina five, and Georgia three.

When vacancies happen in the representation from any state, the Executive authority thereof shall issue writs of election to fill such vacancies.

The House of Representatives shall chuse their Speaker and other officers; and shall have the sole power of impeachment.

Sect. 3. The Senate of the United States shall be composed of two senators from each state, (chosen by the legislature thereof,) for six years; and each senator shall have one vote.

Immediately after they shall be assembled in consequence of the first election, they shall be divided as equally as may be into three classes. The seats of the senators of the first class shall be vacated at the expiration of the second year, of the second class at the expiration of the fourth year, and of the third class at the expiration of the sixth year, so that one-third may be chosen every second year; (and if vacancies happen by resignation, or otherwise, during the recess of the Legislature of any state, the Executive thereof may make temporary appointments until the next meeting of the Legislature, which shall then fill such vacancies.)

No person shall be a senator who shall not have attained to the age of thirty years, and been nine years a citizen of the United States, and who shall not, when elected, be an inhabitant of that state for which he shall be chosen.

The Vice-President of the United States shall be President of the senate, but shall have no vote, unless they be equally divided.

The Senate shall chuse their other officers, and also a President pro tempore, in the absence of the Vice-President, or when he shall exercise the office of President of the United States.

The Senate shall have the sole power to try all impeachments. When sitting for that purpose, they shall be on oath or affirmation. When the President of the United States is tried, the Chief Justice shall preside: And no person shall be convicted without the concurrence of two-thirds of the members present.

Judgment in cases of impeachment shall not extend further than to removal from office, and disqualification to hold and enjoy any office of honor, trust or profit under the United States; but the party convicted shall nevertheless be liable and subject to indictment, trial, judgment and punishment, according to law.

Sect. 4. The times, places and manner of holding elections for senators and representatives, shall be prescribed in each state by the legislature thereof; but the Congress may at any time by law make or alter such regulations, except as to the places of chusing Senators.

The Congress shall assemble at least once in every year, and such meeting shall (be on the first Monday in December,) unless they shall by law appoint a different day.

Sect. 5. Each house shall be the judge of the elections, returns and qualifications of its own members, and a majority of each shall constitute a quorum to do business; but a smaller number may adjourn from day to day, and may be authorized to compel the attendance of absent members, in such manner, and under such penalties as each house may provide.

Each house may determine the rules of its proceedings, punish its members for disorderly behaviour, and, with the concurrence of two-thirds, expel a member.

Each house shall keep a journal of its proceedings, and from time to time publish the same, excepting such parts as may in their judgment require secrecy; and the yeas and nays of the members of either house on any question shall, at the desire of one-fifth of those present, be entered on the journal.

Neither house, during the session of Congress, shall, without the consent of the other, adjourn for more than three days, nor to any other place than that in which the two houses shall be sitting.

Sect. 6. The senators and representatives shall receive a compensation for their services, to be ascertained by law, and paid out of the treasury of the United States. They shall in all cases, except treason, felony and breach of the peace, be privileged from arrest during their attendance at the session of their respective houses, and in going to and returning from the same; and for any speech or debate in either house, they shall not be questioned in any other place.

No senator or representative shall, during the time for which he was elected, be appointed to any civil office under the authority of the United States, which shall have been created, or the emoluments whereof shall have been encreased during such time; and no person holding any office under the United States, shall be a member of either house during his continuance in office.

Sect. 7. All bills for raising revenue shall originate in the house of representatives; but the senate may propose or concur with amendments as on other bills.

Every bill which shall have passed the house of representatives and the senate, shall, before it become a law, be presented to the president of the United States; if he approve he shall sign it, but if not he shall return it, with his objections to that house in which it shall have originated, who shall enter the objections at large on their journal, and proceed to reconsider it. If after such reconsideration two-thirds of that house shall agree to pass the bill, it shall be sent, together with the objections, to the other house, by which it shall likewise be reconsidered, and if approved by two-thirds of that house, it shall become a law. But in all such cases the votes of both houses shall be determined by yeas and nays, and the names of the persons voting for and against the bill shall be entered on the journal of each house respectively. If any bill shall not be returned by the President within ten days (Sundays excepted) after it shall have been presented to him, the same shall be a law, in like manner as if he had signed it, unless the Congress by their adjournment prevent its return, in which case it shall not be a law.

Every order, resolution, or vote to which the concurrence of the Senate and House of Representatives may be necessary (except on a question of adjournment) shall be presented to the President of the United States; and before the same shall take effect, shall be approved by him, or, being disapproved by him, shall be repassed by two-thirds of the Senate and House of Representatives, according to the rules and limitations prescribed in the case of a bill.

Sect. 8. The Congress shall have power

To lay and collect taxes, duties, imposts and excises, to pay the debts and provide for the common defence and general welfare of the United States; but all duties, imposts and excises shall be uniform throughout the United States;

To borrow money on the credit of the United States;

To regulate commerce with foreign nations, and among the several states, and with the Indian tribes;

To establish an uniform rule of naturalization, and uniform laws on the subject of bankruptcies throughout the United States;

To coin money, regulate the value thereof, and of foreign coin, and fix the standard of weights and measures;

To provide for the punishment of counterfeiting the securities and current coin of the United States;

To establish post offices and post roads;

To promote the progress of science and useful arts, by securing for limited times to authors and inventors the exclusive right to their respective writings and discoveries;

To constitute tribunals inferior to the supreme court;

To define and punish piracies and felonies committed on the high seas, and offences against the law of nations;

To declare war, grant letters of marque and reprisal, and make rules concerning captures on land and water;

To raise and support armies, but no appropriation of money to that use shall be for a longer term than two years;

To provide and maintain a navy;

To make rules for government and regulation of the land and naval forces;

To provide for calling forth the militia to execute the laws of the union, suppress insurrections and repel invasions;

To provide for organizing, arming, and disciplining, the militia, and for governing such part of them as may be employed in the service of the United States, reserving to the States respectively, the appointment of the officers, and the authority of training the militia according to the discipline prescribed by Congress;

To exercise exclusive legislation in all cases whatsoever, over such district (not exceeding ten miles square) as may, by cession of particular States, and the acceptance of Congress, become the seat of the government of the United States, and to exercise like authority over all places purchased by the consent of the legislature of the state in which the same shall be, for the erection of forts, magazines, arsenals, dock-yards, and other needful buildings; — And

To make all laws which shall be necessary and proper for carrying into execution the foregoing powers, and all other powers vested by this constitution in the government of the United States, or in any department or officer thereof.

Sect. 9. The migration or importation of such persons as any of the states now existing shall think proper to admit, shall not be prohibited by the Congress prior to the year one thousand eight hundred and eight, but a tax or duty may be imposed on such importation, not exceeding ten dollars for each person.

The privilege of the writ of habeas corpus shall not be suspended, unless when in cases of rebellion or invasion the public safety may require it.

No bill of attainder or ex post facto law shall be passed.

No capitation, or other direct, tax shall be laid, unless in proportion to the census or enumeration herein before directed to be taken.

No tax or duty shall be laid on articles exported from any state. No preference shall be given by any regulation of commerce or revenue to the ports of one state over those of another: nor shall vessels bound to, or from, one state, be obliged to enter, clear, or pay duties in another.

No money shall be drawn from the treasury, but in consequence of appropriations made by law; and a regular statement and account of the receipts and expenditures of all public money shall be published from time to time.

No title of nobility shall be granted by the United States: — And no person holding any office of profit or trust under them, shall, without the consent of the Congress, accept of any present, emolument, office, or title, of any kind whatever, from any king, prince, or foreign state.

Sect. 10. No state shall enter into any treaty, alliance, or confederation; grant letters of marque and reprisal; coin money; emit bills of credit; make any thing but gold and silver coin a tender in payment of debts; pass any bill of attainder, ex post facto law, or law impairing the obligation of contracts, or grant any title of nobility.

No state shall, without the consent of the Congress, lay any imposts or duties on imports or exports, except what may be absolutely necessary for executing its inspection laws; and the net produce of all duties and imposts, laid by any state on imports or exports, shall be for the use of the Treasury of the United States; and all such laws shall be subject to the revision and controul of the Congress. No state shall, without the consent of Congress, lay any duty of tonnage, keep troops, or ships of war in time of peace, enter into any agreement or compact with another state, or with a foreign power, or engage in war, unless actually invaded, or in such imminent danger as will not admit of delay.

II.

Sect. 1. The executive power shall be vested in a president of the United States of America. He shall hold his office during the term of four years, and, together with the vice-president, chosen for the same term, be elected as follows.

Each state shall appoint, in such manner as the legislature thereof may direct, a number of electors, equal to the whole number of senators and representatives to which the state may be entitled in the Congress: but no senator or representative, or person holding an office of trust or profit under the United States, shall be appointed an elector.

(The electors shall meet in their respective states, and vote by ballot for two persons, of whom one at least shall not be an inhabitant of the same state with themselves. And they shall make a list of all the persons voted for, and of the number of votes for each; which list they shall sign and certify, and transmit sealed to the seat of the government of the United States, directed to the president of the senate. The president of the senate shall, in the presence of the senate and house of representatives, open all the certificates, and the votes shall then be counted. The person having the greatest number of votes shall be the president, if such number be a majority of the whole number of electors appointed; and if there be more than one who have such majority, and have an equal number of votes, then the house of representatives shall immediately chuse by ballot one of them for president; and if no person have a majority, then from the five highest on the list the said house shall in like manner chuse the president. But in chusing the president, the votes shall be taken by states, the representation from each state having one vote; a quorum for this purpose shall consist of a member or members from two-thirds of the states and a majority of all the states shall be necessary to a choice. In every case, after the choice of the president, the person having the greatest number of votes of the electors shall be the vice-president. But if there should remain two or more who have equal votes, the senate shall chuse from them by ballot the vice-president.)

The Congress may determine the time of chusing the electors, and the day on which they shall give their votes; which day shall be the same throughout the United States.

No person except a natural born citizen, or a citizen of the United States, at the time of the adoption of this constitution, shall be eligible to the office of president; neither shall any person be eligible to that office who shall not have attained to the age of thirty-five years, and been fourteen years a resident of within the United States.

In case of the removal of the president from office, or of his death, resignation, or inability to discharge the powers and duties of the said office, the same shall devolve on the vice-president and the Congress may by law provide for the case of removal, death, resignation or inability, both of the president and vice-president, declaring what officer shall then act as president, and such officer shall act accordingly, until the disability be removed, or a president shall be elected.

The president shall, at stated times, receive for his services, a compensation, which shall neither be encreased nor diminished during the period for which he shall have been elected, and he shall not receive within that period any other emolument from the United States, or any of them.

Before he enter on the execution of his office, he shall take the following oath or affirmation:

"I do solemnly swear (or affirm) that I will faithfully execute the office of president of the United States, and will to the best of my ability, preserve, protect and defend the constitution of the United States."

Sect. 2. The president shall be commander in chief of the army and navy of the United States, and of the militia of the several States, when called into the actual service of the United States; he may require the opinion, in writing, of the principal officer in each of the executive departments, upon any subject relating to the duties of their respective offices, and he shall have power to grant reprieves and pardons for offences against the United States, except in cases of impeachment.

He shall have power, by and with the advice and consent of the senate, to make treaties, provided two-thirds of the senators present concur; and he shall nominate, and by and with the advice and consent of the senate, shall appoint ambassadors, other public ministers and consuls, judges of the supreme court, and all other officers of the United States, whose appointments are not herein otherwise provided for, and which shall be established by law. But the Congress may by law vest the appointment of such inferior officers, as they think proper, in the president alone, in the courts of law, or in the heads of departments.

The president shall have power to fill up all vacancies that may happen during the recess of the senate, by granting commissions which shall expire at the end of their next session.

Sect. 3. He shall from time to time give to the Congress information of the state of the union, and recommend to their consideration such measures as he shall judge necessary and expedient; he may, on extraordinary occasions, convene both houses, or either of them, and in case of disagreement between them, with respect to the time of adjournment, he may adjourn them to such time as he shall think proper; he shall receive ambassadors and other public ministers; he shall take care that the laws be faithfully executed, and shall commission all the officers of the United States.

Sect. 5. The president, vice-president and all civil officers of the United States, shall be removed from office on impeachment for, and conviction of, treason, bribery, or other high crimes and misdemeanors.

III.

Sect. 1. The judicial power of the United States, shall be vested in one supreme court, and in such inferior courts as the Congress may from time to time ordain and establish. The judges, both of the supreme and inferior courts, shall hold their offices during good behaviour, and shall, at stated times, receive for their services, a compensation, which shall not be diminished during their continuance in office.

Sect. 2. The judicial power shall extend to all cases, in law and equity, arising under this constitution, the laws of the United States, and treaties made, or which shall be made, under their authority; to all cases affecting ambassadors, other public ministers and consuls; to all cases of admiralty and maritime jurisdiction; to controversies to which the United States shall be a party; to controversies between two or more States, between a state and citizens of another state, between citizens of different States, between citizens of the same state claiming lands under grants of different States, and between a state, or the citizens thereof, and foreign States, citizens or subjects.

In all cases affecting ambassadors, other public ministers and consuls, and those in which a state shall be party, the supreme court shall have original jurisdiction. In all the other cases before mentioned, the supreme court shall have appellate jurisdiction, both as to law and fact, with such exceptions, and under such regulations as Congress shall make.

The trial of all crimes, except in cases of impeachment, shall be by jury; and such trial shall be held in the state where the said crimes shall have been committed; but when not committed within any state, the trial shall be at such place or places as the Congress may by law have directed.

Sect. 3. Treason against the United States, shall consist only in levying war against them, or in adhering to their enemies, giving them aid and comfort. No person shall be convicted of treason unless on the testimony of two witnesses to the same overt act, or on confession in open court.

The Congress shall have the power to declare the punishment of treason, but no attainder of treason shall work corruption of blood, or forfeiture except during the life of the person attainted.

IV.

Sect. 1. Full faith and credit shall be given in each state to the public acts, records, and judicial proceedings of every other state. And the Congress may by general laws prescribe the manner in which such acts, records and proceedings shall be proved, and the effect thereof.

Sect. 2. The citizens of each state shall be entitled to all privileges and immunities of citizens in the several states.

A person charged in any state with treason, felony, or other crime, who shall flee from justice and be found in another state, shall, on demand of the executive authority of the state from which he fled, be delivered up, to be removed to the state having jurisdiction of the crime.

(No person held to service or labour in one state, under the laws thereof, escaping into another, shall, in consequence of any law or regulation therein, be discharged from such service or labour, but shall be delivered up on claim of the party to whom such service or labour may be due.)

Sect. 3. New states may be admitted by the Congress into this union; but no new state shall be formed or erected within the jurisdiction of any other state; nor any state be formed by the junction of two or more states, or parts of states, without the consent of the legislatures of the states concerned as well as of the Congress.

The Congress shall have power to dispose of and make all needful rules and regulations respecting the territory or other property belonging to the United States; and nothing in this Constitution shall be so construed as to prejudice any claims of the United States, or of any particular state.

Sect. 4. The United States shall guarantee to every state in this union a Republican form of government, and shall protect each of them against invasion; and on application of the legislature, or of the executive (when the legislature cannot be convened) against domestic violence.

V.

The Congress, whenever two-thirds of both houses shall deem it necessary, shall propose amendments to this constitution, or, on the application of the legislatures of two-thirds of the several states, shall call a convention for proposing amendments, which, in either case, shall be valid to all intents and purposes, as part of this constitution, when ratified by the legislatures of three-fourths of the several states, or by conventions in three-fourths thereof, as the one or the other mode of ratification may be proposed by the Congress; Provided, that no amendment which may be made prior to the year one thousand eight hundred and eight shall in any manner affect the first and fourth clauses in the ninth section of the first article; and that no state, without its consent, shall be deprived of its equal suffrage in the senate.

VI.

All debts contracted and engagements entered into, before the adoption of this Constitution, shall be as valid against the United States under this Constitution, as under the confederation.

This constitution, and the laws of the United States which shall be made in pursuance thereof; and all treaties made, or which shall be made, under the authority of the United States, shall be the supreme law of the land; and the judges in every state shall be bound thereby, any thing in the constitution or laws of any state to the contrary notwithstanding.

The senators and representatives beforementioned, and the members of the several state legislatures, and all executive and judicial officers, both of the United States and of the several States, shall be bound by oath or affirmation, to support this constitution; but no religious test shall ever be required as a qualification to any office or public trust under the United States.

VII.

The ratification of the conventions of nine States, shall be sufficient for the establishment of this constitution between the States so ratifying the same.

The Constitution of the United States

Done in Convention, by the unanimous consent of the States present, the seventeenth day of September, in the year of our Lord one thousand seven hundred and eighty-seven, and of the Independence of the United States of America the twelfth. In witness whereof we have hereunto subscribed our Names.

GEORGE WASHINGTON, President
And Deputy from Virginia.

New-Hampshire.	John Langdon, Nicholas Gilman.	Delaware.	George Read, Gunning Bedford, Junior. John Dickinson. Richard Bassett. Jacob Broom.
Massachusetts.	Nathaniel Gorham. Rufus King.		
Connecticut.	William Samuel Johnson, Roger Sherman.	Maryland.	James M'Henry, Daniel of St. Tho. Jenifer. Daniel Carrol.
New-York.	Alexander Hamilton.		
New-Jersey.	William Livingston. David Brearley. William Paterson. Jonathan Dayton.	Virginia.	John Blair, James Madison, Junior.
		North-Carolina.	William Blount, Richard Dobbs Spaight, Hugh Williamson.
Pennsylvania.	Benjamin Franklin. Thomas Mifflin, Robert Morris, George Clymer, Thomas Fitzsimons, Jared Ingersoll, James Wilson, Gouverneur Morris.	South-Carolina.	John Rutledge. Charles Cotesworth Pinckney. Charles Pinckney, Pierce Butler.
		Georgia.	William Few, Abraham Baldwin.

Attest, William Jackson, Secretary.

Articles in addition to, and Amendment of the Constitution of the United States of America, proposed by Congress, and ratified by the Legislatures of the several States, pursuant to the fifth Article of the original Constitution.

Article (I)

Congress shall make no law respecting an establishment of religion, or prohibiting the free exercise thereof; or abridging the freedom of speech, or of the press; or the right of the people peaceably to assemble, and to petition the Government for a redress of grievances.

Article (II)

A well regulated Militia, being necessary to the security of a free State, the right of the people to keep and bear Arms, shall not be infringed.

Article (III)

No Soldier shall, in time of peace be quartered in any house, without the consent of the Owner, nor in time of war, but in a manner to be prescribed by law.

Article (IV)

The right of the people to be secure in their persons, houses, papers, and effects, against unreasonable searches and seizures, shall not be violated, and no Warrants shall issue, but upon probable cause, supported by Oath or affirmation, and particularly describing the place to be searched, and the persons or things to be seized.

Article (V)

No person shall be held to answer for a capital, or otherwise infamous crime, unless on a presentment or indictment of a Grand Jury, except in cases arising in the land or naval forces, or in the Militia, when in actual service in time of War or public danger; nor shall any person be subject for the same offence to be twice put in jeopardy of life or limb; nor shall be compelled in any criminal case to be a witness against himself, nor be deprived of life, liberty, or property, without due process of law; nor shall private property be taken for public use, without just compensation.

Article (VI)

In all criminal prosecutions, the accused shall enjoy the right to a speedy and public trial, by an impartial jury of the State and district wherein the crime shall have been committed, which district shall have been previously ascertained by law, and to be informed of the nature and cause of the accusation; to be confronted with the witnesses against him; to have compulsory process for obtaining witnesses in his favor, and to have the Assistance of Counsel for his defence.

Article (VII)

In Suits at common law, where the value in controversy shall exceed twenty dollars, the right of trial by jury shall be preserved, and no fact tried by a jury, shall be otherwise re-examined in any Court of the United States, than according to the rules of the common law.

Article (VIII)

Excessive bail shall not be required, nor excessive fines imposed, nor cruel and unusual punishments inflicted.

Article (IX)

The enumeration in the Constitution, of certain rights, shall not be construed to deny or disparage others retained by the people.

Article (X)

The powers not delegated to the United States by the Constitution, nor prohibited by it to the States, are reserved to the States respectively, or to the people.

Article (XI)

The judicial power of the United States shall not be construed to extend to any suit in law or equity, commenced or prosecuted against one of the United States by Citizens of another State, or by Citizens or Subjects of any Foreign State.

Article (XII)

The Electors shall meet in their respective states, and vote by ballot for President and Vice-President, one of whom, at least, shall not be an inhabitant of the same state with themselves; they shall name in their ballots the person voted for as President, and in distinct ballots the person voted for as Vice-President, and they shall make distinct lists of all persons voted for as President, and of all persons voted for as Vice-President, and of the number of votes for each, which lists they shall sign and certify, and transmit sealed to the seat of the government of the United States, directed to the President of the Senate; — The President of the Senate shall, in the presence of the Senate and House of Representatives, open all the certificates and the votes shall then be counted; — The person having the greatest number of votes for President, shall be the President, if such number be a majority of the whole number of Electors appointed; and if no person have such majority, then from the persons having the highest numbers not exceeding three on the list of those voted for as President, the House of Representatives shall choose immediately, by ballot, the President. But in choosing the President, the votes shall be taken by states, the representation from each state having one vote; a quorum for this purpose shall consist of a member or members from two-thirds of the states, and a majority of all the states shall be necessary to a choice. (And if the House of Representatives shall not choose a President whenever the right of choice shall devolve upon them, before the fourth day of March next following, then the Vice-President shall act as President, as in the case of the death or other constitutional disability of the President.) — The person having the greatest number of votes as Vice-President, shall be the Vice-President, if such number be a majority of the whole number of Electors appointed, and if no person have a majority, then from the two highest numbers on the list, the Senate shall choose the Vice-President; a quorum for the purpose shall consist of two-thirds of the whole number of Senators, and a majority of the whole number shall be necessary to a choice. But no person constitutionally ineligible to the office of President shall be eligible to that of Vice-President of the United States.

Article XIII

Section 1. Neither slavery nor involuntary servitude, except as punishment for crime whereof the party shall have been duly convicted, shall exist within the United States, or any place subject to their jurisdiction.

Section 2. Congress shall have power to enforce this article by appropriate legislation.

Article XIV

Section 1. All persons born or naturalized in the United States, and subject to the jurisdiction thereof, are citizens of the United States and of the State wherein they reside. No State shall make or enforce any law which shall abridge the privileges or immunities of citizens of the United States; nor shall any State deprive any person of life, liberty, or property, without due process of law; nor deny to any person within its jurisdiction the equal protection of the laws.

Section 2. Representatives shall be apportioned among the several States according to their respective numbers, counting the whole number of persons in each State, excluding Indians not taxed. But when the right to vote at any election for the choice of electors for President and Vice President of the United States, Representatives in

Congress, the Executive and Judicial officers of a State, or the members of the Legislature thereof, is denied to any of the male inhabitants of such State, being twenty-one years of age, and citizens of the United States, or in any way abridged, except for participation in rebellion, or other crime, the basis of representation therein shall be reduced in the proportion which the number of such male citizens shall bear to the whole number of male citizens twenty-one years of age in such State.

Section 3. No person shall be a Senator or Representative in Congress, or elector of President and Vice President, or hold any office, civil or military, under the United States, or under any State, who, having previously taken an oath, as a member of Congress, or as an officer of the United States, or as a member of any State legislature, or as an executive or judicial officer of any State, to support the Constitution of the United States, shall have engaged in insurrection or rebellion against the same, or given aid or comfort to the enemies thereof. But Congress may by a vote of two-thirds of each House, remove such disability.

Section 4. The validity of the public debt of the United States, authorized by law, including debts incurred for payment of pensions and bounties for services in suppressing insurrection or rebellion, shall not be questioned. But neither the United States nor any State shall assume or pay any debt or obligation incurred in aid of insurrection or rebellion against the United States, or any claim for the loss or emancipation of any slave; but all such debts, obligations and claims shall be held illegal and void.

Section 5. The Congress shall have power to enforce, by appropriate legislation, the provisions of this article.

Article XV

Section 1. The right of citizens of the United States to vote shall not be denied or abridged by the United States or by any State on account of race, color, or previous condition of servitude.

Section 2. The Congress shall have power to enforce this article by appropriate legislation.

Article XVI

The Congress shall have power to lay and collect taxes on incomes, from whatever source derived, without apportionment among the several States, and without regard to any census or enumeration.

Article (XVII)

The Senate of the United States shall be composed of two Senators from each State, elected by the people thereof, for six years; and each Senator shall have one vote. The electors in each State shall have the qualifications requisite for electors of the most numerous branch of the State legislatures.

When vacancies happen in the representation of any State in the Senate, the executive authority of such State shall issue writs of election to fill such vacancies; *Provided,* That the legislature of any State may empower the executive thereof to make temporary appointments until the people fill the vacancies by election as the legislature may direct.

This amendment shall not be so construed as to affect the election or term of any Senator chosen before it becomes valid as part of the Constitution.

Article (XVIII)

(Section 1. After one year from the ratification of this article the manufacture, sale, or transportation of intoxicating liquors within, the importation thereof into, or the exportation thereof from the United States and all territory subject to the jurisdiction thereof for beverage purposes is hereby prohibited.

(Sec. 2. The Congress and the several States shall have concurrent power to enforce this article by appropriate legislation.

(Sec. 3. This article shall be inoperative unless it shall have been ratified as an amendment to the Constitution by the legislatures of the several States, as provided in the Constitution, within seven years from the date of the submission hereof to the States by the Congress.)

Article (XIX)

The right of citizens of the United States to vote shall not be denied or abridged by the United States or by any State on account of sex.

Congress shall have power to enforce this article by appropriate legislation.

Article (XX)

Section 1. The terms of the President and Vice President shall end at noon on the 20th day of January, and the terms of Senators and Representatives at noon on the 3d day of January, of the years in which such terms would have ended if this article had not been ratified; and the terms of their successors shall then begin.

Sec. 2. The Congress shall assemble at least once in every year, and such meeting shall begin at noon on the 3d day of January, unless they shall by law appoint a different day.

Sec. 3. If, at the time fixed for the beginning of the term of the President, the President elect shall have died, the Vice President elect shall become President. If a President shall not have been chosen before the time fixed for the beginning of his term, or if the President elect shall have failed to qualify, then the Vice President elect shall act as President until a President shall have qualified; and the Congress may by law provide for the case wherein neither a President elect nor a Vice President elect shall have qualified, declaring who shall then act as President, or the manner in which one who is to act shall be selected, and such person shall act accordingly until a President or Vice President shall have qualified.

Sec. 4. The Congress may by law provide for the case of the death of any of the persons from whom the House of Representatives may choose a President whenever the right of choice shall have devolved upon them, and for the case of the death of any of the persons from whom the Senate may choose a Vice President whenever the right of choice shall have devolved upon them.

Sec. 5. Sections 1 and 2 shall take effect on the 15th day of October following the ratification of this article.

Sec. 6. This article shall be inoperative unless it shall have been ratified as an amendment to the Constitution by the legislatures of three-fourths of the several States within seven years from the date of its submission.

Article (XXI)

Section 1. The eighteenth article of the amendment to the Constitution of the United States is hereby repealed.

Sec. 2. The transportation or importation into any State, Territory, or possession of the United States for delivery or use therein of intoxicating liquors, in violation of the laws thereof, is hereby prohibited.

Sec. 3. This article shall be inoperative unless it shall have been ratified as an amendment to the Constitution by conventions in the several States, as provided in the Constitution, within seven years from the date of the submission hereof to the States by the Congress.

Article (XXII)

Section 1. No person shall be elected to the office of the President more than twice, and no person who has held the office of President, or acted as President, for more than two years of a term to which some other person was elected President shall be elected to the office of the President more than once. But this Article shall not apply to any person holding the office of President when this Article was proposed by the Congress, and shall not prevent any person who may be holding the office of President, or acting as President, during the term within which this Article becomes operative from holding the office of President or acting as President during the remainder of such term.

Sec. 2. This article shall be inoperative unless it shall have been ratified as an amendment to the Constitution by the legislatures of three-fourths of the several States within seven years from the date of its submission to the States by the Congress.

Article (XXIII)

Section 1. The District constituting the seat of Government of the United States shall appoint in such manner as the Congress may direct:

A number of electors of President and Vice President equal to the whole number of Senators and Representatives in Congress to which the District would be entitled if it were a State, but in no event more than the least populous State; they shall be in addition to those appointed by the States, but they shall be considered, for the purposes of the election of President and Vice President, to be electors appointed by a State; and they shall meet in the District and perform such duties as provided by the twelfth article of amendment.

Section 2. The Congress shall have power to enforce this article by appropriate legislation.

Article (XXIV)

Section 1. The right of citizens of the United States to vote in any primary or other election for President or Vice President, for electors for President or Vice President, or for Senator or Representative in Congress, shall not be denied or abridged by the United states or any State by reason of failure to pay any poll tax or other tax.

Section 2. The Congress shall have power to enforce this article by appropriate legislation.

THE DECLARATION OF INDEPENDENCE

In Congress, July 4, 1776.
A Declaration by the Representatives of the United States of America,
In General Congress Assembled.

WHEN in the Course of human Events, it becomes necessary for one People to dissolve the Political Bands which have connected them with another, and to assume among the Powers of the Earth, the separate and equal Station to which the Laws of Nature and of Nature's God entitle them, a decent Respect to the Opinions of Mankind requires that they should declare the causes which impel them to the Separation.

We hold these Truths to be self-evident, that all Men are created equal, that they are endowed by their Creator with certain unalienable Rights, that among these are Life, Liberty, and the Pursuit of Happiness — That to secure these Rights, Governments are instituted among Men, deriving their just Powers from the Consent of the Governed, that whenever any Form of Government becomes destructive of these Ends, it is the Right of the People to alter or to abolish it, and to institute new Government, laying its Foundation on such Principles, and organizing its Powers in such Form, as to them shall seem most likely to effect their Safety and Happiness. Prudence, indeed, will dictate that Governments long established should not be changed for light and transient Causes; and accordingly all Experience hath shewn, that Mankind are more disposed to suffer, while Evils are sufferable, than to right themselves by abolishing the Forms to which they are accustomed. But when a long Train of Abuses and Usurpations, pursuing invariably the same Object, evinces a Design to reduce them under absolute Despotism, it is their Right, it is their Duty, to throw off such Government, and to provide new Guards for their future Security. Such has been the patient Sufferance of these Colonies; and such is now the Necessity which constrains them to alter their former Systems of Government. The History of the present King of Great-Britain is a History of repeated Injuries and Usurpations, all having in direct Object the Establishment of an absolute Tyranny over these States. To prove this, let Facts be submitted to a candid World.

He has refused his Assent to Laws, the most wholesome and necessary for the public Good.

He has forbidden his Governors to pass Laws of immediate and pressing Importance, unless suspended in their Operation till his Assent should be obtained; and when so suspended, he has utterly neglected to attend to them.

He has refused to pass other Laws for the Accommodation of large Districts of People, unless those People would relinquish the Right of Representation in the Legislature, a Right inestimable to them, and formidable to Tyrants only.

He has called together Legislative Bodies at Places unusual, uncomfortable, and distant from the Depository of their public Records, for the sole Purpose of fatiguing them into Compliance with his Measures.

He has dissolved Representative Houses repeatedly, for opposing with manly Firmness his Invasions on the Rights of the People.

He has refused for a long Time, after such Dissolutions, to cause others to be elected; whereby the Legislative Powers, incapable of Annihilation, have returned to the People at large for their exercise; the State remaining in the mean time exposed to all the Dangers of Invasion from without, and Convulsions within.

He has endeavoured to prevent the Population of these States; for that Purpose obstructing the Laws for the Naturalization of Foreigners; refusing to pass others to encourage their Migrations hither, and raising the Conditions of new Appropriations of Lands.

He has obstructed the Administration of Justice, by refusing his Assent to Laws for establishing Judiciary Powers.

He has made Judges dependent on his Will alone, for the Tenure of their Offices, and the Amount and Payment of their Salaries.

He has erected a Multitude of new Offices, and sent hither Swarms of Officers to harrass our People, and eat out their Substance.

He has kept among us, in Times of Peace, Standing Armies, without the consent of our Legislatures.

He has affected to render the Military independent of and superior to the Civil Power.

He has combined with others to subject us to a Jurisdiction foreign to our Constitution, and unacknowledged by our Laws; giving his Assent to their Acts of pretended Legislation:

For quartering large Bodies of Armed Troops among us:

For protecting them, by a mock Trial, from Punishment for any Murders which they should commit on the Inhabitants of these States:

For cutting off our Trade with all Parts of the World:

For imposing Taxes on us without our Consent:

For depriving us, in many Cases, of the Benefits of Trial by Jury:

For transporting us beyond Seas to be tried for pretended Offences:

For abolishing the free System of English Laws in a neighbouring Province, establishing therein an arbitrary Government, and enlarging its Boundaries, so as to render it at once an Example and fit Instrument for introducing the same absolute Rule into these Colonies:

For taking away our Charters, abolishing our most valuable Laws, and altering fundamentally the Forms of our Governments:

For suspending our own Legislatures, and declaring themselves invested with Power to legislate for us in all Cases whatsoever.

He has abdicated Government here, by declaring us out of his Protection and waging War against us.

He has plundered our Seas, ravaged our Coasts, burnt our Towns, and destroyed the Lives of our People.

He is, at this Time, transporting large Armies of foreign Mercenaries to compleat the Works of Death, Desolation, and Tyranny, already begun with circumstances of Cruelty and Perfidy, scarcely paralleled in the most barbarous Ages, and totally unworthy the Head of a civilized Nation.

He has constrained our fellow Citizens taken Captive on the high Seas to bear Arms against their Country, to become the Executioners of their Friends and Brethren, or to fall themselves by their Hands.

He has excited domestic Insurrections amongst us, and has endeavoured to bring on the Inhabitants of our Frontiers, the merciless Indian Savages, whose known Rule of Warfare, is an undistinguished Destruction, of all Ages, Sexes and Conditions.

In every stage of these Oppressions we have Petitioned for Redress in the most humble Terms: Our repeated Petitions have been answered only by repeated Injury. A Prince, whose Character is thus marked by every act which may define a Tyrant, is unfit to be the Ruler of a free People.

Nor have we been wanting in Attentions to our British Brethren. We have warned them from Time to Time of Attempts by their Legislature to extend an unwarrantable Jurisdiction over us. We have reminded them of the Circumstances of our Emigration and Settlement here. We have appealed to their native Justice and Magnanimity, and we have conjured them by the Ties of our common Kindred to disavow these Usurpations, which, would inevitably interrupt our Connections and Correspondence. They too have been deaf to the Voice of Justice and of Consanguinity. We must, therefore, acquiesce in the Necessity, which denounces our Separation, and hold them, as we hold the rest of Mankind, Enemies in War, in Peace, Friends.

We, therefore, the Representatives of the UNITED STATES OF AMERICA, in GENERAL CONGRESS, Assembled, appealing to the Supreme Judge of the World for the Rectitude of our Intentions, do, in the Name, and by Authority of the good People of these Colonies, solemnly Publish and Declare, That these United Colonies are, and of Right ought to be, FREE AND INDEPENDENT STATES; that they are absolved from all Allegiance to the British Crown, and that all political Connection between them and the State of Great-Britain, is and ought to be totally dissolved; and that as FREE AND INDEPENDENT STATES, they have full Power to levy War, conclude Peace, contract Alliances, establish Commerce, and to do all other Acts and Things which INDEPENDENT STATES may of right do. And for the support of this Declaration, with a firm Reliance on the Protection of divine Providence, we mutually pledge to each other our Lives, our Fortunes, and our sacred Honor.

Signed by ORDER AND IN BEHALF *of the* Congress,

JOHN HANCOCK, President.

ATTEST.
CHARLES THOMSON, Secretary.

(SIGNERS OF THE DECLARATION OF INDEPENDENCE)

John Hancock

New-Hampshire.	*Josiah Bartlett,*
	Wm. Whipple,
	Matthew Thornton.

Massachusetts-Bay. *Saml. Adams,*
John Adams,
Robt. Treat Paine,
Elbridge Gerry.

Rhode-Island and Providence, &c. *Step. Hopkins,*
William Ellery.

Connecticut. *Roger Sherman,*
Saml. Huntington,
Wm. Williams,
Oliver Wolcott.

New-York. *Wm. Floyd,*
Phil. Livingston,
Frans. Lewis,
Lewis Morris.

New-Jersey. *Richd. Stockton,*
Jno. Witherspoon,
Fras. Hopkinson,
John Hart,
Abra. Clark.

Pennsylvania. *Robt. Morris,*
Benjamin Rush,
Benja. Franklin,
John Morton,
Geo. Clymer,
Jas. Smith,
Geo. Taylor,
James Wilson,
Geo. Ross.

Delaware. *Caesar Rodney,*
Geo. Read,
Tho M:Kean.

Maryland. *Samuel Chase,*
Wm. Paca,
Thos. Stone,
Charles Carroll, of
Carrollton.

Virginia. *George Wythe,*
Richard Henry Lee,
Ths. Jefferson,
Benja. Harrison,
Thos. Nelson, jr.
Francis Lightfoot Lee,
Carter Braxton.

North-Carolina. *Wm. Hooper,*
Joseph Hewes,
John Penn.

South-Carolina. *Edward Rutledge,*
Thos. Heyward, junr.
Thomas Lynch, junr.
Arthur Middleton.

Georgia. *Button Gwinnett,*
Lyman Hall,
Geo. Walton.

THE GETTYSBURG ADDRESS
November 19, 1863.

Fourscore and seven years ago our fathers brought forth on this continent a new nation, conceived in liberty, and dedicated to the proposition that all men are created equal.

Now we are engaged in a great civil war, testing whether that nation, or any nation so conceived and so dedicated, can long endure. We are met on a great battlefield of that war. We have come to dedicate a portion of that field as a final resting-place for those who gave their lives that that nation might live. It is altogether fitting and proper that we should do this.

But, in a larger sense, we cannot dedicate — we cannot consecrate — we cannot hallow — this ground. The brave men, living and dead, who struggled here, have consecrated it far above our poor power to add or detract. The world will little note nor long remember what we say here, but it can never forget what they did here. It is for us, the living, rather, to be dedicated here to the unfinished work which they, who fought here, have thus far so nobly advanced. It is rather for us to be here dedicated to the great task remaining before us — that from these honored dead we take increased devotion to that cause for which they gave the last full measure of devotion; that we here highly resolve that these dead shall have not died in vain; that this nation, under God, shall have a new birth of freedom; and that government of the people, by the people, for the people, shall not perish from the earth.

APPENDIX K

ERRORS IN LOGIC

Thinking is often muddled by faulty reasoning, particularly when the mind misuses or misunderstands facts by omitting key data or distorting the issues. The ten most common errors in logic are as follows:

1. **Bandwagon** — the faulty notion that everyone else is doing, thinking, or saying something. This fallacy assumes that the actions of the majority should govern the behavior of everyone.
Example: On this road everybody drives over the speed limit, so it must be safe.

2. **Red herring** — drawing attention to another issue in order to escape making an important decision.
Example: I can't waste my time worrying about recycling when the real threat to the world is a nuclear catastrophe.

3. **Equivocation** — using a word in the wrong sense.
Example: It is his right to abstain from voting. Therefore his decision must be right.

4. **Non sequitur** — an illogical conclusion that does not precede from a given statement.
Example: The Arapaho are deserving of federal aid, so they will probably receive the grant.

5. **False analogy** — a faulty assumption that because things resemble each other in some respects, they must be alike in other ways.
Example: David and Jake are both 150-pound swimmers, so either one would make a good choice for team captain.

6. **Generalization** — a conclusion that lacks evidence to support it.
Example: Too many young people are choosing accounting for a career.

7. **Attacking the person** — a statement that attacks the person rather than the issue.
Example: We can't take Wendell's advice on lawncare because he is known for being conceited.

8. **Circular thinking** — an assertion that restates the original issue without adding any new data.
Example: The club has a reputation for snobbery because they are choosy about the people they admit.

9. **Either . . . or** — a statement which allows only two alternatives.
Example: We must decide whether to commit the city to a new landfill or build an incinerator as a means of dealing with solid waste.

10. **Faulty cause and effect** — a false assumption that because one situation follows another, the first must have caused the second.
Example: Our new office manager has caused nothing but trouble. Since her appointment to the job, three secretaries have quit.

ROMAN NUMERALS

ARABIC	ROMAN	ARABIC	ROMAN	ARABIC	ROMAN
1	I	21	XXI	500	D
2	II	22	XXII	600	DC
3	III	23	XXIII	700	DCC
4	IV	24	XXIV	800	DCCC
5	V	25	XXV	900	CM
6	VI	29	XXIX	1,000	M
7	VII	30	XXX	1,111	MCXI
8	VIII	40	XL	1,500	MD
9	IX	50	L	2,000	MM
10	X	60	LX	3,000	MMM
11	XI	70	LXX	4,000	$M\overline{V}$
12	XII	80	LXXX	5,000	$\overline{V}$
13	XIII	90	XC	6,000	$\overline{V}M$
14	XIV	99	XCIX	10,000	$\overline{X}$
15	XV	100	C	20,000	$\overline{XX}$
16	XVI	111	CXI	100,000	$\overline{C}$
17	XVII	150	CL		
18	XVIII	200	CC		
19	XIX	300	CCC		
20	XX	400	CD		

NATIONAL, TRADITIONAL, AND RELIGIOUS HOLIDAYS

I. National and Traditional Holidays.

New Year's Day	January 1
Twelfth Night	January 5
Robert E. Lee's Birthday	January 12
Martin Luther King, Jr.'s Birthday	January 15
Lincoln's Birthday	February 12
St. Valentine's Day	February 14
Washington's Birthday	February 22
St. Patrick's Day	March 17
First day of spring	March 20
April Fool's Day	April 1
Arbor Day	April 29
May Day	May 1
Mother's Day	2nd Sunday in May
Memorial Day	May 30
Father's Day	3rd Sunday in June
Flag Day	June 14
First day of summer	June 20
Independence Day	July 4
Bastille Day (French Independence Day)	July 14
Labor Day	1st Monday in September
Grandparent's Day	September 11
First day of autumn	September 22
American Indian Day	September 30
Columbus Day	October 12
United Nations Day	October 24
Halloween	October 31
Veterans Day	November 11
Election Day	Tuesday after the first Monday in November
Thanksgiving Day	4th Thursday in November
First day of winter	December 21
Kwanzaa	December 26
New Year's Eve	December 31

Note: Daylight Savings begins on the first Sunday in April and ends on the last Sunday in October.

II. Christian Holidays

Epiphany/Twelfth Day	January 6
Epiphany Sunday (Three Kings Day)	between January 2 and January 8
Race Relations Sunday	1st Sunday in February
World Day of Prayer	1st Friday in March
Annunciation Day	March 25
Shrove Tuesday (Mardi Gras begins)	Tuesday before Lent
Lent	forty days before Easter
Ash Wednesday	1st day of Lent (7th Wednesday before Easter)
Palm Sunday	Sunday before Easter
Maundy Thursday	Thursday before Easter
Good Friday	Friday before Easter
Easter	1st Sunday after the first full moon that occurs on or after March 21
Easter Monday	Monday after Easter
Ascension Day	forty days after Easter
Whitsunday (Pentecost)	7th Sunday after Easter
Trinity Sunday	Sunday after Whitsunday (Pentecost)
Corpus Christi Day	Thursday after Trinity Sunday
St. John the Baptist Day/ Midsummer's Day	June 24
World Communion Sunday	first Sunday in October
World Food Day	October 16
Reformation Sunday	fourth Sunday in October
Advent	four Sundays preceding Christmas
All Saints Day	November 1
All Souls Day	November 2
Immaculate Conception	December 8
Human Rights Day	December 10
Christmas Eve	December 24
Christmas Day	December 25

III. Jewish Holidays

Purim	14th day of Adar
Passover	eight days beginning the 14th of Nisan
Shavuot	6th and 7th days of Sivan
Rosh Hashana (Jewish New Year)	1st and 2nd days of Tishri
Yom Kippur	10th day of Tishri
Sukkot	15th to the 22nd day of Tishri
Simhat Torah	23rd day of Tishri
Hanukkah	25th day of Kislev

IV. Canadian Holidays

Victoria Day	Monday before May 25
Canada Day	1st Monday in July
Labour Day	1st Monday in September
Thanksgiving	2nd Monday in October
Remembrance Day	November 11
Boxing Day	December 26

TRAFFIC SIGNS

COLORS OF SIGNS

RED: Stop, yield, do not enter or wrong way.

YELLOW: General warning.

ORANGE: Construction & maintenance warning.

BLACK: Regulatory.

BROWN: Public recreation areas and parks.

BLUE: Motorist services guidance.

GREEN: Distance, direction and information.

WHITE: Regulatory.

SERVICE AND GUIDE SIGNS

ONLY ONLY

SLOW MOVING VEHICLE

DO NOT ENTER

STOP

MERGE

YIELD

CAMPING CAMPING

TRAIL

BIKE ROUTE

HOSPITAL

CATTLE XING

SIGNAL AHEAD

PED XING

R×R

DIVIDED HIGHWAY

TWO WAY TRAFFIC

HILL

DO NOT PASS

NO PASSING ZONE

NO U TURN

NO RIGHT TURN

BIKE XING

DEER XING

SLIPPERY WHEN WET

SCHOOL ZONE

NO LEFT TURN

KEEP RIGHT

COMPUTER TERMS

algorithm
The sequence of steps required to complete a process or solve a problem.

application
The software that creates and modifies documents, e.g. word processing, spreadsheet, database, graphics, and page-makeup.

ASCII
Standard representation of characters that all computers can read; American Standard Code for Information Interchange.

back-up
A spare copy of a disk.

BASIC
A simplified computer language; Beginners' All-purpose Symbolic Instruction Code.

baud
A unit of transmission speed, usually one bit per second.

binary
A two-part number system used by computers.

bit
The smallest unit of data; binary digit.

boot
To start up a computer by loading software into the memory.

box
An enclosed part of a screen which contains a message.

buffer
A temporary storage place for data.

bug
A fault in a program.

byte
A group of bits functioning as a unit.

cancel button
An onscreen oval which offers the choice of deleting a command.

character
Any letter, number, or symbol, e.g. n, b, 7, 3, &, (, [, __, /, =, ⁹, ..

chip
An integrated circuit composed of electrical elements housed in silicon.

click
Press and release a mouse button to activate a pointer or some aspect of a program.

clipboard
A segment of memory that stores copied data.

closing
Deactivating a box on the screen.

command
Any instruction to a computer.

control panel
A feature which allows the operator to change the volume, alter the blinks of the cursor, or set time and date.

copying
Duplicating data and replacing it elsewhere, such as on a clipboard.

crash
Unexplained stoppage or error which may result in loss of data.

cursor
An electronic icon that points out the location of the last inserted character.

cutting
Selecting data to be either deleted or transferred.

data base
An efficiently organized group of facts.

debug
To remove faults from a program.

desk accessories
Programs that are always available from the menu.

desktop
The computer's working environment.

dialog box
An onscreen box requesting input from the operator.

directory
The contents of a disk or folder.

disk
A magnetic circular sheet where a computer stores information.

disk drive
A mechanism that reads and writes data on disks.

document
A single collection of data, such as a spreadsheet or mailing list.

DOS
The system that allows a computer to operate a disk drive; **d**isk **o**perating **s**ystem.

dot matrix
A pattern of dots which forms a character.

dots per inch (dpi)
The measure of dots in a line one inch long which appear onscreen or on printed copy. (Also given in dots per square inch or **dpsi**.)

download
To store information from another computer.

drag
To move an object onscreen by means of a mouse.

edit
To alter a document by adding, deleting, or rearranging data.

error
A fault in a program.

file
A collection of information grouped for convenience.

finder
The program that runs all applications.

floppy disk
A removable disk used for data storage.

folder
A group of documents.

font
A group of letters and numbers of the same size and style, e.g. Avant Garde, Bookman, Eras, Quorum or Rockwell.

footer
A section of text at the bottom of a page.

format
To ready a disk to accept data; to initialize.

graphics
Pictures, charts, borders, or images.

hang
A faulty response to commands, usually requiring restarting the system; to fail to respond.

hardcopy
A printed version of data; printout.

hard disk
A fixed disk housed in a casing which stores great amounts of data.

hardware
The computer itself, composed of electronic and mechanical parts.

header
A section of text at the top of a page.

icon
A pictorial representation or symbol, e.g. of a file, bomb, or mouse.

initialize
To ready a disk to accept data; to format.

input
To enter data into a computer.

insertion point
The place onscreen where the last data was entered.

interface
To link one computer with another.

K
A measure of computer memory equaling 1024 characters or about 170 words; a kilobyte.

letter-quality
Print production that resembles high quality typesetting.

lock
To prevent changes on a disk; write-protect.

loop
Repeated instructions.

mainframe
A system combining a series of computers.

meg
A measure of computer memory equaling 1,048,576 characters or about 175,000 words; a megabyte.

memory
Chips or circuits that store information electronically.

menu
A list of commands from which to choose.

microcomputer
A very small computer.

modem
A mechanism that sends information from one computer through telephone lines to another computer; a **mo**dulator-**dem**odulator.

monitor
A video screen which displays data.

mouse
A hand-held control device.

network
A system of computers which communicate with each other.

output
Data from a computer which is utilized by another device, such as a printer.

page-makeup
The creation of finished page layout.

pasting
Inserting data into a document from a clipboard.

pica
A measure equal to 1/6 of an inch.

pixel
The smallest dot of light on a screen.

port
A point where cables connect computers to printers or other devices.

printout
A printed version of data; hardcopy.

program
A set of instructions; software.

programmer
A person who creates software.

public domain
Products that anyone can copy.

RAM
Short-term computer memory; **r**andom-**a**ccess **m**emory.

ROM
Long-term computer memory; **r**ead-**o**nly **m**emory.

save
Transfer or store memory to a disk.

scroll
To move data up and down the screen in order to see what is above or below.

SCSI
A system that transfers data rapidly from one device to another; **s**mall **c**omputer **s**ystem **i**nterface (pronounced "scuzzy").

spooler
A piece of software which allows the user to continue working while printing is in progress.

spreadsheet
An arrangement of numbers into columns.

style
A variation in a font, e.g. **bold,** *italic,* underlined, outline, or shadow.

system
The program that allows a computer to start up and accept software.

template
A document that is saved and reused, such as a letterhead.

tractor feed
Revolving wheels which force paper through a carriage.

utility
A program that performs a simple task, such as count words.

virus
Deliberate sabotage of a program.

word processor
A program that enables a user to create text.

A TIME LINE OF LITERATURE

?-A.D. 428	Ancient Literature	
1750 B.C.		**Hammurabi codifies Babylonian laws**
1350-1250 B.C.	Moses receives the Ten Commandments	
1200 B.C.	*Gilgamesh*	
ca. 1000 B.C.	*Song of Deborah*	
900-801 B.C.	Homer composes the *Iliad* and the *Odyssey*	
ca. 950 B.C.	Solomon's poems and sayings composed	
ca. 940 B.C.	David's *Psalms; Genesis* written	
800-701 B.C.	Solomon's sayings collected	
776 B.C.		**First Olympic games**
750-700 B.C.	Homer's *Iliad* and *Odyssey* written in manuscript form	
ca. 600 B.C.	Sappho's poetry	
600-501 B.C.	Aesop's "Fables"; wisdom of Solon, Confucius, Buddha, Zoroaster, Lao-tse, the Jewish prophets	
ca. 500 B.C.	*Ramayana*	
458 B.C.	Aeschylus's *Oresteia*	
ca. 450 B.C.	Herodotus's *Histories*	
443 B.C.	Sophocles's *Antigone*	
431 B.C.	Euripides's *Medea*	**Hippocrates practices medicine**
ca. 429-27 B.C.	Sophocles's *Oedipus Rex*	
ca. 415 B.C.	Euripides's *Trojan Women*	
411 B.C.	Aristophanes's *Lysistrata*	
405 B.C.	Aristophanes's *The Frogs*	
ca. 400 B.C.	the Pentateuch or Torah assembled	
396 B.C.	Plato's "Apologia"	
387 B.C.	Plato's *Symposium*	
ca. 350 B.C.	*Mahabharata* begun	**Praxiteles sculpts Greek statuary**
307 B.C.	Library at Alexandria established	
ca. 255 B.C.	Septuagint begun in Greek	
205 B.C.	Plautus's *Miles Gloriosus*	
167 B.C.	Terence's *Andrea*	
165 B.C.	*Book of Daniel*	
65-54 B.C.	Catullus's poetry	
60 B.C.	Lucretius's "De Rerum Natura"	
70-19 B.C.	Virgil's *Aeneid*	
55 B.C.	Cicero's "De Oratore"	
54 B.C.	Caesar's "De Bello Gallico"	
47 B.C.	Ptolemy's library burned	
46 B.C.		**Leap Year introduced in the calendar**
45 B.C.-A.D. 8	Horace's poetry	
39 B.C.-A.D. 17	Livy's histories	
2 B.C.	Ovid's *Art of Love*	
A.D. 5	Ovid's *Metamorphoses*	
58	Paul's Letters to the Corinthians	

65	Mark's Gospel	
68	Josephus's "History of the Jewish War"	
85	Matthew and John's Gospels	
330		**St. Peter's Church erected in Rome**
360	Scrolls being replaced by bound books	
423	Palestinian Talmud compiled	

428-1100	**Old English (Anglo Saxon) Period**	
ca. 450-700	*Beowulf, The Wanderer, The Seafarer* composed	
ca. 633	The Koran	
ca. 670	Caedmon's *Hymns*	
731	Venerable Bede composes the first history of England, "Ecclesiastical History"	
ca. 750	Li Po's poetry	
760	"The Book of Kells"	
800		**Machu Picchu built**
831	Einhard's Life of Charlemagne	
850	The Edda	
871-899	Alfred the Great's translations; *Anglo-Saxon Chronicle*	
900	*Quem Quaeritis;* "A Thousand and One Nights" begun	
ca. 1000	*Beowulf* written in manuscript form	
1000-1100	Christmas and Easter Cycle plays	
ca. 1050	Omar Khayyam's poems composed	
1086	*Domesday Book*	

1100-1350	**Anglo-Norman Period**	
1100	*Chanson de Roland*	
1100-1204	*Niebelungenlied*	
ca. 1136	Geoffrey of Monmouth's "History of the Kings of Britain"; Abelard writes of his love for Heloise	
1163		**Notre Dame cathedral begun in Paris**
1176	Reynard the Fox fables	
1215	*Magna Charta*	
ca. 1307-1321	Dante's *Divine Comedy*	
1328	Chester cycle of plays written	
ca. 1335	Petrarch's poetry	
1348	Boccaccio's *Decameron*	

1350-1500	**Middle English Period**	
1350-1400	*Sir Gawayne and the Green Knight*	
ca. 1360	*The Pearl*	
ca. 1362	*Piers Plowman*	

ca. 1370	Chaucer's *The Book of the Duchess*	
		Steel crossbow used as a weapon
ca. 1375	Robin Hood stories appear	
ca. 1387	Chaucer's Prologue to the *Canterbury Tales*	
1456	Gutenberg prints the Bible	
1469	Malory's *Morte D'Arthur*	
ca. 1477	Caxton brings printing press to England	

1500-1660	**The Renaissance**	
ca. 1500	*Everyman*	
1503		**Da Vinci paints the *Mona Lisa***
1516	More's *Utopia*	
1525	Tyndale translates the New Testament	
1531	Eliot's *The Book Named the Governor*	
1532	Machiavelli's *The Prince*	
1535	Coverdale translates the Bible	**Cartier explores St. Lawrence River**
1549	*Book of Common Prayer*	
1555		**Michelangelo sculpts the Pieta**
ca. 1560	*Gammer Gurton's Needle*	
1577	Holinshed's *Chronicles*	
1580	Montaigne's *Essays*	
ca. 1588	Marlowe's *Doctor Faustus*	
1590	Spenser's *Faerie Queene*	
ca. 1590	Shakespeare's *The Comedy of Errors*	
1592	Shakespeare's *Richard III*	
1595	Shakespeare's *Midsummer Night's Dream*	
1596	Shakespeare's *Romeo and Juliet*	
1597-1600	Shakespeare's *Merchant of Venice, Henry IV, Henry V, Merry Wives of Windsor, Julius Caesar, Much Ado About Nothing, As You Like It, Twelfth Night*	
1599	Globe theater built	
1601	Shakespeare's *Hamlet*	
1602		**Bodleian Library opens at Oxford**
1602-1604	Shakespeare's *Troilus and Cressida, All's Well That Ends Well, Measure for Measure*	
1604	Shakespeare's *Othello*	
1605	Cervantes's *Don Quixote;* Shakespeare's *Macbeth, King Lear*	
1606	Jonson's *Volpone*	
1607	Shakespeare's *Antony and Cleopatra*	**English settle in Jamestown, Virginia**
1608		**Quebec founded**
1609	Shakespeare's *Sonnets*	

1609-1611	Shakespeare's *Cymbeline, Winter's Tale, Tempest*	
1611	King James Bible	
1612	Bacon's *Essays;* Shakespeare's *Henry VIII*	
1614	Webster's *Duchess of Malfi*	
1616	Captain John Smith's *A Description of New England*	
1623	First Folio of Shakespeare's plays	
1628		**Taj Mahal built**
1630-1647	Bradford's *History of the Plymouth Plantation*	
1630-1649	Winthrop's *History of New England*	
1632	Second Folio of Shakespeare's plays	
1633	John Donne's *Poems*	
1636		**Harvard established**
1639	First printing press in America	
1640	*Bay Psalm Book*	
1650	Anne Bradstreet's *The Tenth Muse*	
		Beginning of modern musical harmony
1660-1798	**Neo-Classic Period**	
1660-1669	Pepys' *Diary*	
1667	Milton's *Paradise Lost*	
1670	Moliere's *Le Bourgeois Gentilhomme*	**Hudson Bay Company chartered**
1678	Bunyan's *Pilgrim's Progress, Part I*	
1709-1711	Addison and Steele's *The Tatler*	
1711-1712	Addison and Steele's *The Spectator*	
1719	Defoe's *Robinson Crusoe*	
1721		**Postal service begins between London and New England**
1726	Swift's *Gulliver's Travels*	
1733	Pope's *Essay on Man*	
1740	Richardson's *Pamela*	
1741	Edwards's "Sinners in the Hands of an Angry God"	
1749	Fielding's *Tom Jones*	
1751	Gray's *Elegy Written in a Country Churchyard*	
1753		**British Museum chartered**
1755	Johnson's Dictionary	
1766	Goldsmith's *The Vicar of Wakefield*	
1773	Goldsmith's *She Stoops to Conquer;* Phillis Wheatley's *Poems*	
1775	Sheridan's *The Rivals*	
1776	Jefferson's *Declaration of Independence*	

1777	Sheridan's *School for Scandal*	**Stars and Stripes adopted as official U.S. flag**
1782	Crevecoeur's *Letters from an American Farmer*	
1783-1785	Noah Webster's grammar book	
1786	Burns's *Poems*	
1789	Blake's *Songs of Innocence*	
1791	Paine's *The Rights of Man*	
1797	Coleridge's *Kubla Khan*	

1798-1832	**Romantic Period**	
1798	Wordsworth and Coleridge's *Lyrical Ballads*	
1805	Scott's *Lay of the Last Minstrel*	
1807	Lamb's *Tales from Shakespeare*	
1810	Scott's *Lady of the Lake*	
1813	Austen's *Pride and Prejudice*	**The waltz sweeps European ballrooms**
1814	Scott's *Waverley*	
1816	Byron's *Prison of Chillon*	
1817	Mary Shelley's *Frankenstein;* Bryant's *Thanatopsis;* Keats's *Poems*	
1818	Scott's *Heart of Midlothian*	
1820	Scott's *Ivanhoe;* Irving's *Sketch Book;* Keats's *Lamia*	
1821	Lamb's *Essays of Elia;* Bryant's *Poems;* Cooper's *The Spy;* Shelley's *Adonais;* Byron's *Cain*	
1826	Cooper's *Last of the Mohicans*	
1828	Webster's *An American Dictionary*	
1829		**Typewriter patented**
1831	Poe's *Poems*	

1832-1901	**The Victorian Era**	
1832	Richardson's *Wacousta*	
1834	Hugo's *The Hunchback of Notre Dame*	
1836	Dickens's *Pickwick Papers*	
1837	Dickens's *Oliver Twist;* Hawthorne's *Twice-Told Tales*	
1838	Dickens's *Nicholas Nickleby*	**Literary Garland published**
1839	Poe's "Fall of the House of Usher"	
1840	Cooper's *Pathfinder;* Poe's *Tales of the Grotesque and Arabesque*	
1841	Emerson's *Essays;* Longfellow's *Ballads and Other Poems;* Cooper's *Deerslayer;* Poe's "Murders in the Rue Morgue"	**New York *Tribune* in publication**
1842	Browning's *Dramatic Lyrics;* Tennyson's *Poems*	
1843	Dickens's *A Christmas Carol;* Dumas's *The Three Musketeers*	

1844	Dumas's *The Count of Monte Cristo*	
1845	Poe's *The Raven*	
1846	Hawthorne's *Mosses from an Old Manse;* Melville's *Typee*	
1847	Emily Brontë's *Wuthering Heights;* Charlotte Brontë's *Jane Eyre;* Longfellow's *Evangeline;* Thackeray's *Vanity Fair*	
1848	Marx and Engels's "Communist Manifesto"	
1849	Dickens's *David Copperfield*	**David Livingstone crosses the Kalahari Desert**
1850	Elizabeth Barrett Browning's *Sonnets from the Portuguese;* Hawthorne's *Scarlet Letter;* Tennyson's *In Memoriam*	
1851	Hawthorne's *House of Seven Gables;* Melville's *Moby Dick*	
1852	Stowe's *Uncle Tom's Cabin*	
1854	Thoreau's *Walden*	
1855	Whitman's *Leaves of Grass;* Longfellow's *Hiawatha*	
1857	Flaubert's *Madame Bovary*	
1859	Tennyson's *Idylls of the King;* Dickens's *Tale of Two Cities* and *Great Expectations;* English translation of *The Rubaiyat of Omar Khayyam;* Darwin's *Origin of Species*	
1860		**Baseball becomes a popular sport**
1861	Eliot's *Silas Marner*	
1862	Hugo's *Les Misérables*	
1864	Lincoln's *Gettysburg Address*	
1865	Carroll's *Alice's Adventures in Wonderland;* Whitman's *Drum Taps*	
1866	Dostoevsky's *Crime and Punishment*	
1867	Twain's "The Celebrated Jumping Frog of Calaveras County"; Marx's *Das Kapital*	**British North America Act takes effect**
1868	Alcott's *Little Women*	
1869	Harte's "The Outcasts of Poker Flat"	
1870	Harte's "The Luck of Roaring Camp"	**Heinrich Schliemann excavates Troy**
1871	Darwin's *Descent of Man*	
1872	Verne's *Around the World in Eighty Days*	
1873	Tolstoy's *Anna Karenina*	
1876	Twain's *Tom Sawyer*	
1878	Hardy's *Return of the Native;* James's *Daisy Miller*	
1879	Ibsen's *A Doll's House*	
1880	Harris's *Uncle Remus;* Maupassant's *Stories;* Wallace's *Ben-Hur*	**Bingo invented**

1882	Twain's *The Prince and the Pauper*	
1883	Twain's *Life on the Mississippi*; Stevenson's *Treasure Island*	
1884	Twain's *Huckleberry Finn*	
1885	Gilbert and Sullivan's *The Mikado*	
1886	Hardy's *The Mayor of Casterbridge*; Stevenson's *Dr. Jekyll and Mr. Hyde*	**Statue of Liberty dedicated**
1888	Kipling's *Plain Tales from the Hills*	
1889	Twain's *A Connecticut Yankee in King Arthur's Court*	
1890	Dickinson's *Poems*; Ibsen's *Hedda Gabler*; Wilde's *The Picture of Dorian Gray*	
1891	Hardy's *Tess of the D'Urbervilles*; Garland's *Main-Travelled Roads*; Doyle's *Adventures of Sherlock Holmes*	**Toulouse-Lautrec produces posters**
1894	Kipling's *Jungle Book*	
1895	Crane's *The Red Badge of Courage*; Wells's *The Time Machine*; Yeats's *Poems*	
1897	Kipling's *Captains Courageous*; Wells's *The Invisible Man*; Rostand's *Cyrano de Bergerac*; Stoker's *Dracula*	
1898	Wells's *The War of the Worlds*; James's *The Turn of the Screw*	
1900	Conrad's *Lord Jim*	
1901-1914	**Age of Realism**	
1901	Kipling's *Kim*; Washington's *Up from Slavery*	
1902	Potter's *Peter Rabbit*	
1903	London's *The Call of the Wild*	
1904	Barrie's *Peter Pan*; O. Henry's *Cabbages and Kings*; London's *Sea Wolf*; Chekhov's *The Cherry Orchard*; Freud's *The Psychopathology of Everyday Life*	
1906	Sinclair's *The Jungle*	**First radio broadcast in the U.S.**
1910	Conrad's *Heart of Darkness*	
1911	Wharton's *Ethan Frome*	
1912	Millay's *Renascence*; Shaw's *Pygmalion*; Synge's *Playboy of the Western World*	
1913	Cather's *O Pioneers!*	
1914-	**Modern Era**	
1914	Amy Lowell's *Sword Blades and Poppy Seeds*; Lindsay's *The Congo and Other Poems*; Burroughs's *Tarzan of the Apes*	
1915	Maugham's *Of Human Bondage*; Masters's *Spoon River Anthology*	

1916	Joyce's *Portrait of the Artist as a Young Man;* Sandburg's *Chicago Poems;* Twain's *The Mysterious Stranger*	**John Dewey advances modern educational theory**
1917	Eliot's *The Love Song of J. Alfred Prufrock*	
1918	Cather's *My Antonia*	
1919	Anderson's *Winesburg, Ohio;* Hesse's *Demian*	
1920	Eliot's *Poems;* Wharton's *The Age of Innocence*	
1921	Strachey's *Queen Victoria;* Pound's *Poems 1918-1921*	
1922	Eliot's *The Waste Land;* Lewis's *Babbitt;* Joyce's *Ulysses;* Hesse's *Siddhartha*	
1924	Forster's *A Passage to India;* Melville's *Billy Budd*	
1925	Dreiser's *An American Tragedy;* Fitzgerald's *The Great Gatsby;* O'Neill's *Desire Under the Elms;* Ferber's *So Big*	**Crossword puzzles fashionable**
1926	Hemingway's *The Sun Also Rises*	
1927	Woolf's *To the Lighthouse;* Wilder's *The Bridge of San Luis Rey*	
1928	Remarque's *All Quiet on the Western Front;* Benet's *John Brown's Body*	**Mickey Mouse's debut**
1929	Faulkner's *The Sound and the Fury;* Hemingway's *A Farewell to Arms;* Wolfe's *Look Homeward Angel*	
1930	Faulkner's *As I Lay Dying*	
1931	Buck's *The Good Earth*	
1932	Huxley's *Brave New World;* Wilder's *Little House in the Big Woods*	
1933	Yeats's *Collected Poems;* Hilton's *Lost Horizon*	
1934	Hilton's *Good-bye Mr. Chips*	**F.B.I. shoots John Dillinger, Public Enemy No. 1**
1936	Mitchell's *Gone with the Wind*	
1937	Steinbeck's *Of Mice and Men* and *The Red Pony;* Dinesen's *Out of Africa;* Tolkien's *The Hobbit*	
1938	Wilder's *Our Town;* Steinbeck's *The Grapes of Wrath;* Daphne Du Maurier's *Rebecca*	
1939	Huxley's *Brave New World*	
1940	Hemingway's *For Whom the Bell Tolls;* Wright's *Native Son;* Hamilton's *Mythology*	**Irving Berlin composes "White Christmas"**
1941	Maclennan's *Barometer Rising*	
1943	Frost's *Come In*	
1945	Williams's *The Glass Menagerie;* Wright's *Black Boy;* Hersey's *A Bell for Adano*	
1946	Hersey's *Hiroshima;* Orwell's *Animal Farm*	

1947	Williams's *A Streetcar Named Desire*; Warren's *All the King's Men*; *The Diary of Anne Frank*; Mitchell's *Who Has Seen the Wind*
1948	Paton's *Cry, The Beloved Country*; Michener's *Tales of the South Pacific*
1949	Gunther's *Death Be Not Proud*; Orwell's *1984*; Miller's *Death of a Salesman*
1950	Bradbury's *Martian Chronicles*
1951	Salinger's *Catcher in the Rye*; McCullers's *A Member of the Wedding*
1952	Beckett's *Waiting for Godot*; Hemingway's *The Old Man and the Sea*; White's *Charlotte's Web*
1953	Richter's *A Light in the Forest*; Bradbury's *Fahrenheit 451*; Miller's *The Crucible*
1954	Golding's *Lord of the Flies*; Tolkien's *Lord of the Rings*
1955	Williams's *A Cat on a Hot Tin Roof*
1956	O'Neill's *A Long Day's Journey into Night*; Kantor's *Andersonville*; Churchill's *History of the English-Speaking Peoples*; Dennis's *Auntie Mame*
1957	Agee's *A Death in the Family*; Dr. Seuss's *The Cat in the Hat*; Kerouac's *On the Road*
1958	Pasternak's *Dr. Zhivago*; Cummings's *95 Poems*; MacLeish's *J.B.*
1959	Michener's *Hawaii*; Richler's *The Apprenticeship of Duddy Kravitz*
1960	Hellman's *Toys in the Attic*; Jarrell's *The Woman at the Washington Zoo*; Updike's *Rabbit, Run*; Knowles's *A Separate Peace*; Singer's *The Magician of Lublin*
1961	Heller's *Catch-22*; Lee's *To Kill a Mockingbird*
1962	Albee's *Who's Afraid of Virginia Woolf*; Porter's *Ship of Fools*; Williams's *The Night of the Iguana*; Solzhenitsyn's *One Day in the Life of Ivan Denisovich*
1964	Hemingway's *A Moveable Feast*; Lowell's *For the Union Dead*; King's "Why We Can't Wait"
1965	Albee's *Tiny Alice*; O'Connor's *Everything That Rises Must Converge*; Capote's *In Cold Blood*; White's *Once and Future King*

Menotti composes *Amal and the Night Visitors* (1951)

U.S.S.R. launches Sputnik (1957)

Verrazano Bridge opens in New York (1964)

1966	Malamud's *The Fixer;* Katherine Anne Porter's *Collected Stories;* Rawlings's *The Yearling;* Mao Tse-tung's "Quotations of Chairman Mao"; Cohen's *Beautiful Loser*	
1967	Styron's *Confessions of Nat Turner;* Pinter's *The Homecoming*	
1968	Barth's *Lost in the Funhouse*	
1969	Fowles's *The French Lieutenant's Woman;* Crichton's *The Andromeda Strain;* Hellman's *An Unfinished Woman*	**Neil Armstrong walks on the moon**
1970	Hemingway's *Islands in the Stream;* Bach's *Jonathan Livingston Seagull;* Davies's *Fifth Business*	
1971	Rice and Webber's *Jesus Christ, Superstar;* Zindel's *The Effect of Gamma Rays on Man-in-the-Moon Marigolds;* Vonnegut's *Slaughter-house-Five;* Plath's *The Bell Jar;* Wouk's *Winds of War*	
1972	Adams's *Watership Down*	
1973	Welty's *The Optimist's Daughter*	
1976	Haley's *Roots;* Styron's *Sophie's Choice*	**First supersonic jet service across the Atlantic ocean**
1977	McCullough's *The Thorn Birds;* Charnin's *Annie*	
1978	White's *Book of Merlyn;* Michener's *Chesapeake;* Wouk's *War and Remembrance*	
1980	Alain Boublil's dramatization of *Les Miserables*	
1982	Walker's *The Color Purple*	
1985	Atwood's *The Handmaid's Tale*	
1987	Wolf's *The Bonfire of the Vanities*	
1989		**Berlin Wall opened**
1990	Updike's *Rabbit at Rest*	

INDEX

INDEX

Picture Credits